*For Marian, without whom it would be life
without spice, and for Alex and Niki, of whom
I am constantly amazed and very proud.*

Acknowledgments

I would like to acknowledge the assistance of Catherine (Cass) Bayley, who years ago told me to stop bothering her and start writing, and then introduced me to Bones. For their invaluable assistance and insights for this book, I would also like to acknowledge Harry Barberian; Harm Rosenboom, and his much better-looking wife, Donna, of the Burlington Fish Market; the American Lamb Council; and Don Fancourt of Schneider's Meats in Kitchener.

Home Bistro

Creating the Best of Restaurant Cuisine in Your Kitchen

David Kingsmill

KEY PORTER  BOOKS

Cataloguing in Publication Data

Kingsmill, David
   Home bistro : creating the best of restaurant cuisine in your kitchen

ISBN 1-55013-702-6

1. Cookery, International. I. Title.

TX725.A1K55 1996   641.59   C96-930469-2

The publisher gratefully acknowledges the assistance of the Canada Council and the
Ontario Arts Council.

David Kingsmill can be reached at kingsmil@spectranet.ca or at 75662.2715@
compuserve.com.

Key Porter Books Limited
70 The Esplanade
Toronto, Ontario
Canada M5E 1R2

Printed and bound in Canada

96 97 98 99 6 5 4 3 2 1

Contents

Introduction

Let's get one thing out of the way right now: If you really want to cook as well as the chef in your favorite restaurant, you probably can. If you love food and like to cook, you have the same qualifications the chef had when he or she decided to become a chef. Really. These people aren't eggs thrown against a sacred culinary wall and miraculously hatched by the sun, for Pete's sake.

All you need are recipes that tell you *why* you are doing something as well as *how*; some critical tips, such as how to buy ingredients; and a little encouragement. First, the encouragement, by way of a reality check.

Myth #1: Cooking in a restaurant is stimulating, challenging, even an art—the opposite of home cooking.

Reality: Cooking in a successful restaurant is ninety-five percent routine with little ingenuity. Once the menu is set by the executive chef, the only one with the right to originality, each dish must be made consistently. That means the recipe never changes. If you, the customer, like the veal chop, it had better be exactly the same the next time or you will be disappointed and might not come back. The executive, or head, chef might want to slather prunes on the chop before grilling it, but if you don't like prunes, the chef can't put them on and stay in business. Restaurants depend upon repeat customers, and repeat customers come from the surrounding neighborhood. A restaurant must serve what the neighborhood wants to eat, not what the chef wants to cook.

At home, you can cook what you damn well please, and you can change your mind—or your recipe—on a whim. That's the artistic aspect of cooking. But even in your own home, you'll have to learn a few rules of common taste and acceptance if you wish to please most of your guests. If you are going to serve fast food, for instance (although I can't think why you would want to), you have to plan the menu around the formula used by all successful fast-food joints: "Fat, salt, sugar, and you don't need teeth to eat it." Do that, wear a tacky polyester uniform, and you can't go wrong.

Myth #2: Restaurant chefs can turn anything into a work of art.

Reality: Even the best chef would find it hard to turn out a consistently good meal with poor ingredients. The converse is true, too: a mediocre chef can turn out a great meal with great ingredients. Good chefs demand good raw materials. And they know how to buy. That is the main difference between you and a restaurant chef: buying.

Start with the best ingredients, and you can create great meals.

Myth #3: People go to restaurants, again and again, because of the food.

Reality: Wrong. When I first became a restaurant critic, people would jump me from dark corners and scream: "You've got to try this restaurant I went to last night. It was to die for. It was fabulous."

I would ask what they had to eat.

No one could tell me right away. "Let's see," they would say, "I had the, um, duck, this duck salad thing. And then I had...oh, I don't know, some sort of pasta..."

Very few could tell me what their dinner companions had, even after much thought. So what made the place so terrific?

Simple. They had a great time. The *mood* was made perfect by warm surroundings, and was not disturbed by the *service*, which was there but not there, if you know what I mean. The menu had something everyone liked, so the *food* was good. And the *price* didn't leave them with a bad taste in their mouths.

Mood, service, food and price to match.

Myth #4 (a corollary to Myth #3): People come to dinner at your place because you are such good company.

Reality: Maybe, if you're a very bad cook. If you cook well, they probably come for the food. Sorry about that.

Almost everyone remembers his or her first date at a restaurant, whether it was a drive-in hamburger joint or Chez Moolah. Marriage is proposed in restaurants, anniversaries marked and graduations celebrated. It is hard to not eat in restaurants when on vacation and hard to forget the sometimes strange meals in them. (It may be even harder to forget the price: in the late 1980s a customer made the mistake of asking for French fries with his meal at a famous restaurant in Paris. According to French restaurant critic Christian Millau, fries didn't come with the meal, but the restaurateur obliged—and charged him an extra four hundred francs, some eighty dollars.)

In almost all of North America, you need a license to cut hair, but you don't need a license to open a restaurant, and anyone can call himself or herself a chef, despite the cursing by the Culinary Federation of America and the Canadian Federation of Chefs and Cooks (formerly the Canadian Federation of Chefs de Cuisine).

As a result, you get some seriously crazy restaurateurs. One I know used to kick people out of his restaurant if they didn't like the way he cooked duck (rare). Another insisted upon playing his violin badly at everyone's table, even when the customers clearly didn't have tin ears, hated his playing, and asked him to buzz off.

So, if you want to act like a genuine restaurateur, just be yourself—you couldn't possibly be more outrageous than the pros.

Could you run a restaurant? It depends upon how you define the word.

McDonald's is a restaurant. Your office cafeteria is a restaurant. So is the neighborhood deli, the truck-stop diner, the hot-dog cart and the three-thousand-dinners-a-day hotel. When it comes right down to it, however, all these restaurants still rely on the same things, in proportion to the promises they imply with their menus, prices, decor and ingredients:

Mood, service, food and price to match.

This book takes the basic premises of specific types of restaurants and incorporates them into home-entertaining settings, so you can run a home restaurant every now and then without the restaurateur's hassles, worries and sixteen-hour days. When you study how successful restaurants operate, you find common denominators, regardless of size, type or location. That, at least, is what Harry Barberian discovered when writing an insider's manual to pass on to his sons.

Barberian has been a well-known restaurateur for more than forty years in both Canada and the United States. He has owned, opened and successfully run more than twenty operations during his career, including Barberian's in downtown Toronto since 1959 and Petite Marmite in Palm Beach, Florida. It is also safe to say he is a pack rat. For as long as he has been in the business, he has been clipping newspapers, saving letters and transcribing conversations with every successful restaurateur he has met; his files used to fill two garages until he donated them to a university. But several years ago, after enduring a serious medical problem, he sat down and wrote a restaurant operations manual to help his two sons and wife run the restaurants without him. What eventually evolved was a study of restaurant success. Where others theorized or analyzed failures in retrospect, Barberian analyzed success, and in doing so he found common denominators in all the successful restaurants he visited over those years.

The next time you go to your favorite restaurant take a stopwatch and look around. It's probably your favorite for the same reasons other restaurants have become successful. To wit:

- The manager and staff are happy to see you.
- It's comfortable and friendly. Occasionally, the staff will give you a drink or bring you an appetizer or dessert on the house—something that makes you feel special.
- You can smell the food from the kitchen, and the smell is wonderful.
- The salt and pepper shakers are clean. So are your knives, forks and spoons. So is the washroom.
- Your first course will be on the table twenty minutes after you have had a drink, read the menu and ordered. And all the meals ordered at your table will come at the same time. The second course will arrive twenty minutes later, and the third course twenty minutes after that. To overcome this time constraint, the kitchen has to be able to finish cooking everything on the menu within that time frame, which means much of what you order has

been partially prepared beforehand. To put it another way, risotto takes thirty minutes to cook but in your favorite restaurant it should come twenty minutes after you've ordered. The chef is not a mind reader, so he cooks it partially ahead of time and then finishes cooking it when you order (as the risotto recipes in the Trattoria section will show you). On the other hand, Frogs' Legs Meunière take only a few minutes to bread, fry and sauce.

- The staff will not rush you with the check. You will be free to linger.
- The waiter never walks into or out of the kitchen empty-handed.

True, I have not mentioned the food. It's a given that the best ingredients are used, it looks wonderful on the plate, it smells terrific and tastes just as good. But take a look at the menu. The highest price in each category on the menu is never more than double the lowest price. And really, all the prices in each category are within the same general range.

The portions are always the same. The way each dish is cooked is always the same. The restaurant never runs out of anything.

You looked at the salt and pepper shakers to make sure they were clean because a properly trained and supervised staff will always keep them clean. If they are dirty, it means the staff is inexperienced, or not trained and supervised sufficiently, or overworked. Inevitably it is the management's fault, and bad management leads to staff turnover, burnout, unhappy employees...and eventually unhappy customers, even if they aren't consciously aware of the problem.

Now put yourself in the restaurateur's shoes for just a moment; think about restaurant guests and guests in your own home, and you will understand why some restaurateurs commit murder.

When you get down to it, people want to cook or run a restaurant so they can serve something spectacular and be rewarded with a smile, a moan or a smile-moan combo. (And untold wealth, of course; but since you can't charge guests in your home, forget about that.) Most guests are a pain because they obstruct this wish fulfillment. You cannot put a decent menu together without someone being a vegetarian, lactose intolerant, gout susceptible or living in mortal fear of "hamburger disease."

And then there's Michael, who doesn't like pasta. Just doesn't like it. "I don't know...there's something squishy about it." Everyone likes pasta. Not Mike, but you've got to invite him. He's a great guy and a very funny dinner guest, even if he is a moron about pasta.

Old-fashioned etiquette is dead. Long gone are the days when dinner guests ate everything put in front of them, even if they hated it. Now they not only don't eat, they also tell you they hate it. Put those same people in a restaurant, however, and they will not only eat everything, but also tell the host the meal was fine. They will never come back because they hated it but they hate confrontation with strangers in authority more.

To make matters worse, the media's obsession with health has given everyone, especially those without a medical degree, the right to offer professional dietary advice. You can't buy whipping cream in the supermarket without a complete stranger asking your cholesterol count. And just try to order a coffee double double in a doughnut shop. It's a doughnut shop, not a health spa, okay?

Of course, all this has the unsettling effect of putting unfettered creativity into a straitjacket of culinary correctness, and you wind up making something harmless not to offend. And that, unfortunately, is what most restaurants do, and one reason why four out of five fail within three years.

If you love to cook, however, such a grasp at mediocrity is self-defeating, because *the* reason to hold a dinner party is so you can *troll for compliments*. With "safe" food, however, you are not going to land the whale, you are going to snag the guppy. And despite the fact that this book is designed to make you a home restaurateur, let's get real: you aren't charging your guests to eat and you don't want them back the next night.

If you wimp out and cook something *safe*, your guests will say, "Oh (fill in your name), the meal is absolutely divine, just wonderful! How did you manage it?" Then before you can answer, they will move on to the sociopolitical *debate du jour*. It's enough to deflate a soufflé. Now, you could do without guests and make whatever you want—calories and allergies be damned. But, you'll have to admit, there's little challenge in trolling for your own compliments, and empty restaurants are depressing.

So here's the trick. With this book, you can feel perfectly safe inviting the gustatorily challenged, because you can throw a dinner party and deflect the blame elsewhere if the meal does not live up to everyone's expectations. Let the Italians or Hungarians choose the menu, not you. Throw an authentic Texas barbecue, and if Henry doesn't like it, blame it on the Texans. Or make a French bistro dinner. If Charlene prefers chunky English chips to your perfect *frites*, blame the French (and then make a mental note that Charlene is an unregenerate heathen). And by all means invite Mike to dinner at your home trattoria, where pasta is bound to be served, "and it must follow, as the night the day, thou canst not then be false to any man."

Voilà. No stress—that elusive value-added aspect everyone promises but nobody delivers.

You're welcome.

Enjoy.

CHAPTER ONE

The Difference Between You and a Chef

The major difference between you and a chef is that the chef knows how to buy food. As Ross Perot says, "Ee-yuts jest that simple."

A chef can tell that the chicken is going to taste good before he roasts it. He knows the steak is going to knock you out before he slaps it on the grill. And he also knows that when the raw product is good, he doesn't need heroics to cook it.

Of course, a chef also has a few tricks up his sleeve. He knows, for example, how to "gourmet up" a vegetable by slapping on a pat of butter flavored with a herb, or how to elevate the taste of a small steak by painting it with a glaze of meat stock. And he can present perfectly symmetrical poached eggs for eggs Benedict because he poaches them the night before, plunges them into ice water, trims the edges and reheats them the next day because he knows egg yolks won't set once they have been partially poached. Now you know, too.

But the important thing to know is that great cooking and great eating do not begin and end in a three-star restaurant with a world-renowned chef. That is simply human conceit. A tomato plucked ripe from a vine in the hot summer sun of Provence, sprinkled with salt and pepper and eaten on the spot is as close as you can get to perfect eating and cooking.

When the first olives of the year are pressed in Tuscany, the fresh green oil is as light as air, and in a ritual as old as the hills around Florence, it is liberally poured on toasted bread rubbed with garlic. This may sound slimy—or worse, trendy—but trust me, it is simple *bruschetta* bliss. Natural bliss.

In The New Greece, a small *ouzeri* in Hania on the island of Crete, when you order fried squid, Stavros sends a small boy to the harbor ten steps away. The boy jigs a line, and when the squid grabs the bait, he pulls it out with one smooth stroke, and just like a North American kid slapping a baseball hard into the pocket of his mitt, grabs the squid with one hand and for five minutes slaps it down on the hot pavement to kill the critter and tenderize the tentacles. The slap, slap, slap is ancient music, ignored by everyone except tourists. The boy disappears into the kitchen and you sip your drink, one part warm ouzo, two parts water, in a rough glass tumbler. The sun beats down on the bleached white church and the brown fort. In minutes a mountain of lightly battered fried squid comes to the table with lemon wedges and the smells of ground pepper and the fresh sea. It melts in your mouth.

Walk into almost any Paris bistro at ten at night and you will hit an aromatic wall of hot garlic tamed by parsley and lemon, sautéed foie gras and beef stock so rich you can almost feel the gelatin sticking to your lips. In winter, bistros are hot and moist from the steam heat, in summer they're cool from the breeze through the open wall of windows facing the narrow dusty streets. Everybody knows everybody. Nobody needs a menu. At Barrière Poquelin in the rue Molière, the salmon is grilled on one side only. At Alan Delforge's la Chaumière en l'Ile on rue Jean-du-Bellay, you can smell the nutty aroma of black butter as each plate of skate wing passes by.

Ingredients, ingredients, ingredients. If skate is not fresh, it exudes ammonia. Really fresh salmon grilled on only one side achieves a succulence both crisp and juicy. Squid straight from the sea is the perfect fast food: fat, salty, sweet, and you don't need teeth to eat it. Good olive oil is like wine; good garlic is peppery, not bitter; real tomatoes are sweet and soft, not woody and acidic.

If you know how and what to buy, and when to buy it, you have a chef's advantage. I am not talking encyclopedic knowledge here, just the basics you use every day—beef, chicken, eggs—plus a bit of common sense. For instance, if you buy a tomato in season, why would you put it in the refrigerator? Think about it. A tomato thrives in the moist warmth of summer. It basks in the sun. It is damaged by frost. Putting a tomato in the refrigerator is like letting winter whistle through the vines. You might as well buy a cardboard tomato. It's the same with other things you use every day. With beef, what's vital is how it is raised and how it is aged; with chicken it's the processing; with fish, it's how and when it is caught, how it is shipped and how it is stored.

As a home cook, you have a distinct advantage over the professional: you don't have to be as sensitive to cost. Remember, the chef must buy food, cook it and price it so people will buy it. Included in the price of each dish is the cost of the labor to produce it, the rent, the insurance, the gas and cleaning bills and a soupçon of profit. A lobster, in high season, costs about $7.99 a pound. The chef will have to charge $25 for a lobster entrée to make a decent profit and pay the bills. How many people will pay that? Not enough to keep the chef in business. You, on the other hand, just pay the $12 for the lobster and serve it to guests ($9 if you know the "Chinese restaurant secret." Wait. Later.) Expensive, but not outrageous.

A restaurant must strike a balance. To be successful, it must provide mood, food, service and a price to match. You can strive for mood, food, a well-timed meal and compliments to match. Really, there's not much difference, except you don't have to serve the same meals night after night, year after year.

Never Trust a Meat Man (and Other Laws of Restaurant Buying)

Scenario #1: You walk up to the fish counter, look at the sole and ask the monger: "Is the sole fresh?"

The fishmonger is going to say (choose the most likely):

a) yes;

b) absolutely yes;

c) certainly, it was in the ocean yesterday;

d) no.

Ask any number of so-called experts about how to judge the quality of the food you buy, and you will undoubtedly get a lot of useful information. But *when* you ask is as important as *whom* you ask.

For instance, a fish retailer can tell you exactly what to look for to ensure a fish is fresh. That's her job, right? Right. But will she?

Sure. On the telephone.

After years of being a food writer, phoning people in the food business, it became obvious that just about everyone loves being asked to share expertise. I was always amazed by both the knowledge and enthusiasm of the answers I received. One monger went on and on about the sex life of crabs, and I stopped listening. Years later I learned that the female crab cannot mate with her shell on; she must shed it. Which is where we get soft-shell crabs. The fish expert was trying to educate me, and I was too stupid to realize that the sex life of a blue crab in Chesapeake Bay has determined the employment and food preference of countless millions of Americans for two centuries.

Asking in person, however, is another matter. It's not that the fishmonger is being suddenly dishonest, but he has changed from Olympian expert to seller, and commerce clouds everything. He is as likely to explain how to judge freshness by analyzing the fish he's holding up as tell you straight out that it has been a long time out of water.

Now, this may seem cynical. It is. But it brings me to that most common refrain of restaurateurs: "Never trust a meat man."

When buying anything, a good chef always embraces a universal conspiracy theory to stay sharp.

It's commerce again. For every chef who knows how to judge meat, there is one who knows how to *order* but not to judge. And the meat men know it.

To get an order, the conspiracy theory goes, the meat men deliver terrific cuts at a very competitive price. Over the course of time, however, the quality seems to slip: the cuts at the bottom of the box are inferior; the boxes get a little light. Smart restaurateurs know they must weigh everything as it comes in the back door. Everything. And everything must be inspected and counted before it is accepted—produce, fruit, meat, even paper towels.

If designating one person's time—and salary—to checking is impractical, the meat men know. And when they know, the restaurateur is ripe for the taking. Cynical? Slanderous? Well, consider the frustrated restaurateur who told the renowned Harry Barberian about the inconsistent quality of his deliveries—meat, produce, everything. He was sure he was being ripped off but couldn't prove it. Harry told him to buy a weigh scale and put it beside the back door, where the deliveries were made. He did. His problems were solved. The salesperson went straight back to the distribution warehouse and told the boss the restaurateur was weighing everything. The proof? No one tried to short him again. (By the way, the scale didn't work. The restaurateur couldn't afford a working scale, so he bought a broken one for peanuts at an auction.)

Whenever confronted with a sign or a salesperson claiming a thing is fresh, go immediately into conspiracy mode. How? Read on.

CHAPTER TWO

Miscellaneous Stuff You Should Know, or How to Buy Food Like a Chef

CHICKEN

Take a good chicken and roast it until the fragrance kicks the brain where memories of farm mothers hide, and the fat crackles and caramelizes in the heat, and the skin turns crisp and golden. You have created the perfect main course. No sauce. No stuffing. You don't even have to truss the bird. (It may look oddly splayed when you take it from the oven, but that aroma drives out any mean thoughts about artistic merit.) Simplicity itself.

A chef knows that to achieve simple perfection, you must start with a chicken that has the potential to produce maximum flavor and texture. Where does that potential come from? The most important consideration is how the bird is *processed*.

What you want is a chicken that has undergone a "soft scald" to remove the feathers and then has been "air-chilled" (also known as "dry-chilled" or "dry-packed").

You want a chicken that looks and feels slightly greasy, not a smooth, shiny white-skinned object sitting in a pink pool on a foam tray.

The popular buzzwords in recent years have been "farm-raised, free-range, organic," indicating that the bird is raised without pesticides or antibiotics and allowed to run around and peck for food in a farmyard. Is this the ticket to great taste? A chicken's home life is secondary, and if it is not processed well, a free-range chicken will taste just like a supermarket bird.

At the beginning of the process, chickens are scalded to loosen the feathers for plucking. Most are put through a hot scald, which does that job well but cooks the outer layer of skin right off the bird. That is why supermarket birds are smooth, shiny and white: the outer layer, the epidermis, which contains a significant amount of the great taste, is gone.

The best way to process a chicken is to put it through a "soft" or "cool" scalding process, which takes a little longer. It loosens the feathers but does not cook off the outer layer of skin.

Almost all supermarket chicken is water-chilled. This means the cleaned and gutted chicken is thrown into a tub of water chilled to just above the freezing point. The chicken soaks up water so easily that most places have laws limiting the water content to five percent of body weight. This, as you may imagine, is neither an easy nor inexpensive regulation to follow—or to enforce.

Although processing is the key factor in the quality of chicken, how the bird is raised can also determine flavor.

Some claim that you can spot a free-range, corn-fed chicken by its yellower skin. Pecking corn in the farmyard is certainly one way to color the skin. One processor put marigold petals in the chicken feed; it made the skin go yellower, too.

But let's get real here. How many chickens do you think strut around the barnyard in the middle of winter? The vast majority of the chicken we eat is produced indoors—and always has been. Animal-rights advocates complain that this factory farming is cruel, and suggest that we return to the good old days when Mom and Pop let the critters roam free, preserving their dignity right up to the day when Pop would take a rusty ax and, if his aim was good, neatly sever their heads. If his aim wasn't so good, or the ax was rustier than usual ...

The good old days? Nonsense. North Americans have been eating roast chicken only since the Great Depression. Before then, chickens were raised for egg production, and when the hens stopped laying, for stewing or fertilizer. With the Depression, North America needed a source of cheap protein, and chicken was the answer. In 1900, eighty percent of egg production was in commercial factory farms.[*] Today, it is about ninety percent. In other words, we have never relied on Mom and Pop for chicken or eggs. The climate does not permit it. Moreover, our chicken consumption is huge. One efficient plant can process two hundred thousand chickens. How many free-range farms would be needed to supply such a plant, even for a day? It has always been thus.

Having said all that, organic chicken that is processed well can give you a taste advantage, which has more to do with the type of feed than with the antibiotics or growth stimulants in the feed or the stress of being raised in a barn with several thousand relatives. You can usually translate "organic" to mean that the folks raising the chicken have thought long and hard about how to do it and might well be feeding the bird good stuff. But if they then hot-scald and water-chill the organic chicken,

---

[*]*Foods and Food Production Encyclopedia*, Douglas M. Considine and Glenn D. Considine (Van Nostrand Reinhold, 1982).

they are wasting time and money. The only true test is in the cooking. If the bird tastes superb, it may be worth the extra cost. Remember the brand name or farm and stick with it. All "organic" birds are not created equal.

So, how do you ensure consistency? The best chefs get their birds at the farm gate: they either buy live directly from the farmer or have the birds killed to their specifications. Chefs can also deal with suppliers who have cultivated food sources that enhance their product, and therefore their profits. Good suppliers will comb the world for anything their restaurant clients will pay good money for. You do not have access to the farm or the pros, but you can read and ask questions. First, look for the term air-chilled on the package. If you can't find it, ask your butcher. If he or she has been trained in the local supermarket you will get a look like you're from Mars.

Here are two relatively accessible sources.

Food professionals consider kosher chickens to be consistently the best-tasting chickens commonly available in North America. The reason lies in the processing. Kosher chickens are typically put through a very cool scalding process, so cool that some pin feathers are not dislodged, which is a reassuring sign of a well-processed bird. The outer skin remains untouched; therefore all the natural taste remains. Kosher chickens are also often but not always air-chilled. The other feature of kosher chickens is that they are salted, set aside for a short time to draw out some of the blood, and then singed before the processing is finished. This can produce a saltier bird, but you can take this into consideration when cooking.

In the United States, the good news is that a major processor is now air-chilling chicken. The bad news is that the processor, to fight salmonella and other contaminant transference, puts the birds through three scalding processes.*

The news is a lot better in Canada. One of the country's largest processors, Maple Leaf, is soft-scalding and air-chilling about ten percent of its production under the Prime label. The birds are also aged for twenty-four hours in the air chiller, which goes that extra mile to produce great-tasting chicken.

Other processors are also moving into this area. It costs more to process birds this way, and the birds will cost you more. But they're worth it.

Chickens are named by age and weight. The younger the bird, the more tender the flesh, the theory goes—but this is not always true.

CAPONS

These are male chickens that undergo castration at four weeks. Capons grow up completely unaware they are supposed to crow at dawn or fight anything that comes between them and their would-be wives. As a result of their stress-free life,

*48 Hours CBS, Wednesday, February 9, 1994.

by the time they are seven months old, they are between six and nine pounds of succulent roasting flesh with an abundance of easily melted fat under the skin.

ROASTING CHICKENS

These are usually processed at fourteen to eighteen weeks and weigh four to seven pounds. They are terrific for, yup, roasting.

BROILERS

These are about seven to nine weeks old and weigh between one and a half and four pounds. They can be barbecued, grilled, roasted, spitted, kebabed—an all-round terrific bird. The French call the smallest of these *poussins*.

STEWING CHICKENS

Really old, up to seven pounds and good for (yup) stews. Restaurants will use them for stock if the price is right, which it rarely is.

ROCK CORNISH GAME HEN

Great name. Sounds like you had to shoot it yourself. These little guys, weighing one to two pounds, are the invention of Jacques Makowsky, a New York artist turned Connecticut poultry farmer who crossed a Cornish game cock with a Plymouth Rock hen. He called the small, plump result a Rock Cornish game hen and introduced it to an unsuspecting market in 1950. Their unique feature—and the reason for their extraordinary expense—is their diet of cranberries and acorns, which give the little chickens a gamy flavor.

GUINEA HEN

The best are bred from the original gray-feathered French stock in Ontario; they are known as Pintelle and Pintade. The hens are much more tender than the cocks, weigh between two and three pounds and have a dry flesh. (It is, therefore, imperative not to overcook guinea hens.)

SQUAB

Your basic one-pound, pale-meat, domestic pigeon. You can overcook them to cardboard in the blink of an eye.

QUAIL

The half-pound tiny domesticated cousin of the wild quail is a white-fleshed bird that most people find too fussy to cook and eat. The tiny, sharp bones also bother most. But these little guys are a restaurant dream—fast cooking, easily stuffed and impressive to serve for the very reason most people won't cook them at home.

But as soon as you try the recipe in the Greek *Ouzeri* section, you'll be hooked on them. Their eggs are also fabulous for hors d'oeuvres, and can be purchased (either raw or cooked and canned) in Greek or Asian supermarkets.

Finally, a word to animal-rights advocates who complain about factory farming.

Chickens, like most of us, are not rocket scientists. If chickens are not on earth to supply food for fox and man, what are they doing here?

It is an utter waste for a human being to spend time championing the spurious case of chickens. Get real. Chickens don't vote. Do something useful— champion the rights of live humans to enjoy dead chickens in the privacy of their own homes. As it is, until you taste an organically raised, soft-scalded, air-chilled roast chicken, you will never know what Auntie Em was feeding Dorothy just before the twister. You will forever be mendaciously and ignorantly content with poultry mediocrity, which can lead to ambivalence about chickens as a fabulous food source, which can lead to boredom, which can lead to feelings of inadequacy, which often impel humans to seek something to justify their lives, namely championing the rights of profoundly stupid chickens.

Enough written. Go forth and eat well.

EGGS

Any experienced chef will tell you that the hardest meal to cook is breakfast.

Think about it. How do you like your fried eggs? Over easy? Over hard? Sunny-side up and runny? Not runny? Do you like a crisp edge around the whites? And boiled eggs...two, three, four or five minutes? Scrambled soft and creamy or cooked till they're bouncy?

Eggs are the heart of cooking; you eat them raw in eggnog, half done in Caesar salad, fully cooked in an egg salad sandwich. You can't make a meringue without them, soufflés rise because of them, and bread crusts shine from an egg wash. You can make pasta without eggs, but why would you want to? They thicken classic sauces, common gravies, French creams and custard.

There ought to be a monument the size of the Arc de Triomphe to the humble egg, but all we have is the ridiculous image of a cracked Humpty.

Everybody knows how to cook eggs. The trick for a restaurant chef is to offer cooked eggs in ways that people do not usually do them at home, like poached with a flourish (Benedict, Florentine) that moves the egg beyond the expertise of the Sunday morning fry cook.

Like all simple foods, eggs are taken for granted and usually badly cooked.

Eggs. Chicken eggs. White ones, brown ones, peewee, small, medium, large, extra large, double yolkers, Grade A ...

What if you discovered that egg quality starts to deteriorate within seconds of being laid?* How long do you think it's been since the eggs in your supermarket have been out of the chicken? How long does a carton of eggs sit in your refrigerator before you use the last one?

Unless you live on a chicken farm, you may never know what a beautiful thing an egg can be, but you should learn to judge how unfresh the eggs you are buying are.

Crack an egg onto a plate. The yolk of a fresh egg sits in the middle of the white, and it sits up high. The white of a fresh egg is not clear, but milky. An egg white is comprised of thick and thin elements. The proportion of thick to thin is sixty–forty in a fresh egg. In an old egg, there is more thin than thick, and it runs all over the plate. The yolks of older eggs are likely to break when you crack them into a pan because the white, being thin, does not hold the yolk together.

Despite what the alarmists say, eggs are not dangerous. Billions are laid every day, and billions are eaten every day. How many people do you know who get sick from them in a year? Okay, now how many people do you know who die from the drinking water while on vacation? Chances are those same recently deceased enjoyed a breakfast of eggs before they succumbed.

The idiocy culminated in 1993, when some cracked bureaucrat in New Jersey, no doubt egged on by a politician (puns intended), proposed a law that would ban restaurants from serving eggs sunny-side up. Fortunately, the law was ridiculed into oblivion by the public and press.

To get the freshest, find a farmer. Failing that, look at the egg carton for the best before date. Eggs are sold within thirty-two days, and it takes, on average, two days to get the egg from the chicken, through the cleaning, sizing and grading process, to the carton. Count back thirty days from the date on the carton and you get the date when the eggs were packaged.

Beef

Your local supermarket may advertise fresh meats and promote lean beef, but a good chef doesn't want either. A chef wants a side of beef hung in a cooler, for twenty-eight days or longer, until a quarter inch of mold covers the outside, the carcass has shrunk, and the meat has developed a distinctive (and, to the knowledgeable, addictively attractive) stink. This is called *aging* in North America, *mortification* to the French, and makes great taste for all.

The carcass is hung whole because its sheer weight stretches the tendons and fibers. The mold is cut away, along with the underlying layer of "fresh" flesh.

---

*Much of the information in the next few pages comes from *On Food and Cooking: The Science and Lore of the Kitchen*, Harold McGee (Collier Macmillan, 1984).

When you factor in shrinkage—up to twenty-five percent of the body weight—and the cost of aging for almost a month, the beef is going to cost at least fifty percent more than supermarket cuts. Supermarket beef is aged only for as long as it takes to move it from the slaughterhouse to a central warehouse and then to the supermarket in refrigerated trucks. As one meat manager told me, "We're not sure it's dead when it comes in the back door."

A really good cut of beef will also cost you more because it is *not* lean.

Have you ever wondered why a great steakhouse steak is always better than the one you cook at home, even when the restaurant sells you its secret spices? It's the marbling in the meat. "Marbling" is a nice way of saying riddled with fat. The more the marbling, the better—and more expensive—the steak. We're not talking slabs of fat here. The best meat has a fine threading of fat throughout, like a cobweb woven into the muscle.

In the United States, a uniform grading system for beef identifies the level of marbling and determines the prices. An experienced meat buyer inspecting a hanging carcass looks at the eye of the round, both for size (the larger the better) and fine marbling (the more the merrier). If the eye of the round, a tough cut, is well marbled, the buyer knows the rest of the carcass will be tasty and tender. U.S. Prime beef has the most thin lines of interwoven fat. (In a steak, the marbling is obvious to the naked eye.) The next grade down is U.S. Choice, which also makes for a fine steak. Third grade is U.S. Select, which will have only slight visible marbling. This is typically the supermarket beef.

An overlap of marbling is allowed between the grades. Look carefully. You don't want to pay Choice prices for Select beef.

In Canada, Grade AAA, or Triple A, corresponds to U.S. Choice. Grade AA, or Double A, corresponds to U.S. Select; Canada Grade A beef is below U.S. standards for marbling.

Marbling is important because the flavor of beef is in the fat, and the marbling makes the steak tender. That sense of soft, chewable juiciness we experience is directly attributable to the amount of fat. You cannot fight Mother Nature. Human beings need and love fat. This is not a habit that can be changed. When McDonald's created the McLean burger, it took out just a bit of the fat and told us that we could change our burger habits for the healthier. No way. The McLean was a flop. So were all the other chains' attempts to reduce fat in their food.

Marbling depends on both the feed and the breed. Limousin cattle are prized by the French because they naturally develop a substantial marbling without a lot of outside fat, which just gets trimmed away. In North America, feeding corn to beef cattle during the last few weeks before slaughter produces the desirable amount of marbling.

Alberta breeds and feeding practices radically changed in the '70s and '80s to produce leaner, "healthier" beef—in other words, beef without marbling.

Alberta then lost much of their lucrative California export market, along with taste and texture. Supermarket beef sales dropped during this period as well, not, I think, because people believed the food evangelists' picture of nutritional Armageddon but because they didn't enjoy the new beef very much, which made it easier to substitute fish and chicken. During the same period, steakhouses selling U.S. Prime beef continued to flourish.

No law requires processors or butchers to sell graded beef. Many prefer ungraded, or "no roll," beef. (Grade stamps are put on the carcass with a roller, much like a paint roller but smaller.) In practice, the major benefit of a grading system is for ordering. Purveyors of beef to the restaurant trade do not come to the back door with samples, just an order sheet and clipboard. The chef orders U.S. Choice. It is delivered stamped U.S. Choice, or it is sent back. The down side is that there is a great range of marbling within each grade. The best U.S. Choice is the same as low-end Prime, but a heck of a lot cheaper. If you can judge by sight, rather than by relying on the grade, you can get a better cut at a cheaper price.

So, when you are buying a steak in a butcher shop, for example, choose the one with most marbling and a creamy white layer of fat around the edge. The suet around a prime rib roast or the fat separating the tail from the tenderloin and sirloin portions of a porterhouse should flake apart at the touch. The edging of fat around a steak adds flavor; if you are worried about ingesting that much fat, cut it off after cooking. You'll get the added taste and aroma without the cholesterol.

A well-aged steak looks as if you could gently pull it apart. It is not dense, impenetrable or porcelainlike. This is due to the stretching of the connective tissues. An experienced chef holds a raw steak between the thumb and forefinger. If the fingertips meet easily when pressed together, the chef knows the meat will yield just as easily to the teeth when cooked. Unfortunately, supermarkets don't allow customers to pinch the meat before buying it.

You would have to walk into an aging refrigerator where beef has been hung for twenty-one days or more to know what well-aged beef smells like. It has a rich, dense, even sweet aroma. Despite its strength, it is not repulsive. You won't gag inhaling the aroma. You will never forget it, either. Do not be put off by beef that has an odor, unlike good fish, which has none. A human nose is a highly sensitive instrument that has evolved over millions of years to keep homo sapiens alive. If the meat has a repulsive smell, avoid it, as you would avoid anything your nose (and brain) tells you to avoid.

Color is not a good indicator of taste. A very dark red or even brownish color may be evidence of good aging, bacterial invasion, bruising at slaughter, or inconsistent temperature storage. The most common reason for darkness, however, is oxidation, which means the meat has been hanging around after it was cut from the carcass. Oxidation does not mean the meat is bad, but the finest steakhouses will not sell steak cut more than twelve hours before it hits the grill, because steak starts to lose flavor as soon as it is cut and trimmed. To most people, a brownish steak or roast doesn't appeal, so supermarkets wrap beef in loose paper or oxygen-permeable plastic wrap to retard the color change. (Unscrupulous grocers used to dye the meat, but this has been outlawed. Instead, supermarkets use special lights at the meat counter to make the beef look redder.)

The rump roast is from (you guessed it) the hind end. The strength of flavor directly corresponds to the amount of exercise the various muscles of the animal get. The hindquarters, including the rump, of course, are heavily used; therefore more blood flows to those areas, and this increases their flavor dramatically.

The tenderloin (filet, filet mignon, chateaubriand) lies along the spine, and does not get flexed much at all.

The rump has more flavor. The tenderloin has a less beefy flavor, but it is buttery tender, because it has few connective tissues. The rump is tough because it has a lot of strong connective tissue as well as muscle.

The trick to cooking tough cuts of meat is to break down the connective tissues without cooking out all the flavor. Connective tissues begin to break down at 140°F (60°C) but get dry and stringy at temperatures hotter than 160°F (71°C). So, to make the tough connective tissues edible, meat should be cooked to at least 140° but not more than 160°F (60° and 71°C). Easy, right? No— because of the gelatin factor.

Meat becomes dry when the internal gelatin is cooked out. Gelatin is a natural enzyme, which turns to liquid if cooked for a long time at high temperatures. It begins to liquefy at 170°F (77°C), and in that state gives meat a rich, silky texture. Great stuff, gelatin. You want it all to stay in the meat. So, to break down but not petrify the connective tissues yet bring out but not liquefy the gelatin—in other words, to perfectly cook a tough cut of meat—cook it at 165° to 170°F (73° to 77°C), and certainly never above 190°F (90°C).

Don't panic about these seemingly low temperatures. Trichina, the trichinosis worm that pork eaters fear, is killed at 137°F (58°C); most other pathogens at 140°F (60°C); even the most resistant salmonella strains are killed at 160°F (71°C). Meat cooked at 161°F (72°C) is absolutely safe to eat because the temperature is sufficient to kill surface bacteria, worms and trichina.

Rare roast beef has an internal temperature of 130° to 145°F (54° to 63°C); medium rare beef is between 145° and 155°F (63° and 68°C); medium-well between 155° and 170°F (68° and 77°C); and well done beef between 170° and 180°F (77° and 82°C). Aha! you say, the internal temperature of rare roast beef is less than 140°F (60°C), the bacteria killing temperature. True, but it doesn't mean rare roast beef is unsafe. The temperature on the exterior, where bacteria and pathogens gather, is between 170° and 180°F (77° and 82°C), well above the safe level.

In a hamburger, the exterior meat (where bacteria grow) is mixed up with the interior meat. So treat the whole burger as though it has been exposed to the air. Hamburger should be cooked at least medium to well. Having said that, the so-called "hamburger disease" is very rare and almost never the fault of the restaurant. The trouble is usually traced to meat packaging and processing plants. Practical proof of this is steak tartar, tenderloin that is ground to order and eaten raw. The trick is grinding it to order, which avoids potential problems.

Pierre de Serre is a scientist and the inventor of the Smart Pot, a device like a slow cooker with a very accurate temperature control. In his larger institutional version of this, he can cook a roast of beef. He places the roast in a heavy plastic bag and immerses it in water that is exactly the temperature the meat should be when it is finished. Immerse the roast in a bath set at 155°F (68°C) and it comes out rare. As the temperature never rises higher than 155°F (68°C), the meat will never overcook or undercook, and can be kept at that temperature almost indefinitely. You (or a restaurant or institution) can cook a roast overnight, then leave it all day in its bath, and the roast remains perfectly cooked. Shrinkage is also minimal, unlike in oven roasting.

Pierre's only problem is us human beings, who hate change and therefore persist in cooking meat in the most inefficient way possible, by heating it in air, the worst possible conductor of heat.

The trick is to buy the right grade and cut of beef and then apply the right amount of heat for the right length of time. Simple. But don't be fooled about the buying aspect. Two of the biggest myths in meat cookery should be blown to bits right now, so you won't be tempted to be cheap.

Myth #1: You can tenderize meat in various ways.

Despite what old wives and old cooks will tell you, you cannot tenderize a piece of meat with chemicals (MSG, commercial tenderizers), naturally occurring acids (papaya, pineapple) or marinades (wine–acid combinations). The chemical and natural tenderizers and the acid in wine marinades eat protein— but only on the surface of the meat. They make the outside mushy, but never penetrate the interior. And the chemical tenderizers don't achieve much until they reach 140°F (60°C). Not much point to them, is there?[*]

You can make meat more tender by physically altering its composition before cooking—by grinding, flattening or pounding it. You can also make a piece of meat seem more tender by physically altering it after it is cooked. (Slicing tough meat against the grain in thin slices makes it easier to chew, and thus it appears to be more tender.)

---

[*]On Food and Cooking: The Science and Lore of the Kitchen, Harold McGee (Collier Macmillan, 1984), p. 108.

Myth #2: When you sear meat quickly, you seal in the juices.

The people who say this also tell you that after you have seared both sides of a steak, you should cook the second side until you see specks of blood coming through the seared crust. It's rare at that point.

Excuse me? If the juices have been sealed in, how can they come out to let you know your steak is cooked?

Searing caramelizes the surface of the meat and makes it taste much better. Good taste is the only reason to sear meat.

Steakhouse steaks come from three areas of the steer: the sirloin, the short loin and the rib sections. Some have bones, some don't, but the bones add flavor to a cut.

SIRLOIN

From the sirloin—the back of the beast, one section up from the rump or round—come, naturally, the sirloin steaks, of which there are many types: flat bone, pin bone and wedge bone are the prime names, but supermarkets usually call them all "sirloin steak." The best sirloin includes a filet portion on one side of the bone and the sirloin on the other. Some have a tail, some do not—butcher's choice. (The tail is delicious, but tougher.) A "top sirloin" (or "Iowa cut") is boneless and cut from the tougher round area near the top part of the sirloin.

SHORT LOIN

The favorites from this area are porterhouse, T-bone, New York and club steaks.

The porterhouse is a large steak cut from the short loin end nearest the sirloin. It has a bone with the filet on one side, the sirloin on the other and a strip steak above the sirloin. It is often sold with the tail, which is separated by a layer of suet; this gives the steak added flavor. If you take away the bone, tail and filet, you have a New York strip steak, aka Kansas City, strip, shell, key strip or hotel steak.

The T-bone has the filet on one side of the bone that gives it its name and the top loin on the other side; it can come with or without a tail. It is cut from the center of the short loin.

Club steaks are cut from the short loin nearest the rib section. They are very succulent steaks. They have no tenderloin or tail and only a slight bone. (Most steakhouses don't serve this steak because it is too often confused with the inferior rib steak in the public mind.) For home buyers, it's a very nice cut. A 1-inch (2.5 cm) thick club steak weighs between ½ and ¾ lb (225 and 340 g).

RIB

A rib steak is actually a cut of a standing rib roast with a tail. It is usually liberally marbled, and a good one will fall apart in your mouth. Take away the bone and tail and you have the original Delmonico or country club steak. (Some butchers call the sirloin section of a sirloin steak a Delmonico, but it is not as tender.)

FILET

The filet or tenderloin runs down the back under the spine between the sirloin and the short loin. Because this part of the beast moves very little, it is the most tender. The way it is trimmed in North America, however, it lacks a covering of fat and therefore a distinctive beefy taste.

At the sirloin end of the long, boneless strip of meat is a flap best used as a lovely breakfast fry-up or ground for great hamburger. Next up are the five tournedos. The fat center section is cut into two pieces for chateaubriand. In North America the next section produces three or four good-size filets mignons (what the French call tournedos). At the end are the tenderloin tips.

VEAL

Some people swear that veal is the finest meat going, but I have never developed an enthusiasm for it. First, it doesn't have much fat and therefore lacks flavor and natural tenderness. Second, it costs too much. Nevertheless, schnitzel wouldn't be schnitzel without it, and both at Jeremiah Tower's Stars in San Francisco and at Splendido in Toronto, I have had veal chops that melted in the mouth. Both restaurants buy prime veal. I use only two cuts of veal, the scallopini and the loin chop.

Veal is meat from calves. The best is from calves eight to twelve weeks old weighing 150 to 250 lb (70 to 115 kg). They are called "vealers" in the trade, but the tony term is "milk fed," because they haven't yet been weaned. The flesh is white to very light pink, and the bones are soft and very red inside. The flesh should look velvety and moist but never watery.

Not all veal is milk fed. Provimi veal comes from calves raised and fed under licence. The term indicates a diet of *pro*teins, *vi*tamins and *mi*nerals. Provimi veal is consistently good because the feeding is consistent. Restaurateurs like consistency, and that is the attraction of Provimi veal.

Older calves, weighing upwards of 400 lb (180 kg), also produce veal, albeit darker in color and less desirable in taste and texture, because the calves have been grain fed after weaning at twelve weeks.

Because veal has little connective tissue and little fat, it is generally not aged more than seven days.

For scallopini, the trick is to find a butcher who knows how to cut meat from the boneless leg.

The better the animal, the better the scallopini; but if the scallopini are not cut across the grain, it won't matter how good the animal was. If the scallopini curl up like shoe leather in the rain when cooked, the butcher did not cut properly.

A veal loin chop must be of the highest quality you can afford. Try to get a chop cut from the rib end; it looks like a rib chop with a thin, 4-inch (10-cm) bone and a large round of meat called the loin eye. The sirloin end of the veal loin produces chops that look like T-bone steaks; while you get a tenderloin piece on one side of the bone, as well as the loin eye, this chop does not cook as evenly. Keep the bone on—it gives added taste. To make the chop a "restaurant cut," take the back of a chef's knife and scrape away the fat and the layer of tougher meat, leaving the bone bare. (This is called Frenching the bone; you can do it to lamb rib chops, as well.)

LAMB

Of all the meat sold in North America, lamb challenges the buyer's expertise most. Should you buy frozen or chilled New Zealand lamb? Do you buy U.S. lamb, and if so, Washington State or mid-west? Should you buy fresh lamb, regardless of where it is raised, fed, bred or finished? And then there's Salt Spring Island lamb from British Columbia—is that the ultimate?

Lamb dramatically changes in flavor according to its age and what it has been fed. The breed largely determines the fat content, and therefore the taste.

If you are not a regular lamb eater, a general guideline is to buy grain fed local fresh spring lamb.

Lamb is what it eats, especially in the two weeks before it is slaughtered. And what it becomes is as much a matter of aroma as taste.

New Zealand and Australian lamb is grazed on grass, supplemented with hay, silage or forage crops; this makes it cheap to produce. Grass, however, produces a strong flavor and a strong aroma in cooking. Lamb must be slaughtered very young to suit the North American market for mild lamb. The rib, loin chops, racks and legs of such young lambs are small.

Some U.S. lamb, especially of the west and northwest, is milk and grain fed, then finished with two weeks of grain. This usually produces a mild-tasting lamb with a pleasant, not overpowering cooking aroma, and producers can allow the sheep to grow larger before slaughtering them. The breeds are larger than New Zealand breeds, too. Chops and legs are generally larger, which can be attractive to a chef.

Saltspring Island, in the Strait of Georgia between Vancouver Island and British Columbia mainland, has a double attraction. The continuous fog rolls in over the pastureland on the island and deposits a seasoning of salt on the grass.

The sheep almost marinate themselves from the inside out as they munch away. (Mustard goes so well with lamb, it is a pity sheep won't eat wild mustard.)

Washington State lamb is milk fed, then grazed on grass much like the salty pastures of Salt Spring Island. Some is shipped before slaughter to be finished elsewhere, often on grain. The result is a mild, wonderfully aromatic lamb that, because of breed and size, has a large rack.

Lamb from New Zealand comes to North America flash frozen or, more recently, "chilled," an almost-but-not-quite-frozen state, about 32°F (0°C). Meat freezes at 28°F (-2°C). Chilling does not allow tissue damage caused by the expansion of water as it freezes into crystals. New Zealand is, however, the world's largest lamb exporter—and they know their business: their freezing is state of the art, and the product first rate.

Fresh lamb does not necessarily mean it was raised near you. In Ontario, for example, any lamb slaughtered in the province is labeled "fresh Ontario lamb," although it was probably grown in central United States. (The Ontario lamb industry is almost extinct.) If you can get a lamb straight from the farm gate, so much the better; you cannot get fresher than that.

A "spring lamb" is defined as a sheep less than a year old. Typically, however, especially around Easter, the sheep is between six and twelve weeks and about 30 lb (13.5 kg), yielding a small (depending upon the breed), tender, mild-flavored and mildly aromatic meat.

Mutton is sheep more than a year old. In some countries, people eat mutton up to five years old.

Like beef, lamb can be aged a week or more, but aging intensifies taste and aroma, which defeats the purpose of buying young lamb. Moreover, spring lamb is very tender, especially the rib eyes and loin chops. And let's get real here: it's hard enough to find a butcher in North America who ages beef, let alone lamb, should your tastes run to gamy.

PORK

Pork production and grading standards are absolutely rigid, so it's easy to get good pork. Once a reputable supplier is found, a chef just orders the appropriate cut and size. Pork does not benefit from aging as beef and chicken do. If it has been fed well, preferably on corn, treated well, that is, without bruising, and processed well, it will be good.

You can judge pork by sight. The best is fresh and uniformly pale pink to pale red in color, but never red. The meat is smooth and has a fine marbling of firm, white fat. The outer skin is thin, white and pliable, free of hair stubble and not wrinkled. Good pork has no sign of blood or discoloration in the meat or skin.

Reject pork with any sign of blood in the meat and skin, which indicates poor processing. Blood in the bone usually indicates a younger pig. A suckling pig is about three weeks old, weighs 10 to 20 lb (4.5 to 9 kg), and has been fed nothing but mother's milk. It is cooked whole—and is incredibly tender and succulent. A fully grown hog is about six months old and weighs in at 200 to 220 lb (90 to 100 kg), from which comes 130 to 140 lb (60 to 63 kg) of meat. In the middle are the pigs, about four months old and about 120 lb (55 kg).

The home restaurateur might try to get chops from a pig rather than from a hog, either at the farm gate or from a reliable butcher.

One word about trichinosis, the parasite that has scared generations into cooking the hell out of pork. The incidence of trichinosis rises sharply in pigs fed uncooked garbage. In modern pork production, however, pigs are not slopping about in pigsties; they are carefully raised in temperature-controlled barns and their health is continually monitored. Your chances of contracting the trichinosis parasite are negligible. Yet few restaurateurs dare to cook pork less than well done. Some brave chefs leave just a blush of pink in otherwise well-done meat, but even that meets with resistance from a public that distrusts pink pork. To satisfy your guests, it would probably be prudent to cook it well done. The trick is not to overcook it, because pork turns into cardboard quite easily.

TENDERLOIN

The tenderloin runs down the hog's back. As it is not flexed much, it is the most tender part of the animal. The tenderloin called for in these recipes is a full boneless tenderloin with the side muscle removed, about 1 lb (450 g). One end tapers to a flap of meat, which should be folded under and tied to make the whole piece of meat of a uniform thickness for uniform cooking.

LOIN CHOPS VERSUS RIB CHOPS

You can buy loin chops that look like squat, pale T-bone steaks, the filet on one side, the loin on the other. But remember, even though they are on the same chop, the filet section cooks faster and is more tender. For this reason, chefs usually opt for rib chops, which have a little more fat (for more natural flavor and tenderness) and cook evenly and predictably.

RIBS

Spare ribs are from the belly of the beast (where side bacon comes from). There are at least eleven ribs in a full rack. Back ribs are from the loin, at the top of the beast, where Canadian back bacon (gammon) comes from. They have eight ribs to a rack. Country-style ribs are back ribs from the blade end of the loin and have three to six large ribs.

Some people swear spare ribs are the tenderest and tastiest; others insist the bigger back ribs, with the meat from the loin, are better. With good pork ribs, the question is not so much where they come from, but whether you want little ones or big ones, and whether the cost is relevant. In the end you are going to alter the taste with dry rubs and barbecue sauces, and if you cook them correctly, all will be fall-off-the-bone tender and tasty. The trick is long and slow, as you will see later.

BACON

As my friend and crêpe cook Peter Armstrong once remarked, bacon is the most deliciously useless meat. It's almost all fat, often too salty, sometimes smoked poorly, but almost always delicious.

To judge packaged side bacon before you purchase it, read the package label. The best bacon is smoked with natural hardwood smoke. (Most, however, is "smoked" chemically, which is cheaper.) Smoked bacon costs more, so price is often an accurate guideline. The trick with side bacon is to cook it slowly.

Canadian bacon, cut from the loin, is dense, with relatively little fat. It should be warmed up rather than cooked to keep it from becoming tough as leather. Don't be afraid: it has already been cured and smoked. All you have to do is raise its temperature about 140°F (60°C), which isn't hard, considering the thin slices most of us buy.

PORK HOCKS

Ugly, aren't they? Scary. But they taste like juicy ham. In this book, pork hock is used to give a fabulous pork dish, the Mexican *pozole*, taste and body with its gelatin. Gelatin is a natural product, one of three animal proteins produced when heat is applied to meat. The whole trick to cooking meat is to use a temperature high enough to break down the tissues to create gelatin, but not high enough or for long enough to make the connective tissues tough and stringy. In the rib recipes in this book, for example, the ribs are started at a very high temperature to ensure all bacteria is killed, and then they are cooked slowly at a lower temperature so the connective tissues do not toughen. Texas prime rib roasts are cooked the same way—500°F (260°C) to start, and then the oven is turned off. Eight hours later, the chefs carve a perfect medium rare roast for the people on the ranch. Escoffier taught chefs this cooking method, and they taught others, who taught others, right down to the culinary schools that are training chefs today. In beef stock, for instance, you get the desirable body in the broth from the gelatin in the beef bones cooked for twelve hours or more (I cook them for twenty-four). You can buy "leaves" of gelatin in any supermarket. Put a leaf in a quarter cup of water to dissolve it, then add it to a dish to firm it up. Few people realize, however, that most commercial gelatin is made from the skin of pork.

The pork hock has it all. It has a gelatinous texture from the skin and a fabulous flavor from the fat. A shrine should be erected to the humble pork hock, right alongside the Temple of the Egg, the Cathedral of Cream and the Basilica of Butter.

LOBSTER AMERICANUS . . . AND MORE

When I was a mild-mannered restaurant critic, I noticed that in every Chinese restaurant I reviewed, my lobster had only one claw. It used to drive me crazy. Who stole the claw? Was I the butt of some joke?

Then I noticed something else: the lobster in Chinese restaurants was priced considerably lower than lobster in any other kind of restaurant.

Years went by. Then the editor of a national hotel and restaurant magazine let me in on the secret. I was so happy I asked him to become my daughter's godfather. He accepted.

Lobsters are not only prehistoric and ugly-looking, they are also vicious, cannibalistic and antisocial beasts. They think nothing of tearing the claw off a fellow lobster that comes too close. (You see? Lobsters deserve to be boiled alive and eaten by higher life forms!) The claws grow back, but much smaller than the originals. Fishermen call these "culls."

Steak and seafood restaurants serve lobster whole, so they buy unmolested ones, as do fishmongers, who display live beasts in glass-sided tanks. The Chinese, however, chop them into pieces with a cleaver and stir-fry them. The Chinese do not need the symmetry of two giant claws, so they buy the culls, which are at least a dollar a pound less than the big-clawed beauties. Moreover, Chinese restaurants are plentiful and cook a hell of a lot of lobsters. Why is this a serious consideration? In a tank in a fish shop, lobsters slowly eat themselves from the inside. No sense trying to feed them anything; they're on strike and won't eat proffered food. Therefore, the quicker they get from the lobster pot to the boiling water, the better. Culls make the trip faster than others, unless you buy directly from the Maine or Maritime Canadian pens.

Atlantic lobsters are caught during two seasons—spring and summer, and November and December. (We eat turkey at Christmas. The French eat lobster, so we send them ours.) In season, the prices usually drop, so this is the time to serve whole boiled lobster with drawn Scotch butter at dinner parties. You can often get culls with decent-sized claws.

At other times of the year, lobster can be bought frozen. Canadian east coast processors are allowed to harvest canners, lobsters that weigh less than a pound. Their meat is canned (cooked) and frozen. In a $16 can, you get the meat of about six or seven canners, so the price is very good. (Only twenty to twenty-five percent of a lobster's weight is meat; the rest is shell.) Canners are terrific for salads and lobster rolls, one of the richest sandwiches ever invented. (For two sandwiches: 2 tbsp (30 mL) minced shallots, 2 tbsp (30 mL) butter, 4 oz (110 g) lobster, ½ tsp (2 mL) cayenne or hot Hungarian paprika, 1 tsp (5 mL) lemon juice, mayonnaise to bind, and salt and pepper to taste. Sauté shallots in butter until soft; warm up lobster in butter; stir in the remaining ingredients and serve on a hot-dog bun.)

Small lobsters, called chicken lobsters, are cooked, frozen in brine and packaged in a plastic pouch. These "Popsicles" can be found in supermarket freezers. The Japanese prefer the chicken lobsters for their looks and consistency of taste. I prefer the frozen canned lobsters for their value.

Those who are squeamish about cooking live lobster can purchase its relatives—scampi, langoustine, lobsterette and spiny lobster—dead and frozen for easy, guilt-free cooking. The exception is the crayfish, a freshwater species that does not travel well. Crayfish are sold live. They are very expensive and rarely found far from where they live, breed and are harvested.

Of course, lobsters are sold by fishmongers, who sell more than just lobsters. They sell fish, which you will want to buy occasionally, too.

It's easy to judge the freshness of fish. Just breathe in; your nose will tell you whether it's fresh. Other signs are equally obvious. The eyes should be clear and sparkling, the gills should be red and fresh-looking, and the flesh should be firm, not spongy and squooshy.

And how do you find a good fishmonger? Walk into a fish store and look for the following signs.
1) Does it smell fishy? If so, leave.
2) Is the store stocked with whole fish? The head, tail and skin should be intact, but the fishmonger should gut the fish for you.
3) Does the fishmonger pick the fish up by the gills? Picking it up any other way risks breaking the spine, which can release blood into the flesh. That can create a bitter flavor.

To prolong freshness, buy the whole gutted fish with the head on. Just the moment before you cook the fish, remove the head and skin. And when skinning, sprinkle your hands with salt first for a better grip. If you are skinning a fish filet, a scaled trout, for instance, pan fry flesh-side-down first, to prevent curling.

Chef Paul Prudhomme, the Cajun wizard of K-Paul's restaurant in New Orleans, and really the voice and heart of Creole and Cajun regional American cooking, has a rule when he is faced with less than fresh fish: don't use herbs. Herbs bring out the fishiness. Use spices on older fish. Spices will mask a pronounced fishy taste. Use herbs only on fresh fish.

Chefs' Tips for Sundry Ingredients

Garlic: To peel a clove of garlic quickly, set it flat and whack it with the side of the knife; then shake off the paperlike skin. This trick works only with fresh garlic: a bulb firm to the hard squeeze and tightly closed. Old garlic is bitter. So is burned garlic. The pungency comes from the membranes between the thin layers within each clove. If you don't break the membranes, you won't get the strong taste and aroma. A whole baked clove is mild, squishy and exotic, not strong or off-putting, and it won't advertise itself on you the next day. A whole, peeled  clove is slightly stronger. Crushing the clove under a knife makes the taste stronger still. Then comes crushing and chopping. Finely chopped garlic gives the fullest garlic hit.

Mushrooms: These fungi offer the human body virtually no nutrients, minerals or vitamins. They are impervious to food evangelists, dieticians and nutritionists. Their only use is to impart flavor. So get rid of those tasteless button mushrooms wrapped in cellophane and find mushrooms with taste. Some, such as morels and chanterelles, will cost you a fortune. Others, such as portobello, shitake or oyster mushrooms, are much less expensive and give dishes an extraordinary depth, which is what they're good at. Before you sauté them, wipe them free of dirt. Don't wash them under water, as they will absorb it. And don't bother peeling them. You've got enough to do.

Parsley: Curly, or English, parsley is that bushy, crisp "head" in supermarket vegetable displays. The second time you look for it, it will be the limp, slimy thing on the bottom of your vegetable crisper. Parsley is tricky. Don't buy it until you need it, and put the stems in a glass of cool salted water on the kitchen counter to keep it crisp.

Added to a fish stock, Bercy sauce or sauce marnier, curly parsley will turn the sauce green. It does the same to butter in parsleyed potatoes, making it unattractive to drizzle over the spuds after cooking. Parsley stalks, however, add the parsley flavor without turning a sauce or butter green. Add the stalks to the dish during cooking, then remove. Just before serving, add the chopped leafy parts.

Flat or Italian parsley is used in all Italian recipes. Chinese parsley, also called coriander or cilantro, is a distinctive, almost licorice-tasting herb used in Tex-Mex, Mexican and Asian, especially Indian, cuisines.

Pepper: Pepper grows on large bushes and is green when ripe. Most pepper berries, however, are picked just before they're ripe. They are dried—the best are sun-dried—until they turn black and crinkly. Peppercorns left on the bush beyond the ripe stage are picked by hand, placed in containers or sacks and washed until bacteria loosen the hulls and the water washes the hulls away. In India, people trample the peppercorns, like the French stomp grapes, to complete the hulling.

Black peppercorns are the most aromatic, but they lose their qualities quickly. You should have a good mill to grind them. (You should also find a reliable spice merchant, because even whole peppercorns deteriorate, especially when stored and handled carelessly.)

White peppercorns are stronger and hotter. They are also harder to find and generally more expensive. They, too, should be freshly ground, so buy a second pepper mill.

Green peppercorns can be purchased pickled or preserved. Those packed in the Far East often carry a taste of garam masala, which is unsuitable for the cream sauces of western cuisines. Green peppercorns are used whole as a garnish. To cook with them, crush them between your fingers for best taste. For the recipes in this book, buy only peppercorns packed in the English, French, German or North American styles.

When a recipe calls for crushed peppercorns, don't use the grinder. Place the peppercorns between layers of plastic film or tea towels and whack them with a mallet or the bottom of a saucepan. Crushed peppercorns have a distinct, rough and raw taste that is crucial for béarnaise sauce and butter.

These days, restaurant waiters come around with huge pepper mills and ask you if you want some pepper ground onto a dish of food you have not yet tasted. I suggest you either shoot the waiter or bring your own grinder to adjust the seasoning—if necessary—*after* you have tasted the dish.

Potatoes: New potatoes are the first, tiny growth of a season, of which there could be several, depending upon where you live. They are identifiable by their thin, flaky skins, which are just forming.

A Burbank russet is a baking potato, produced by a guy named Burbank. It is McDonald's current choice for fries, and should be yours, too, if you can find it. Any russet (all Idaho baking potatoes are russets) will do for a French fry as long as it is fresh and hard.

Zest: The outer skin of an orange, lemon or lime. If it is called for in a marinade, don't worry too much about avoiding the bitter white part (pith). Chefs don't; why should you?

Tomato: Never store a tomato in the refrigerator. Ruins it.

Lettuce: Hubert A. Des Maraise IV, executive chef of the Ocean Grand in Palm Beach, Florida, advises dipping the head of lettuce in ice water, trimming the stem and storing it head side up in the refrigerator to give it a longer life.

Balsamic vinegar: Balsamic vinegar is fabulously aromatic and wonderful-tasting. The best is aged for decades and can become as thick as molasses. (Your wallet has to be as thick to buy it.) Good, cheaper versions are available. In the event you can't get any, Claude Troisgros, owner of C.T. Restaurant in New York City, suggests substituting red wine vinegar mixed with soy sauce.*

Cooking with wine and spirits: When a recipe calls for wine, Scotch or brandy, don't omit it. Use a decent wine—not necessarily an expensive one, but a decent one. You should want to drink it as well as eat it. When cooking with white wine I'm a California jug Chablis guy, and if red is called for, I use a French Beaujolais or a Hungarian Merlot.

Some people who are not wine drinkers balk at buying a bottle to cook with. What doesn't go into the dish isn't drunk, goes off and gets poured down the drain. If you don't want to use wine in a recipe, substitute a dry white French vermouth, even if the recipe calls for a red wine. Vermouth is a fortified wine; it keeps forever, is always reasonably priced and is a terrific cooking wine.

Knives: You are often enticed to buy knives that are guaranteed to last for decades—and they do. They are made of extremely hard steel, which makes them very hard to sharpen. A good chef's knife is made of high-carbon steel, which is softer and easier to sharpen, but doesn't last as long.

Now, you are not going to use your knives as much as a chef does, so they will last a good long time. Like most people, you have or once had a sharpening steel, but gave up—probably because it didn't work on knives made of very hard steel. You stuck the good-looking, useless knives in the drawer. A dull knife is much more dangerous than one with a razor edge. You may nick yourself with a sharp knife, but you could lose a finger with a dull one that you have to lean on to cut with.

A knife seller will tell you a hand-forged knife is better than a stamped one. Well, that's true, but the type of steel is more important. The blade must be strong and unyielding; if you can bend it, it's dangerous. Balance is important, too. A knife should feel comfortable in the hand. Some hand-forged knives are too heavy to be comfortable.

The blade should extend well into the handle. Hardwood handles are pretty, but opt for a heavy-duty plastic one, because it can go in the dishwasher. I will

Nation's Restaurant News, May 23, 1994, page 31.

insist that you never put a knife in a dishwasher, but you are going to do it anyway, because you are in the habit of doing it. A chef is always washing, washing, washing: a knife used to cut something is immediately washed off with a hot soapy water so it can be used again the instant it is needed. Everything—pots, pans, plates—gets the same treatment. It is called *mise en place*, putting or keeping everything in its place. The mark of a professional kitchen is its cleanliness and orderliness. If you are clean and tidy, you can avoid accidents and ensure speedy, precise creation of a dish.

Ramekins: These small ovenproof ceramic or glass dishes are perfect for lobster Scotch butter, crème brûlée, and barbecue dipping sauce. But you will find yourself using them for everything from storing bits of leftover sauces and the kids' canned pasta to warming butter in the microwave. Our cat insists on one for the fish scraps and scallops that Donna from the fish market sends home for him.

Ovenproof soup bowls: Essential for French onion soup, boeuf bourguignon en croûte, Stilton soup—and any other soup. We also use them for leftovers when ramekins are too small.

Candy thermometer: While not absolutely necessary, it will serve you well for pub style fish and chips and real French frites. Besides, it's not expensive.

Pots and pans: Paul Prudhomme of K-Paul's Louisiana Kitchen in New Orleans has probably the best advice on what to buy: "Buy what you can afford."

No matter what you have, you will adapt to it, he says. If your pan hasn't a flat bottom and has hot and cold spots, you'll learn to flip the food around without even thinking about it. He's right. We all start out with aluminum camp fire cookware, and we survive.

The pots and pans in most restaurant kitchens are battered, stained and bottom-burned. Because they take such a beating, the typical pan is heavy-gauge aluminum that can be used on a gas stove, in the salamander (a gas-fired broiler of intense heat) or in the oven. Aluminum is not a great conductor of heat, of course; but as Prudhomme says, the cooks adapt. Try to buy pans with the thickest bottoms you can find.

One step up is stainless steel, again with thick bottoms and with handles that can take any amount of heat. Stainless steel with commercial-strength Teflon surfaces are better still, but more expensive. Heavy-duty copper pots with stainless-steel insides are possibly as posh as you want to go. (I have one small copper pot. I bought it at a garage sale for six dollars because the seller didn't know what she had.)

In cookware, you really do get what you pay for, with the possible exception of "designer cookware," those pots and pans with a catchy name manufactured by a clothes manufacturer, which you should ignore.

The good old cast-iron fry pan is a treasure. Food writers will advise you against cooking cream sauce in one because the pan colors the sauce. They also mutter that cast iron does something horrid to lemon juice. It's probably true—if you use your cast-iron pan only occasionally. A well-seasoned cast-iron pan in constant use does no harm at all unless you drop it on your foot. To season a cast-iron pan, wash it, dry it thoroughly, coat it all over with peanut oil and place it in a 350°F (175°C) oven for two hours. From then on, just wipe it clean after use. Never use detergent on it. If you do, season it again, as above.

Food for the eyes—the chef's art: Whenever you think about how many chops, how many vegetables, how many beets, how many baby potatoes to put on a plate, think odd numbers, principally one, three and five. Human beings instinctively prefer them.

The plate is a chef's canvas, upon which you create a picture with food. This is certainly true of the chefs who compete at the Culinary Olympics. It can take days for a team of chefs to place perfectly sculpted, carved and glazed food on plates—for judging, not eating. Eye appeal is also important for a restaurant—they want you to come back and a "memorable" display might convince you.

In restaurants, "plating" almost always begins as trial and error. The chef then draws a picture or takes a photo of the composition he or she wants and posts it on the bulletin board for the sous chefs. At that point, the creativity stops. As a home restaurateur, you will not have the luxury of replating a meal until it is pleasing to the eye (the dishes will get dirty and the food will get cold). The best you can do is visualize: try to see what the meal should look like, and arrange every plate in exactly the same way. You will make your life easier if you choose your menu with an eye to a simple, easy plate arrangement. Those small frenched rib lamb chops, for instance, are easier to arrange than sliced leg of lamb.

Whether you overload a plate with food is a matter of which restaurant you are bringing home. The measure of all good steakhouses, whether it's Morton's in Chicago, Sparks Steak House in Manhattan or Barberian's in Toronto, is massive amounts of sizzling meat, huge potatoes, monstrous shrimp. In a Greek *ouzeri*, on the other hand, the dishes are nibbles.

Wherever possible, the plate should incorporate contrasting colors, shapes and textures to please the eye. Three colors are better than four. Think odd!

The atmosphere: When you are creating an atmosphere for your home restaurant guests, the sincerest form of flattery is imitation. If your favorite trattoria has red-checked tablecloths, find some red-checked tablecloths. If it has a display of pasta and wine at the entrance to the restaurant, set up a display at the table. Look around. Copy. Like the plates? If you really want to, go out and buy 'em in a restaurant supply store. Many restaurant plates are made by the fine china firms represented in the best china "shoppes," in the same beautiful patterns. But the institutional versions are thicker and heavier, to withstand rigorous handling. If you are in the market for fine china, check out the commercial restaurant versions. They last longer, and few people will spot the difference.

A powerful atmosphere is created by the sense of smell. Tony Marciano, who owns Buonasera in Oakville and in Burlington, has been known to take a small fry pan, sauté some garlic and surreptitiously walk around the dining room with it. People perk up without realizing why. Other restaurateurs put hot bread in front of a fan blowing into the dining room or sear a piece of beef fat and waft it out to the street to entice people in. I visited a friend who lived in an apartment building six or seven stories above a French restaurant called Le Provençal. The delicious garlic aroma coming in the windows had me believing it was my favorite restaurant, although I had eaten there only once.

The best atmosphere, however, is created by generosity. Be at ease, be "at service." Give your guests your best. It always works.

Chapter Three

The Basics

It doesn't matter what country's cuisine you are cooking. All cuisines use stock. With stock in the freezer, along with some compound and simple butters, you can make a meal worthy of any great restaurant at the drop of a hat.

If making your own stock seems too difficult and time-consuming, you can count yourself in the company of most restaurants—the bad ones, the ones that fuel the four-out-of-five restaurant failure rate. These restaurants use powdered stock bases, usually not even good-quality powdered stock bases. I once was hired by a restaurant to save it from bankruptcy. The place had a lot of problems, not the least being the owner's reluctance to pay for staff salaries or food. I didn't need to be much of a detective in the kitchen. To begin with, the "beef stock" base didn't have a hint of beef in it; it was entirely artificial. Yet the owner was particularly proud of the pub's steak-and-kidney pie and its shepherd's pie. Obviously the owner's tastebuds, and those of his few remaining customers, had been removed without their knowledge by some evil surgeon.

The company that made the inferior stock base, however, is thriving, which means it is polluting a lot of restaurants.

Not all stock bases are bad. The best companies make their product with meat and real vegetables, just as a chef would, except in huge quantities and with a measure of beef parts you wouldn't think could become stock. The bases are very expensive, very concentrated and difficult to use in small quantities, which is why they aren't sold at the retail level.

The bottom line is this: you have to make your own stock, especially beef stock, if you want great restaurant quality and taste in your home restaurant. All great restaurants make their own stocks. It is necessary. Period. End of subject.

One cube of *demi-glace* (about 1 tbsp, or 15 mL, of reduced, concentrated beef stock frozen in an ice-cube tray) makes an instant, authentic sauce for two. Melt it with some whipping cream, squeeze some green peppercorns into it, add some salt and pepper, and you have a steak sauce worthy of Maxim's. Melt a cube and paint it on a steak, and you give the meat a blast of richness. Paint a hamburger, and you make it taste like sirloin steak on a bun. French onion soup gratinée is nothing and beef bourguignon is a pallid stew without it.

Stocks are not difficult. You can make a large quantity, reduce it, freeze it in ice-cube trays and plop the cubes in freezer bags for use anytime.

The most important stock is beef stock, also known as brown stock or *estouffade*. It takes the longest time to make, but it is the secret ingredient of great food.

Beef Stock

PREPARATION TIME:
60 MINUTES
COOKING TIME:
10 TO 11 HOURS

Some very good chefs make brown stock in four hours, because by then most of the flavor has been imparted to the water. Escoffier insisted upon at least twelve, to allow the gelatin to seep in. "If you like the gelatin," a chef once said, "just throw a packet of gelatin in it." I tried it. Great trick, but Escoffier turned in his grave. A good brown stock with natural gelatin is a thing of beauty.

A firm rule: never, ever use salt. If you do, the stock will be inedible once you've reduced it, that is, boiled it down.

6 lb	beef bones (with marrow if possible, and as meaty as possible)	2.75 kg
6	carrots, cleaned and roughly chopped	6
2	large onions, peeled and roughly chopped	2
2 tbsp	butter	30 mL
1 lb	stewing beef	450 g
2	stalks celery, cleaned	2
2 lb	veal shank*	900 g
¼ lb	ham	110 g
2	strips bacon	2
¼ cup	parsley	60 mL
4	sprigs thyme	4
4	small bay leaves	4

Preheat oven to 375°F (190°C).

Trim any meat from bones and set aside. Put bones, carrots and onions in a roasting pan and roast in oven until the bones and vegetables are brown, between 45 and 60 minutes.

In a large stock pot, melt butter over medium-high heat and brown stewing beef. Add browned bones, vegetables, trimmed meat and all the other ingredients to the pot, cover with cold water and bring to a boil. Skim off the scum that rises to the surface (it's albumen and will make the stock bitter if you don't remove it). Lower the heat, put a lid half on and simmer stock for 12 to 24 hours, skimming when necessary.

*Or 8 lbs (4 kg) beef bones alone, but the veal shank adds gelatin to the stock.

Strain stock; discard bones and vegetables. Pour stock into a clean pot and reduce to one-third its volume, or until the stock coats the back of cool spoon. Cool, pour into ice-cube trays and freeze. Each cube will make about 1 cup (250 mL) of good strong stock. Your cooking will never be the same again.

Chicken Stock

Chicken stock is a snap. Any time you have a roast chicken or duck or turkey, instead of depositing the bones in the garbage, deposit them in a soup pot with vegetables, pour on cold water until it covers and bring to a boil. Turn down the heat and let it simmer for at least 3 hours, or better still, overnight, and you will always have a supply in the freezer.

If you are making chicken stock from scratch, brown the carrots and onions to give the stock a deeper color. If you are working from a cooked carcass, you don't need to brown the vegetables. And don't throw out that carcass from the take-out barbecue chicken; the bones make a fabulous-tasting stock.

Leftover Chicken Stock

1	cooked chicken carcass (you can also use duck or turkey)	1	
1	large carrot	1	
1	medium onion studded with 2 cloves	1	
1	stalk celery	1	
2	bay leaves	2	
	Sprig of thyme (optional)		
8	whole black peppercorns	8	

PREPARATION TIME:
5 MINUTES
COOKING TIME:
3 HOURS

Put all the ingredients in a stock pot. Pour in enough cold water to cover everything. Bring to a boil. Skim the scum that rises to the top. (The "scum" is albumen, which will make the stock cloudy and bitter.) Lower heat, cover and simmer for 3 hours or overnight. Strain the liquid and taste. If it's bland, concentrate the taste by reducing the stock. (You can never reduce a stock down too far, because all you are doing is removing water. The flavors remain and become concentrated as the volume is reduced. If you boil away all the water, you'll wind up with a mass like a stock cube.) Pour into containers and freeze. Keeps a lot longer than you'll need it to.

Chicken Stock from Scratch

Same as above, except: roughly chop the onion and carrot and brown over medium-low heat in 1 tbsp (15 mL) butter. Add the cleaned, uncooked chicken, and, if you can get them, 2 thoroughly cleaned chicken feet (available in kosher butchers), which will give the stock gelatin. Then follow instructions for Leftover Chicken Stock. This recipe is also good for duck or turkey.

Lamb Stock

This is an uncommon stock, but if you roast a leg of lamb, find inexpensive lamb cuts on special or buy a whole freezer lamb, make a stock and freeze it. It makes all the difference in a shepherd's pie or moussaka.

Proceed as with the beef stock, above, substituting uncooked lamb and lamb bones for beef and veal. If you're working with a leftover leg of lamb, you do not need to brown the bone. Bring to a boil and cook only for 4 hours; you are not going to get any gelatin from the lamb bones.

Cooked Butters

I studied Latin for four long years and can remember only one thing: *Ubi dubi taurus, semper flugitit*, which roughly translates as, "When in doubt, always whip it out." Catullus, the poet, was speaking of serviettes. My regret is that I don't know the Latin for "Butter is fat. Fat is good." I would have made it my motto.

Always buy unsalted butter. It is fresher. If you can, buy cultured unsalted butter.

Salt is a preservative. Salted butter has a supermarket shelf life. This is good for the supermarket, not for the butter. Unsalted butter is not preserved by salt. It has to be made with the freshest cream to be fresh when you buy it. Fresher is better.

Cultured butter has just a touch of natural taste, much like the butter in Paris. It is a matter of how it is manufactured. Nothing better on a croissant left outside your garret door at six in the morning by Chantal, who wears that tight clingy uniform and can't speak a word of English... but I digress. Ah, yes.

I have nothing against salt. In fact, I love salt. This is entirely my mother's fault. But trust me. Salting unsalted butter to taste is much better than letting the processor do it for you.

Béarnaise Butter

This is a compound butter. Other herb butters are simple, that is, just butter whipped with herbs. Think of béarnaise butter as cooked butter, a béarnaise sauce without the egg yolks and the attendant danger of curdling. If you've always loved béarnaise but are hesitant to make it, use this. Egg yolks make Béarnaise sauce silky, so it coats a dish without breaking down. Béarnaise butter will slide off hot steak as fast as a political bagman bellies up to the trough. Béarnaise butter works best underneath a steak or an egg (on the toast, for instance); béarnaise sauce is best on top. The tastes are almost identical.

1 tbsp	butter	15 mL
3 tbsp	minced shallot	45 mL
	(or finely minced spring onion)	
½ cup	white wine	125 mL
½ cup	white wine vinegar	125 mL
30	black peppercorns, crushed	30
¼ cup	dried tarragon leaves	60 mL
1 lb	unsalted butter	450 g
	Salt to taste	

Melt the 1 tbsp (15 mL) butter in a saucepan over medium-low heat and cook shallot until it is soft. Don't let it brown; it will change the color of the sauce. Add wine, wine vinegar, crushed peppercorns and tarragon; bring to a boil. Reduce at a rapid simmer until only 2 tbsp (30 mL) remain. Whisk in butter in small pieces until completely incorporated. Taste and adjust salt. The butter will keep for 6 months in the freezer, 1 month in the refrigerator.

1) Pour into ice-cube trays, refrigerate until set, transfer to freezer bags and freeze. One cube is good for 2 steaks or breakfasts, unless you are a real glutton.
2) Cool butter in refrigerator until solid but malleable. In plastic wrap, roll butter into 2 or 3 logs. Freeze, then cut off rounds for grilled meats or vegetables as required.

Béarnaise Sauce

Think of it as béarnaise butter with egg yolks. As simple as that.

1 tbsp	butter	15 mL
3 tbsp	minced shallot (or finely minced spring onion)	45 mL
½ cup	white wine	125 mL
½ cup	white wine vinegar	125 mL
30	black peppercorns, crushed	30
¼ cup	dried tarragon leaves	60 mL
1 lb	unsalted butter	450 g
2	egg yolks	2
	Salt to taste	

Melt the 1 tbsp (15 mL) butter in a saucepan and sweat the minced shallot until it is soft. Don't let it brown; it will darken the sauce. Add wine, wine vinegar, crushed peppercorns and tarragon; bring to a boil. Reduce at a rapid simmer until only 2 tbsp (30 mL) remain. Remove from heat; let cool to body temperature. Put pot over a double boiler or on a burner over very low heat. Whisk in 2 tbsp (30 mL) butter, then the yolks; whisk until yolks are incorporated. Whisk in the remaining butter, a spoonful at a time, making sure it is incorporated and heated slightly before adding the next spoonful. Adjust for salt. Remember: don't heat the sauce too much or it will curdle.

Dutch (or Lemon) Butter

Same as Béarnaise Butter, but forget the black peppercorns, vinegar and tarragon. Instead, add 2 tsp (10 mL) cayenne pepper. Whip in the butter and then slowly whip in 3 tbsp (45 mL) lemon juice and 1 tsp (5 mL) salt. Great on grilled fish, almost all vegetables and rice. See also page 67 for Hollandaise Sauce recipe.

Shallot Butter

Reduce amount of vinegar in Béarnaise Butter recipe to 3 tbsp (45 mL), sweat 6 tbsp (90 mL) minced shallots in 3 tbsp (45 mL) butter, and omit tarragon. Drop a pat of this on a baked potato or just about any other vegetable.

Sage Butter

Reduce amount of vinegar in Béarnaise Butter recipe to 3 tbsp (45 mL), omit tarragon and add finely chopped fresh sage leaves. Grill a chicken breast and top with this.

Marchand de Vin Butter

¼ cup	red wine	60 mL
1 tbsp	minced shallots	15 mL
1 tbsp	*demi-glace* (beef stock reduced to a thick glaze)	15 mL
10	black peppercorns, crushed	10
¼ cup	butter	60 mL
1 tbsp	minced parsley	15 mL

In a pot over medium-high heat combine wine, shallots, beef glaze and peppercorns. Reduce to 1 tbsp (15 mL). Remove from heat. Cream in butter, then parsley.

Beurre Bercy

Substitute dry French white vermouth for red wine in recipe for marchand de vin butter.

Brown Butter (or Black Butter)

You can't have true sole à la meunière, amandine, skate wing meunière or French vegetables without this.

In a classic sole à la meunière, for instance, a filet of sole is dredged in flour, then quickly fried in very hot clarified butter (recipe below) until brown and crispy on both sides. Deep-fried parsley straight from the oil is spread on top, and brown butter with lemon is poured over to make the parsley crackle as it's served. Simple—and unbelievably fabulous.

For sole almandine, spread butter-toasted almonds over the sole and brown butter over all.

Brown butter with balsamic vinegar gives an incredible whack of taste to steamed broccoli, cauliflower or any green vegetable.

Brown butter with lemon (traditional) or with balsamic vinegar and with capers is poured over skate wing to make the classic bistro dish skate wing meunière.

In fact, with very little effort, you can jazz up any meal with brown butter, the simplest expression of a caring kitchen. It's very simple, just cooked butter with an acidic and herb accompaniment.

Brown Butter for Vegetables

½ lb	unsalted butter	225 g
¼ cup	lemon juice (or balsamic vinegar or wine vinegar)	60 mL
	Salt to taste	

PREPARATION TIME:
1 MINUTE
COOKING TIME:
20 MINUTES

In a small pot over medium-low heat, melt butter and cook until it turns dark brown and has a distinctive nutty aroma. Take it off the heat—you want nutty, not burned butter. Add lemon juice and salt to taste.

Brown Butter for Skate Wing

2 tbsp	unsalted butter	30 mL
1 tbsp	lemon juice	15 mL
1 tbsp	capers	15 mL
2 tbsp	chopped parsley	30 mL

PREPARATION TIME:
1 MINUTE
COOKING TIME:
1 MINUTE
MAKES: SAUCE FOR
1 SKATE WING

Begin 1 minute before skate is done. In a small pot or fry pan over medium-high heat, melt butter and cook, stirring with a wooden spoon now and then, until it is deep brown. Add lemon juice and capers. Keep hot. Just before serving, throw in parsley, then pour over skate.

You can make a black butter for almost any dish that is fried in butter. Just add 2 tbsp (30 mL) fresh butter to the pan after the dish is cooked, let it brown up, add lemon juice or balsamic vinegar or another acid, then add parsley. I wouldn't advise capers on anything other than skate wing.

Clarified Butter

This is really oil, and it can be heated without burning to a higher temperature than regular cooking oils.

1 lb	butter	450 g

In a small pot over low heat, melt butter, then let stand. In about 1 hour, the milk solids will have fallen to the bottom and risen to the top, leaving a clear oil in between. With a spoon, delicately scoop off the top solids and reserve. Carefully pour off the clear oil into another container. Keep the bottom solids, too. In small quantities, milk solids are fabulous on vegetables.

If you let the milk solids turn slightly golden, they impart a slight flavor to the oil and you have Indian *ghee*, which is used in cooking and as the fire killer in Indian cuisine.

Maître d'hôtel Butter

This is one of the classic French butters that chefs have been using for generations to "gourmet up" a grilled steak and vegetables without fuss.

1 cup	unsalted butter	250 mL
3 tbsp	lemon juice	45 mL
¼ cup	finely minced fresh parsley	60 mL
1 tsp	salt	5 mL
1 tsp	freshly ground pepper	5 mL

Cream butter. (Put it in a large bowl; cut, chop and smash it with a fork; then whip the living daylights out of it until it is uniformly soft and pliable.) Add lemon juice a few drops at a time; whip in. Then beat in parsley, salt and pepper. Taste. Adjust salt and pepper to taste. Store in refrigerator for up to a month.

All other simple herb butters

When in season, substitute fresh basil (for pastas, potatoes and white rice), tarragon (for chicken, small birds such as squab and steaks) or chives (for potatoes, cauliflower, rice, peas and beans) for the parsley in maître d'hôtel butter.

CHAPTER FOUR

The Bistro

Bistro Chez Toi

APPETIZERS

Pâté Bonesie 49

Deep Fried Brie 50

Baked Brie in Phyllo with
Cumberland Sauce 51

Escargots Bourguignons,
North American Version 53

Escargots Bourguignons,
French Version 54

Escargots in Blue Cheese
Cream Sauce 55

SOUPS AND SALADS

Vichyssoise 56

Real French Onion Soup 57

Soupe au Pistou 58

Duck Soup with Omelettes 74

Warm Brie Salad with Lardons 59

Bistro Vinaigrette 60

FIRST COURSES

A.J. Liebling Trout 60
Trout poached gently in vinaigrette

Frogs' Legs Niçoise 61
Stew of tomatoes, tarragon,
garlic and demi-glace

Frogs' Legs Meunière 62
Dusted with flour, fried
golden in butter

ENTRÉES

Boeuf à la Bourguignon 62
The classic, served en croûte

Rack of Lamb 66
With three purées and French peas

Magret of Duck 72
With frites and asparagus with
Maltese sauce

Confit of Duck 72
With orange beet purée and
perfect frites

Duck à l'orange 76
With mint spinach purée and
broccoli frizonnes

FRUITS DE MER

Salmon Medici 79
Lightly breaded and butter-fried
salmon filets on béarnaise sauce with
sautéed cherry tomatoes

Poached Salmon Marcel Prévost 80
Poached salmon on a bed of creamed
spinach, garnished with steamed
mussels and white wine sauce

Skate with Black Butter 82
Poached in court bouillon, garnished
with sautéed capers, drizzled with
black butter over parsley

Skate Meunière 84
Poached in court bouillon
and then floured and pan-fried in
butter and topped with fried
parsley and black butter

French cuisine, as a style of restaurant cooking, a symbol of cooking superiority in the Western world, was all but killed by the North American interpretation of *nouvelle cuisine* in the 1970s and '80s.

Nouvelle cuisine, coined by the French restaurant critics Christian Millau and Henri Gault, began as an honest escape from the rigidity of nineteenth-century French cooking doctrine. It wound up in North America as diet food—tiny portions of weird ingredients sculpted and placed on oversize plates garnished with kiwifruit by snooty restaurateurs who, for the most part, possessed no philosophical foundation other than ignorance, incompetence and greed.

French cuisine's evolution is artfully detailed by Rudolph Chelminski in his book *The French at Table* (Morrow, 1985), one of the best ever written on the subject. With apologies to Chelminski, here's what happened.

In 1924, Fernand Point opened La Pyramide in Vienne, a town twenty miles south of Lyons, France. At the time, the great restaurants were in the hotels of Paris and London, and the chefs were the unquestioning disciples of Georges Auguste Escoffier (1847–1935), who had laid down the rules of French cuisine in *Le Guide Culinaire* and *La Cuisine Moderne*. No one questioned them, not even Point. But Point and his friends (notably André Pic of restaurant Pic in Le Pin and Alexandre Dumaine of Le Côte d'Or in Saulie) did not have the resources of the great hotel kitchens or the staff to slavishly follow Escoffier's elaborate recipe accompaniments. They had no choice; they simplified the dishes. They substituted fresh local ingredients that seemed to fit the style. They "lightened up" their menus by offering only one or two main dishes a day, instead of dozens. This was radical.

They broke the rules and were rewarded by the highest form of recognition, the coveted "stars" of the *Guide Michelin*. This gave them a legitimacy not previously bestowed upon chefs outside Paris. Local peasant ingredients cooked perfectly in a bistro atmosphere became accepted, even lauded. It was the beginning.

Fernand Point's contribution to *nouvelle cuisine*, however, went way beyond that. Point, you see, was responsible for training Paul Bocuse, Alain Chapel, Pierre and Jean Troisgros and Jean Banchet, among many others. They, in turn, tweaked Escoffier and Point a little bit more in their own establishments. The result was a far less complicated but no less delicious tribute to the traditional French trinity of butter, cream and eggs.

It was Bocuse and the Troisgros brothers whom the critics Gault and Millau "discovered" and marketed under the banner *nouvelle cuisine*. It was Bocuse and the Troisgros brothers who put the cooking style on the map, promoting in the media the talents of others practising their art. One of the chefs they touted loudest was the brilliant Roger Vergé, who invented "diet food" after he inherited a health spa in the Pyrenees. Vergé's *cuisine minceur* was not *nouvelle cuisine*. It was fat-farm food that tasted great only because Vergé is a certifiable genius. Indeed, *cuisine minceur* is so complicated and ingredient-specific, only Vergé could cook it well. But food writers and critics confused *minceur* and *nouvelle*; and what came to North America in the '70s and '80s was this confusion of basic styles that no one could cook well. All they could do was imitate the hype and charge a fortune.

The public's reaction was to shun all French restaurants, regardless of their culinary stripe, because "French" seemed to mean expensive, pretentious food of little value. (It is still considered a higher-than-average financial risk to openly label a new establishment French.)

But French cuisine will never die completely. It can't. It is the root of all Western cooking because it has been codified and is still taught everywhere.

A bistro today is the middle ground between the Michelin-starred restaurant (although there are rated bistros in France), where lunch is $150 a person, and the brasserie, where the beer is on tap and the croque monsieurs are made by the vendor outside the door on rue St-Séverin, where Sorbonne students gather to riot and watch the Rat Man dangle his fat rodent in tourists' faces.

A brasserie is beer; a bistro is local wines. One mark of a good bistro is its wine cellar; another is its honest food—simple food with twists to reflect the times but with a solid foundation in history. Good bistros know there is nothing wrong with pâté, onion soup and boeuf bourguignon unless they are cooked by scoundrels who pray at the altar of the bottom line rather than serve their customers.

Most of these bistro recipes will be familiar to you. They are all based upon clear classic foundations, tweaked by the innovations of fine chefs who have found ways of improving but not reinventing them.

Most of all, they are proven winners, as long as they are made without cheating on ingredients.

Pâté Bonesie

Starting off a meal with a pot of pâté introduces strong flavors, good bread, a sense of informality and high hopes for what's coming next.

    The thing about bistro pâté is you don't want to know how many calories are in it. Winston's in Toronto produced a pâté that joined chicken livers and butter in an equal marriage. Fabulous. Jack and Charlie's "21" in New York made its *pâté maison* with massive quantities of rendered chicken fat bolstered by vast amounts of heavy cream, cognac and sherry. Everyone loved it. But of them all, I like my wife's the best. Bonesie's pâté is far superior to anything I have ever made.

PREPARATION TIME:
30 MINUTES
COOKING TIME:
2 HOURS
SERVES: 20

4 tbsp	olive oil	60 mL
1	medium onion	1
1	medium shallot	1
6	rashers bacon	6
5	cloves garlic, finely chopped	5
¼ tsp	salt	1 mL
5	grinds fresh pepper	5
1 tsp	dry chervil	5 mL
½ tsp	coriander powder	2 mL
1 tbsp	finely chopped fresh parsley	15 mL
1 tbsp	finely chopped fresh oregano	15 mL
4	fresh sage leaves, finely chopped	4
1¼ lb	chicken livers, cleaned of membranes	570 g
¾ cup	all-purpose flour	180 mL
2	eggs	2
¼ cup	cream	60 mL
½ cup	softened unsalted butter	125 mL
2 tbsp	crushed black peppercorns	30 mL

In a frying pan, heat 1 tbsp (15 mL) olive oil; sauté the onion, shallot and 3 bacon rashers, chopped, for 10 minutes over medium-low heat till onions are limp and translucent but not browned. Add garlic, salt and pepper and herbs and sauté for 5 to 7 minutes, or until the herbs have been absorbed into the mixture. Remove from pan and set aside.

    Add the remaining olive oil to the frying pan and increase heat to medium high. Coat the chicken livers in flour and place them in the frying pan. Brown the livers without burning them, about 3 to 4 minutes on each side, or until the edges appear beige and the livers start to bleed. Remove livers from pan and let cool.

Combine eggs, cream and butter and beat with a wire whisk or electric mixer until well blended.

Heat oven to 350°F (175°C).

Place onion mixture, liver and egg mixture in a food processor and pulse until mixture has a smooth and even texture.

Into an oiled pâté baking dish, sprinkle 1 tbsp (15 mL) peppercorns. (The more finely crushed they are the more peppery the taste.) Pour the liver mixture into the dish. Sprinkle with remaining peppercorns, then cover with remaining bacon rashers.

Cover baking dish and place it in a pan filled with hot water halfway up the pâté dish.

Bake for 1½ hours. Remove from oven and allow to cool. Serve with crusty French bread and butter or your favorite crackers.

Deep Fried Brie

PREPARATION TIME:	12	triangles of Brie or Camembert, about 1 oz (30 g) each	12
1 HOUR			
COOKING TIME:	2	eggs, beaten	2
15 MINUTES		Flour	
SERVES: 4		Fine bread crumbs	
		Vegetable oil for frying, at least 2 inches (5 cm) deep	
	1	bunch parsley, washed and patted dry, stems removed	1

Thirty minutes to 1 hour before serving, coat each Brie triangle in egg, roll in flour, roll again in the egg, then coat completely with fine bread crumbs. (This breading is called *à l'anglaise* in classic French parlance.) Place in the freezer or coldest part of your refrigerator.

Just before serving, heat oil to 375°F (190°C) and heat oven to 150°F (65°C). Straight from the refrigerator or freezer, drop 3 triangles into hot oil and fry until golden. Remove to oven to keep warm. Repeat until all triangles are done. Bring the oil to at least 375°F (190°C). Just before serving, drop all the parsley into the oil for 10 seconds, or until it is so crisp it crumbles to the touch. Put 3 triangles of cheese onto each plate, divide the parsley among the plates, on and around Brie, and serve.

Baked Brie in Phyllo with Cumberland Sauce

Michel Richard, of the L.A. restaurant Citrus, wraps Brie in phyllo pastry and bakes it. Phyllo pastry is a very thin, very delicate strudel pastry used mostly in the Middle East, particularly with Greek appetizers and desserts. You could make it. Don't. Most chefs don't, so why should you? Buy it in the frozen pastry section of your supermarket and follow the instructions on the box.

PREPARATION TIME:
5 MINUTES
COOKING TIME:
15 MINUTES
SERVES: 4

12	triangles of Brie, placed in freezer 1 hour before cooking	12
¼ cup	melted butter	60 mL
48	sheets phyllo pastry, cut to 3 inches (7.5 cm) wide	48
1	egg, beaten Cumberland sauce (recipe follows)	1

Remove Brie from freezer. Working quickly on a flat surface, butter 1 sheet of phyllo, lay a second on top, butter it, add the third, butter it, top with the fourth, butter it. Place 1 triangle of cheese in the bottom right corner of the pastry, about ½ inch (1 cm) up from the base and ½ inch (1 cm) from the right border. Fold it up like a flag: take the bottom right corner and bring it over to the left side of the sheet, take bottom left corner and fold it straight up. Continue folding it over to form a triangle package. Seal the edges and overlapping sheet with the beaten egg. Repeat for each remaining piece of Brie, keeping the unused phyllo pastry moist by covering with a damp tea towel. Place triangles on a baking sheet and bake at 375°F (190°C) for 15 to 20 minutes, or until the phyllo is puffed and golden.

Cumberland Sauce

Most bistros will give you warmed-up cranberry sauce and call it Cumberland, because half the chefs don't know the difference and the other half can't be bothered. All of them know that most of us don't know the difference. This ticks me off. Make this sauce, which is close to Escoffier's version. Thereafter judge all bistros by their Cumberland sauce.

¼ cup	red currant jelly	60 mL
1 tsp	finely minced shallot	5 mL
1 tsp	fine orange zest	5 mL
1 tsp	fine lemon zest	5 mL
3 oz	port wine	90 mL
	Juice of 1 orange	
	Juice of ½ lemon	
1 tsp	dry mustard	5 mL
2 tsp	grated fresh ginger root	10 mL
¼ tsp	cayenne pepper	1 mL

In saucepan over medium-low heat, melt jelly. Stir in remaining ingredients. Cool. Serve at room temperature.

Escargots
(snails by any other name)

They are not "disgusting dirty little creatures," as a woman in a restaurant once described them. She was, undoubtedly, a barbarian. The snail, in fact, is one of the cleanest creatures to live in a shell, feasting on young, tender greens during the spring, summer and fall, and hibernating underground during the winter. When they are collected, the best ones are fed lettuce to really plump them up before they are shipped live or prepared and canned.

Buy the best you can in a can. The most expensive are usually the largest snails, and that's what you want. What, in a can? This advice from the man who has been raving about buying the best and freshest? Trust me. In Europe they can get an apprentice to soak the snails for two hours in vinegar and water, blanch them, remove the little eraser tips, cook them for between three and six more hours with vegetables and herbs splashed with wine, wash the shells in bicarb, then make the butter or sauce and stuff everything back into the shells to heat up again in the oven. That is Europe. This is North America. Buy them in a can. (Don't bother with the extraordinarily expensive ones packed in "champagne."

It's a gimmick.) Wash them thoroughly. For flavor, cover them with cold water, to which you've added a tablespoon of good wine vinegar and a teaspoon of salt, and let them soak for an hour. Buy cleaned shells at a cooking store. Save time, save effort. It's the sauce or butter you're really after, anyway.

Escargots Bourguignons, North American Version

This is the way snails were served when French cuisine was exotic, and Cadillacs had huge fins.

PREPARATION TIME:
90 MINUTES
COOKING TIME:
10 MINUTES
SERVES: 4

¼ cup	butter	60 mL
2	cloves garlic, minced	2
2 tbsp	finely chopped parsley	30 mL
1 tbsp	lemon juice	15 mL
	Pinch cayenne pepper	
	Salt to taste	
24	large snails	24
1 tbsp	white wine vinegar	15 mL
1 tsp	salt	5 mL
24	snail shells	24
24	plugs of fresh French bread, just large enough to be jammed into a snail shell	24

Combine butter, garlic, parsley, lemon juice, cayenne and salt in a saucepan and cook over medium-low heat for 5 minutes. Adjust lemon and salt to taste. Remove from heat and let mixture solidify as you rinse canned snails under running water for 5 minutes. Cover snails with cold water, vinegar and salt; let soak for 1 hour. Remove and pat dry. Place ½ tsp (2 mL) of butter mixture in the bottom of each shell, followed by a snail, more butter, a plug of bread and another smear of the butter mixture. Place shells in an escargot dish, or on a bed of kosher salt, rock salt or sea salt to keep them upright and stable, and bake at 400°F (200°C) for 10 minutes. Serve with French bread to mop up the buttery overflow.

Escargots Bourguignons, French Version

This is the way escargots bourguignons began, not surprisingly accompanied by a good bottle of Burgundy wine.

2	shallots, finely minced	2
1	sprig fresh parsley, or 1 tsp (5 mL) dry	1
1	sprig fresh thyme, or 1 tsp (5 mL) dry	1
1	bay leaf	1
2 tbsp	finely minced mushrooms	30 mL
1 cup	red Burgundy	250 mL
6 tbsp	butter	90 mL
1 tbsp	flour	15 mL
1 tsp	cayenne pepper	5 mL
	Salt to taste	
24	snails	24
24	snail shells	24
24	small plugs of bread	24

Combine the shallots, parsley, thyme, bay leaf, mushrooms and wine in a pot over medium-high heat and reduce liquid by half. Combine 2 tbsp (30 mL) of the butter and flour with a fork thoroughly. (This makes a *beurre manié*). Whisk small pieces of the *manié* into the mixture in the pot until liquid has thickened. Whisk in remaining butter; add cayenne and salt.

Proceed as in the North American version, above, substituting the bourguignon butter for the garlic butter.

Bourguignon butter is also very good on eggs for a weekend breakfast.

Escargots in Blue Cheese Cream Sauce

Pastry shells, like snail shells, should be bought. It's too much fuss to make your own (most restaurants don't), and it's the sauce that counts. Vol-au-vents are small pastry shells into which you stuff several snails. Then you pour on the hot sauce and garnish with chopped parsley. Supermarket vol-au-vents have a long shelf life not because of artificial preservatives but because they contain very little moisture.

PREPARATION TIME:
5 MINUTES
COOKING TIME:
10 MINUTES
SERVES: 4

1 tbsp	butter	15 mL
1	shallot, finely minced	1
½ cup	whipping cream	125 mL
4 oz	blue cheese (Stilton, Gorgonzola, Roquefort), in pieces	115 g
1 tbsp	orange juice	15 mL
12	vol-au-vents	12
36	snails, rinsed, soaked and dried	36
	Minced parsley for garnish	

In a saucepan or pot, melt butter over medium heat and sweat shallot until translucent. Add cream and cheese, stirring until cheese has melted. Add orange juice. Continue cooking over medium heat until sauce thickens, 5 to 10 minutes.

Place 3 vol-au-vents on each appetizer plate. Pack each shell with 3 snails, if possible. Just before serving, pour hot sauce over shells, then dust with minced parsley. Serve immediately.

Vichyssoise

PREPARATION TIME:
30 MINUTES
(+ OVERNIGHT IN
REFRIGERATOR TO
CHILL)
COOKING TIME:
1 HOUR
SERVES: 8

What could be more French, more bistro, eh? Except that it was invented for New Yorkers. Okay, so Louis Diat was French, but the brilliant executive chef was at the Ritz Carlton in New York when he made up this soup. As one of the first great French chefs to take up a ladle in New York, between 1910 and 1951, he also had to endure a thousand morons who said, "Waiter! Take this back. The soup is cold!" (Actually, it's terrific hot, too. After you have puréed the soup, add remaining ingredients, pour into bowls and top with the chopped chives. Louis won't mind.) By the time Diat died, in 1957, he had seen so many bad versions of this, he'd be grateful if you stuck to the original. (Well, almost. Diat didn't use nutmeg, Worcestershire sauce or Tabasco. Those touches came from another ancient New York institution, the "21" Club.)

2 tbsp	unsalted butter	30 mL
2 cups	thinly sliced onions	500 mL
2 cups	thinly sliced leek, white part only	500 mL
1 lb	potatoes (about 5 medium), thinly sliced	450 g
2 ½ cups	chicken stock	625 mL
1 cup	milk	250 mL
2 cups	whipping cream	500 mL
½ tsp	salt	2 mL
½ tsp	nutmeg	2 mL
1 tsp	Worcestershire sauce (optional)	5 mL
1 tsp	Tabasco (optional)	5 mL
	Chopped chives for garnish	

In a large pot over medium heat, melt butter. Add onions and leek and cook until they are slightly brown. Add potatoes and chicken stock; bring to a boil. Cover the pot, turn down heat and keep the soup at a low boil for 45 minutes.

Put soup through a food mill, food processor or very fine sieve to purée the vegetables. Return to pot. Add milk, ½ cup (125 mL) of the cream and salt; bring to a boil. Remove from heat and chill, preferably overnight.

Before serving, add enough of the remaining cream to reach the consistency you like (it's your restaurant, after all). Add nutmeg, Worcestershire sauce and Tabasco. Pour into soup bowls, sprinkle chopped chives over top and serve.

Real French Onion Soup

PREPARATION TIME:
30 MINUTES
COOKING TIME:
1 HOUR
SERVES: 4

Before it was demolished in the late 1960s, Paris had a huge market district called Les Halles, which only came alive in the middle of the night. It was a city within a city, trapped by time and food. Almost every imaginable edible was trucked into Les Halles in the hours before dawn. The smells of wet gray soot, diesel fumes coughed from a hundred trucks and wafting acrid brown tobacco smoke mixed with the scent of beef stock bubbling in *soupe à l'oignon gratinée* from the cafés that fed and watered the habitués of the city trapped in the night.

The market is gone, but bistros such as Au Pied de Cochon, at 6 rue Coquillière, remain, still open twenty-four hours, still serving *soupe à l'oignon gratinée*, along with such other Les Halles staples as grilled pigs' trotters, pork shank and oysters.

Perhaps no other French dish has been butchered more than onion soup. Why? The vast majority of restaurateurs are too cheap to add the port wine or Banyuls, the sweet fortified wine from the south of France. And they don't think a dash of nutmeg is significant. Some get fancy, or lazy, and use mild Spanish or Bermuda onions, rather than the common, strong cooking onions of the market around them. Worse, they use canned broth or cheap powdered soup base or even dehydrated onion-soup mix. These cooks should be shot for defiling a basic breath of life. To be truly French, use Banyuls. Chances are you will not find it, so use tawny port (as opposed to ruby or vintage port), instead. That's not defiling, just necessity.

6 cups	thinly sliced cooking onions	1.5 L
¼ cup	butter	60 mL
1 tbsp	flour	15 mL
4 cups	beef stock	1 L
½ tsp	nutmeg	2 mL
¼ cup	tawny port or Banyuls	60 mL
4	rounds of bread, the same size as the mouth of the ovenproof soup bowls Salt and pepper to taste	4
½ lb	Emmentaler cheese, grated	225 g

Preheat oven to 300°F (150°C).

In a large pot over medium-low heat, sauté onions in butter until golden. With a wooden spoon, mix in flour and stir for 2 to 3 minutes to cook the flour. Add stock, bring to a boil, then lower heat and simmer for 1 hour. Add the nutmeg; simmer for 5 minutes. Add port and remove from heat.

While the soup is simmering, bake bread rounds until they are toasted and dry, about 20 minutes. Remove from oven and set aside.

Turn oven to 450°F (230°C); add salt and pepper and 2 tbsp (30 mL) of the grated cheese to each of 4 soup bowls. Divide soup among them. Top each with a bread round. Divide remaining cheese among bowls and bake for 5 minutes, or until the cheese melts. Turn on broiler and crisp up the cheese. Serve, bistro style, with Burgundy. It's a meal in itself.

Soupe au Pistou

PREPARATION TIME:
15 MINUTES
MAKES: 2 CUPS

Pistou is really the French version of pesto. The French don't deny it's originally from Genoa, but they give it a difference. Some versions, like this one, include tomatoes. And instead of pine nuts, which often make their way into pesto, I use walnuts.

Soupe au pistou is vegetable soup with pasta by any other name, except that when you are about to serve it, you plop in a dollop of garlic, basil and Parmesan paste that blows the roof of your mouth off. Take any good vegetable soup recipe and add thin pasta noodles. Then add at least 1 tbsp (15 mL) of *pistou* to each bowl just before you serve it.

It is best if you use a mortar and pestle to pound the garlic, salt and basil into a paste, but you can use a food processor if you wish. The salt acts like sandpaper to break down the garlic and basil. The salt taste comes from the Parmesan, so resist the urge to use more salt in the first step.

10	cloves garlic, peeled	10
1 tsp	salt	5 mL
½ cup	finely chopped fresh basil leaves	125 mL
1	large tomato, peeled, seeded and chopped	1
6 tbsp	extra-virgin first cold pressed olive oil	90 mL
½ cup	grated Parmesan	125 mL
¼ cup	finely chopped walnuts	60 mL

Pound the garlic, salt and basil in a mortar with a pestle (or in a wooden salad bowl with the back of a spoon, or in the food processor) until you have a paste. Pound in the tomato. Blend in the olive oil. (At this point, mixture can be put in small containers and frozen. It will keep for months.)

Add cheese and chopped walnuts. Spoon into soup just before serving.

Warm Brie Salad with Lardons

The idea for this salad came from a small French bistro in Kensington Market in Toronto, called Café la Gaffe. The café was a lot like the bistros I had been able to afford when I was broke in Paris in the early 1970s—hot and wet in the winter, filled with smoke, and the scents of garlic and hot stock smacked you in the face when you walked into the long, narrow, multitiered room.

PREPARATION TIME:
20 MINUTES
COOKING TIME:
5 MINUTES
SERVES: 8

3	bunches fresh spinach (about 2 ¼ lb, or 1 kg)	3
½ lb	slab unsliced side bacon	225 g
½ cup	white wine vinegar	125 mL
24	toasted bread rounds, 2 inches (5 cm) across by ½ inch (1 cm) thick	24
5	garlic cloves, peeled	5
1 ½ lb	French Brie, at room temperature	680 g
	Bistro Vinaigrette (recipe below)	

Thoroughly wash spinach leaves in several batches of cold water to remove grit; stem the spinach, then rip larger leaves into fork-size pieces. Dry thoroughly and set aside.

Cut bacon into strips 1 ½ inch (4 cm) long and ¼ inch (5 mm) thick. Put slices in a large fry pan with the wine vinegar. Evaporate vinegar over medium heat; then turn heat down and gently brown the bacon on all sides. Remove, drain and set aside.

Rub the bread rounds with garlic, spread Brie on each and place on a cookie sheet.

Warm Bistro Vinaigrette in a pan over low heat.

To assemble, warm 8 large bowls. Place cookie sheet of bread rounds under the broiler until the cheese begins to melt. Remove from oven. Toss spinach with vinaigrette until it is thoroughly coated, then divide among the bowls. Place 3 rounds of Brie toast in each bowl, sprinkle with bacon and serve.

Bistro Vinaigrette

½ cup	vegetable oil	125 mL
¼ cup	olive oil	60 mL
3 tbsp	lemon juice	45 mL
3 tbsp	cider vinegar	45 mL
1 tbsp	orange juice	15 mL
2	garlic cloves, finely chopped	2
1	shallot, finely chopped	1
1 tbsp	Dijon mustard	15 mL
1 tbsp	liquid honey	15 mL
1 tsp	each dried chervil, dried parsley, dried oregano, dried thyme, fresh dill	5 mL

Combine all ingredients in a jar and shake until blended. Set aside for at least 2 hours.

A.J. Liebling Trout

PREPARATION TIME:
5 MINUTES
COOKING TIME:
5 MINUTES
SERVES: 8

Abbott Joseph Liebling, Joe to his friends, A.J. to millions of readers, was one of the *New Yorker*'s most astounding writers. For A.J., food was a passion as well as a sociological study wherever he traveled. He was an unrepentant glutton, a living, breathing food historian. In *Between Meals*, he recalled the glory days of Paris before doctors discovered the human liver. Upon reuniting in 1955 with fellow writer and glutton Yves Mirande, he wrote, "We began with a *truite au bleu*—a live trout simply done to death in hot water, like a Roman emperor in his bath. It was served up doused with enough melted butter to thrombose a regiment of Paul Dudley Whites, and accompanied, as was right, by an Alsatian wine—a Lacrimae Santas Odiliae …"[*]

The French love trout, its subtle flavor, its fine flesh. I do, too, but I would not admit to having made *truite au bleu* lest the Society for the Prevention of Cruelty to Fishy Species comes down on my head with a bass whacker. So here's my cowardly but delicious variation for an hors d'oeuvre.

When you buy a fresh trout, the skin should be really, really slimy. Slime is good. It is what makes the trout turn bluish and curl. Also good.

| 1 | trout (rainbow is nice, but brown or speckled is fine, too) | 1 |

[*]*Liebling Abroad*, A.J. Liebling (Playboy Press, 1981), p. 583.

1 cup	Bistro Vinaigrette (recipe above)	250 mL
	Chopped parsley	
	Lemon wedges	

Gut the fish and clean it thoroughly, if the fishmonger hasn't done it already. In a dish or pan just big enough for the fish, warm the whisked vinaigrette over low heat. When it is just too hot for your finger, slide in the fish. (Head on, head off, who cares—unless you like the cheeks, which I do. They are the "oysters" of the beast.) Poach the fish for about 5 minutes, or until the flesh turns opaque. Remove and allow to cool. Slip off skin and debone.

At this point I could say, "Keep the fish intact so it still looks like a fish," but this is damn difficult. I've never achieved it yet. So just keep the pieces as large as possible, which still isn't easy, because the fish is so tender it falls apart with a breath of air.

Arrange the trout in the center of a small plate and sprinkle parsley on top. Surround with lemon wedges and dessert forks.

Frogs' Legs Niçoise

1	red pepper	1
1 lb	frogs' legs	450 g
1 tbsp	salt dissolved in 4 cups (1 L) cold water	15 mL
2 tbsp	finely chopped onion	30 mL
5 tbsp	butter, and more as needed during cooking	75 mL
6	medium tomatoes, peeled and seeded	6
4	cloves garlic, finely minced	4
2 tsp	hot Hungarian paprika, or 1 tsp (5 mL) cayenne pepper	10 mL
1 tsp	chopped fresh tarragon	5 mL
	Salt to taste	
1 cup	flour	250 mL
2 tsp	salt	10 mL
2 tsp	freshly ground pepper	10 mL
¼ cup	*demi-glace*, melted and hot	60 mL
¼ cup	chopped parsley for garnish	60 mL

PREPARATION TIME:
40 MINUTES

COOKING TIME:
10 MINUTES

SERVES: 4 AS A
FIRST COURSE,
2 AS AN ENTRÉE

Under a hot broiler or over the flame of a gas stove or barbecue, char the skin of the red pepper. Place in a paper bag and keep closed until the pepper cools, about 20 minutes. Remove pepper, slip off peel, cut pepper open and remove membrane and seeds. Dice, then set aside.

Soak frogs' legs in salted water for 30 minutes. Drain and pat dry with a towel.

In a pot, sweat the onion in 1 tbsp (15 mL) of the butter over medium heat until soft. Add tomatoes, garlic, paprika and tarragon; cook until the mixture has thickened. Taste and adjust for salt.

Sift together flour, salt and pepper. Dredge frogs' legs in flour. Over medium-high heat, melt ¼ cup (60 mL) butter in a large fry pan until bubbling hot; fry frogs' legs until golden, adding more butter to the pan as necessary. Add tomato sauce and cook for 3 minutes. Divide meat–tomato mixture among 4 plates. Pour on *demi-glace*. Garnish with chopped parsley.

Frogs' Legs Meunière

PREPARATION TIME:	1 lb	frogs' legs	450 g
40 MINUTES	1 tbsp	salt dissolved in 4 cups (1 L) cold water	15 mL
COOKING TIME:	1 cup	flour	250 mL
10 MINUTES	2 tsp	salt	10 mL
SERVES: 4 AS A	2 tsp	freshly ground pepper	10 mL
FIRST COURSE,	5 tbsp	unsalted butter, and more as needed	75 mL
2 AS AN ENTRÉE		during cooking	
	1 tbsp	lemon juice or tarragon vinegar	15 mL
	2 tbsp	chopped parsley	30 mL

Soak frogs' legs in salted water for 30 minutes. Drain and pat dry. Combine flour, salt and pepper. Dredge legs in seasoned flour and fry in 4 tbsp (60 mL) of the butter until golden all over. Arrange legs on 4 plates. To the butter in the fry pan, add remaining butter and swirl in, cooking until the butter is brown. Add lemon juice and parsley; cook for 30 seconds, then pour over frogs' legs. Serve immediately.

Boeuf à la Bourguignon

MARINATING TIME:
24 HOURS
PREPARATION TIME:
1½ HOURS
COOKING TIME:
5 HOURS
SERVES: 12

When it comes right down to it, the difference between stewing and braising is that a stew has more liquid and smaller pieces of meat. This version is the classic braising, updated only in its presentation, *en croûte*—in individual bowls with a pastry crust baked on top. The aroma when you break through the crust will jolt your brain, the chunks of beef will melt with only the pressure of your tongue, and the stock, wine, brandy, onions and shallots will explode in your mouth.

Really. It is glorious. The value of fat, natural gelatin, slow cooking and marinades has been explained earlier (pp. 17–21), and they all come together in this dish. Paul Prudhomme, the exceptional New Orleans chef, speaks of his cooking as the "layering" of tastes. This dish is a study in layered tastes.

Six tips about bourguignon:

1) Larding is a must.

2) Boil the marinade down to a syrup in Stage 2; otherwise you get a nasty raw wine taste from the wine's tannins. Some recipes may want this raw taste, as if it imparts French sophistication. It doesn't. The wine is there for its intrinsic Burgundian flavor, but that ain't raw.

3) Use wild mushrooms for added flavor. Wild mushrooms are as commonly used in Europe as tasteless button mushrooms are in North America. Who cooks better?

4) This dish must simmer in a broth that barely has any bubbles rising to the surface. The meat dries out at a higher temperature when cooked for this long. The key temperature is 160°F (70°C); see the discussion of cooking temperature in the beef section, pp. 19–20.

5) Cook this dish until a fork passes through the beef like a skewer through butter.

6) Make the whole recipe—it's the same amount of trouble. Besides, the dish will be good in the refrigerator for several days, and it freezes well.

LARDING

You can buy a larding needle for only a few dollars at any cooking store. You need the smaller one, about 8 inches (20 cm) long, not the big one that looks like a carving knife steel. I find the needle indispensable for larding beef, pricking the fat end of eggs for boiling and opening the bathroom door when my kids lock themselves in to play "putting Barbie in a barrel in the Niagara Falls whirlpool."

Larding is simple. The needle has a hinge to trap the bacon strip. Just slide the needle through the beef, dragging the bacon behind. Make sure the bacon is thinner than the hinged end of the needle. When the needle makes it all the way through, snip off the attached bacon, leaving the strip in the beef to act as marbling as the meat cooks.

½ lb	slab bacon fat or salt pork, cut into thin strips, 2 inches (5 cm) by ¼ inch (6 mm)	225 g
¼ cup	brandy	60 mL
6 lb	rump roast, cut into 2-inch (5 cm) cubes	2.75 kg

MARINADE

1 bottle	good red wine, preferably a Burgundy	750 mL
1	carrot, roughly chopped	1
1	onion, peeled, studded with 3 cloves	1
1	stalk celery, roughly chopped	1
1	large shallot, roughly chopped	1
1	leek, white part only	1
2	large garlic cloves, peeled and crushed	2
40	whole coriander seeds	40
2 tbsp	red wine vinegar	30 mL
1 tbsp	olive oil	15 mL
2	sprigs curly parsley	2
	Zest of ½ orange	
1	large bay leaf	1
2 tsp	dried marjoram	10 mL
10	black peppercorns	10
¼ cup	unsalted butter	60 mL
5 cups	beef stock*	1.2 L
1 cup	water	250 mL
½ lb	mushrooms—equal amounts of portobello, oyster and shiitake —wiped clean and stemmed, stems reserved	225 g
12	shallots, peeled	12
10	pearl onions	10
2 tbsp	butter	30 mL
	Salt to taste	
	Puff pastry (buy it from the supermarket freezer)	

*The amount of beef stock may seem like a lot, especially when you've made it from scratch for the first time. But you will have a lot of stock left over from the dish. Think about it—it will have undergone almost the same cooking process all over again, with the result that it is even more intense in flavor, with the added dimension of a wild-mushroom taste and aroma. In short, it is now a sauce. Wonderful over grilled, thinly sliced flank steak. Spoon it on toast and top with an egg fried in butter for breakfast. Heat it, add whipping cream, and you have an incomparable cream sauce for any steak.

STAGE 1 (THE NIGHT BEFORE)

Marinate the strips of bacon in the brandy for 1 hour. Lard the beef pieces with at least 2 strips of bacon in each piece.

In a large bowl, make the marinade. Combine Burgundy, carrot, onion, celery, shallot, leek, garlic, coriander, vinegar, oil, parsley, zest, bay leaf, marjoram and peppercorns. Add the beef, mix it around, cover and marinate overnight in the refrigerator.

STAGE 2 (THE DAY OF)

Remove the beef chunks from the marinade, drain and pat dry. Strain the vegetables and allow to drain. Reserve marinade liquid. Over medium-high heat in a large pot, brown beef chunks in 2 tbsp (30 mL) butter, adding more butter if needed. Remove beef. Add the stems and peelings of the mushrooms, then add the vegetables from the marinade. Fry for 5 minutes. Return beef to pot, then add marinade liquid and boil it down to a syrup, about 30 minutes. Add stock and water, bring to a boil and simmer for 3 hours.

STAGE 3 (THE FINISH)

Preheat oven to 350°F (175°C).

With a slotted spoon, remove the beef from the pot and set aside. Strain the sauce to remove all vegetables; then strain again to clarify the sauce as much as possible. Put meat and sauce in a bowl. Wash the cooking pot.

Chop the mushrooms into bite-size pieces. Peel the shallots and onions. In the washed pot, over medium-low heat, sauté the whole onions and shallots in 2 tbsp (30 mL) butter until they are golden and just caramelized. Add mushrooms and cook for 5 minutes. Return the beef and sauce to the pot and cook in the oven for 1 ½ to 2 hours, until the beef is so tender a fork passes through without resistance. Salt the sauce to taste.

Divide bourguignon among individual ovenproof bowls, top with puff pastry, return to oven and bake until the pastry puffs and browns, about 25 minutes.

Rack of Lamb

PREPARATION TIME:

1 HOUR

COOKING TIME:

20 MINUTES

SERVES: 8

A lamb has thirteen ribs on each side, and the rack is eight or nine of them, depending on the country of origin and butchering. Once the rack is split down the backbone, it becomes two single-rack roasts. The butcher cleans up the backbone area, cuts partway through it at each rib and scrapes off the long rib bones to make them clean and attractive. This is called Frenching and is done with the back of a chef's knife. A single rack from a New Zealand lamb will weigh about 1 lb (450 g). If you are serving a multicourse dinner, half a single rack per person is plenty. If dinner is just the lamb and veggies, a whole single rack per person will knock their socks off. By the way, the rack is often cheaper per pound than individual chops. No, I don't know why.

Nothing could be easier to cook than a rack of lamb, and few main courses are as impressive or delicious.

The marinade flavors and lubricates the rack. Although lamb has a reputation for being fatty, the rack is usually trimmed very close.

Two mustard sauces are suggested here, one a variation on Hollandaise and the other a very fast mustard whipped cream. For a spectacular winter display at the table, serve the rack with three purées, beet, squash and spinach. Lamb goes beautifully with *frites* and any one of the purées, too.

½ cup	good olive oil	125 mL
2 tbsp	dried rosemary	30 mL
2 tbsp	chopped curly parsley	30 mL
½ tsp	salt	2 mL
	Pepper, a good grind or two	
4	single racks of lamb	4
	Sauce (recipes follow)	

Mix oil, rosemary, parsley, salt and pepper in a large bowl. Cut each rack of lamb into 2 pieces, so there are 4 chops per person. Add lamb to oil; coat thoroughly and leave for 1 hour. Remove racks but do not wipe off oil or herbs. Broil 2 inches (5 cm) from broiler, underside first to heat the bones, which will continue to cook the meat from that side when turned over. Or barbecue over medium-hot coals until the outside is dark and the inside is pink, about 10 minutes per side.

Serve racks on individual plates with about 1 tbsp (15 mL) of mustard Hollandaise sauce or lemon-mustard cream sauce napped over each rack. Serve the rest in a sauce boat.

Lemon-Mustard Cream Sauce

2 tbsp	mustard	30 mL
	Salt and pepper to taste	
1 tsp	lemon juice	5 mL
⅔ cup	whipping cream	160 mL

PREPARATION TIME:
3 MINUTES
SERVES: 4

Blend mustard, salt, pepper and lemon juice. With an electric beater, whip in cream until mixture thickens. Keep cool.

Hollandaise Sauce

You do not need a double boiler for Hollandaise, or any other egg-yolk-based sauce. Ignore anyone who tells you it is tricky to make. It isn't. All you need is a good whisk and a pot with a fairly heavy bottom. (Was the double boiler invented before Hollandaise sauce? Of course not.) Just keep the heat low and steady.

PREPARATION TIME:
5 MINUTES
COOKING TIME:
10 MINUTES
SERVES: 4

1 tbsp	lemon juice	15 mL
5 tbsp	butter	75 mL
2	egg yolks	2
	Pepper to taste	

Put the lemon juice in a pot and set over low heat for about 5 minutes, or until it has simmered down to a syrup. (This is a trick that David Burke of Park Avenue Café in Manhattan uses to intensify lemon for a ketchup he puts on, of all things, trout. Lemon essence sauces thicken more easily, because the water has been removed from the juice.)

Remove pot from the heat and whisk in 1 tbsp (15 mL) of the butter. Whisk in the egg yolks, then return pot to burner over low heat. Whisk the yolks until they thicken to the consistency of thick cream. Add the remaining butter, a spoonful at a time, until incorporated (a fancy word for "melted and whisked in") and whisk, whisk, whisk until the sauce is thick enough to be draped over a lamb chop like a heavy quilt. Add pepper as needed.

Taste it. Resist eating it all. Pour into a sauce boat and cover with plastic wrap. Refrigerate if you are not using it for a few hours. Bring it out an hour before serving if you are serving it in the boat. The temperature isn't as important if you are draping it over the chops on the plate.

Mustard Hollandaise

5 tsp	Dijon mustard	25 mL
	Hollandaise Sauce (recipe above)	

Whisk Dijon into Hollandaise. This sauce is good on lamb—and on asparagus and broccoli and fish and …

Maltese Sauce

Escoffier thought this was the finest sauce for asparagus. He used a "blood" orange, a small, sweet, rough-skinned variety with red flecks in the flesh. It gives the sauce a reddish color.

	Double portion Hollandaise Sauce (recipe above)	
	Juice of 1 blood or Valencia orange	
2 tsp	grated orange rind	10 mL

To the Hollandaise sauce, add orange juice and rind. Whisk.

Three Colored Purées

Gingered Butternut Purée

A butternut squash is shaped like a fat bell clapper with a tan skin and orange flesh.

PREPARATION TIME:			
5 MINUTES	1	butternut squash, about 1 lb (450 g)	1
COOKING TIME:	1 ½ tbsp	grated fresh ginger root,	20 mL
45 MINUTES		a 4-inch (10-cm) piece	
	1 tbsp	unsalted butter	15 mL
SERVES: 4	¼ tsp	salt	1 mL

Preheat oven to 400°F (200°C). Split squash lengthwise and remove seeds. Place squash halves, cut side down, in a shallow Pyrex dish and bake for 45 minutes or until very tender. Scoop out insides; mash thoroughly with a fork or pass through a food mill. Add remaining ingredients and mix well.

Orange Beet Purée

4	medium beets, about 1 ½ lb (680 g)	4
	Juice of 1 large orange	

PREPARATION TIME:
   5 MINUTES
COOKING TIME:
   45 TO 90 MINUTES
SERVES: 4

Cut the beet stems about 1 inch (2.5 cm) from the bulb. (Cut closer and the beets will bleed too much.) Rinse, rub off surface grunge and boil for about 45 minutes, or until soft. (The older the beet, the longer it will take. If it takes more than 1 ½ hours, give the greengrocer hell.) Drain beets, let cool, trim off stems and slip off skins. Cut up beets and put through a food mill with medium-sized holes, or mash thoroughly with a fork. You will get about 1 ½ cups (375 mL) puréed beets.

Put the orange juice in a small pan over medium-low heat and boil down to a syrup, scraping the sides down as it reduces. The orange essence gives orange flavor without making the beet purée watery.

Add beets, stir and heat.

Mint Spinach Purée

8	bunches fresh spinach	8
60	fresh mint leaves, roughly chopped	60
	Salt	
2 tbsp	butter	30 mL

PREPARATION TIME:
   5 MINUTES
COOKING TIME:
   5 MINUTES
SERVES: 4

Stem and thoroughly wash spinach. Put it in a pot with the mint leaves, cover tightly and cook over high heat for 5 minutes. Drain well and chop finely. Put in a small pot, add salt and butter, heat and serve.

French Peas

PREPARATION TIME:

5 MINUTES

STANDING TIME:

2 HOURS

COOKING TIME:

5 MINUTES

SERVES: 8

Peas are one of the wonders of summer, picked fresh, plucked quickly from the pod, releasing the sweet smells of chlorophyll and hot earth. Peas have to be cooked almost immediately after they're picked; like corn, their sugar starts to turn to starch right away. But the chances of getting fresh peas these days, especially in the city, are remote. The farmer picks the field one day, drives it to market the next; a large supermarket buys it and puts it on the shelf, where it might remain for several days. Those "fresh" peas could be three, four or more days from the field. So if you break open a pod and the peas smell starchy, it's the scent of the realities of commerce.

Brand-name frozen peas are not bad. What they lack in chlorophyll aroma they more than make up for with a fresh pop in the mouth. These peas are much fresher generally than the ones you buy in supermarkets. The large companies contract farms to grow a pea variety that retains color, nutrients and taste when frozen, which they are within hours—not days—of picking. No respectable chef would admit to using frozen peas, but he or she would not be a traitor to the calling.

The ingredients for this recipe may seem a little odd, but the combination creates a different-tasting dish and rescues aging fresh peas. One source insists that the acids in the lettuce heart, onions and peas create a chemical reaction spread by the butter, but I have never been able to find scientific verification of this theory. Never mind. This is a classic example of how the French, through design or by chance, in culinary endeavor as in politics, raise common elements to majesty.

2 cups	fresh or frozen peas	500 mL
	Heart of 1 iceberg lettuce	
12	pearl onions (or 1 cooking onion, roughly chopped)	12
2 tbsp	butter, melted	30 mL
1 tsp	sugar	5 mL
½ tsp	salt	2 mL

If you are using fresh peas, blanch in boiling salted water for 1 minute. Drain and run cold water over them to stop the cooking process. Frozen peas are ready to use.

The heart of the lettuce is the white, juicy core extending up from the stem. Rip it out by hand (a knife will discolor it), and rip it into small pieces. In a pot just large enough to hold them, mix all ingredients thoroughly. Cover and allow to stand at room temperature for at least 2 hours. Mix with a wooden spoon occasionally.

Just before serving, put the covered pot on medium-high heat just long enough to heat the peas through. Serve.

Minted French Peas

Great with lamb. Add ¼ cup (60 mL) coarsely chopped fresh mint leaves to the pot of French peas to marinate with the rest of the ingredients.

Hollandaise Peas

Sinfully good with a simple barbecued steak. A little goes a long way.

2	cups fresh peas	2
½ cup	Hollandaise Sauce (recipe, p. 67)	125 mL

PREPARATION TIME:
2 MINUTES
COOKING TIME:
2 MINUTES
SERVES: 4

Plunge fresh peas in boiling water for 60 seconds if they are small, 90 seconds if they are larger. Drain. Let cool a little. Bind them with the Hollandaise and serve. For frozen peas: warm in a pan in 1 tbsp (15 mL) water over low heat until they are thawed; remove from heat and bind with the Hollandaise.

THE COMPLEAT FRENCH DUCK DINNER

Ask just about anyone to name two duck dishes, and they will probably say *Duck à l'orange* and Peking Duck. The latter has the reputation of being especially virtuous in this environmentally correct society, because every part of the duck is used. Nothing is wasted. Good for them.

The French have not had as good PR. They don't waste a thing, either. In Gascony, male *moularde* ducks are fattened for their liver (foie gras), the breast meat is skinned, boned and sautéed or roasted like steak (*magret*), and the legs are cured and poached in their own fat (*confit*). The skin that doesn't melt down is chopped and fried to a crisp (*frizonnes*) for salads and garnishes, and the carcass is roasted and made into soup or consommé.

Foie gras is undeniably the richest foodstuff on earth, being mainly fat; but it is also the lightest on the tongue. A slice of foie gras sautéed for mere seconds in a nonstick pan melts in your mouth; it is far lighter in taste and texture than butter. Foie gras and Sauternes are one of the great pairings of food and wine.

Magret is infused with the rich taste of the foie gras but, because it has been boned and skinned, it lacks the fattiness. As all the taste of meat is in the fat, *magret* tastes like steak, not duck, and should be cooked medium-rare like steak.

Confit, on the other hand, is second only to foie gras in fabulous melt-in-the-mouth rich taste and texture. It is also cheaper to make. It's one of the great, original fast foods and lasts for months in the refrigerator. The legs are seasoned, poached, cooled and stored in duck fat to preserve them. Just wipe the fat off a leg, slip the leg 8 inches (20 cm) under a broiler, and in less than five minutes it is done. The roast-duck aroma is addictive, the skin so crisp it shatters between your lips, and the meat dissolves under the slightest pressure of your tongue. One leg. It's all you need.

Two Toronto restaurants, Marcel's Bistro and Le Saint Tropez, both owned by French chef Fabien Siebert, introduced an admirable complete duck dinner during the 1994 fall hunting season. It was much like the dinner here. Here are my versions of *magret*, *confit*, duck soup, *frizonnes* with broccoli and a modern version of *duck à l'orange* that restaurants use instead of the original because it is easier—and you can't really tell the difference. The *magret* recipe is a version of one taught to me by Eli Benchitrit, chef/owner of Provence, a Toronto restaurant.

Magret of Duck

PREPARATION TIME:	2 tsp	clarified butter	10 mL
5 MINUTES	2	duck breasts, skinned and boned	2
COOKING TIME:	2 tbsp	brandy or cognac	30 mL
10 MINUTES	¼ cup	whipping cream	60 mL
SERVES: 2	1 tbsp	pickled green peppercorns*	15 mL
		Salt to taste	

In a skillet or fry pan just large enough to hold the duck breasts, heat butter over high heat. When it begins to smoke, add duck breasts and cook for 1 minute. Turn over and cook for another 1 minute. Pour brandy over breasts, ignite and shake pan until the flames die out. Remove breasts to a heated plate. Pour cream into pan and reduce by half. Remove pan from heat. Squeeze green peppercorns between your fingers to release their full flavor; whisk them into the cream sauce and add salt to taste. Place duck breasts (which should be pink on the inside, like steak) on individual plates. Nap with green peppercorn sauce. Serve with *frites* and French peas.

Confit of Duck

A *confit* is made in three steps: rendering the fat, curing, then poaching and aging.

Rendering the fat: Strip all visible fat and skin from the duck, except from the legs; chop roughly. Fill a stock pot with cold water. Add skin and fat and bring to a boil; lower heat and simmer for at least 1 hour. Remove from heat and cool in the refrigerator or freezer. The rendered fat will rise to the top. Scoop off and

---

*Buy French or North American packed green peppercorns. Those from India are far too strong, and are often packed in mustard oil, which alters the taste.

store. At the bottom of the pot or suspended in the remaining liquid, you will find pieces of skin that have not dissolved. Remove with slotted spoon or pour the liquid through a sieve to capture them. (Fried in a little duck fat or butter, they become *frizonnes*, which, when used like bacon bits, are dynamite on salads and vegetables.)

Curing the duck:

1 tbsp	pickling or kosher salt	15 mL
2 tsp	ground black pepper	10 mL
2 tsp	dried thyme	10 mL
2 tsp	dried rosemary	10 mL
1	bay leaf, crushed	1
¼ tsp	nutmeg	1 mL
¼ tsp	marjoram	1 mL
	Pinch cinnamon	
12	juniper berries, crushed	12
	Duck legs	

Mix salt, spices, herbs and berries in a large bowl; rub mixture well into duck legs. Cover and refrigerate for 24 hours. The salt dries the meat and fat, which is vital for good *confit*; the spices and herbs give it a heavenly aroma. Nevertheless, you must wash off *all* the mixture after the curing process. If you don't, you'll end up serving impossible-to-eat Salt Duck. Also note—the cinnamon is vital, but too much of it will overpower and ruin your *confit*. Wipe every trace of the pickling mixture from every piece of duck with a damp cloth. Make sure you get it all, even from under the skin. Then wash the legs quickly in water to rinse away any dissolved salt. As long as you don't soak the duck, it won't soak up an appreciable amount of water.

Poaching and aging: In a large pot, melt rendered duck fat and bring to 175°F (80°C). Measure the temperature with a thermometer. Gently place duck legs into fat. Bring temperature back to 175°F (80°C) and keep it there for 1 hour. Meanwhile, thoroughly wash and sterilize canning jars just large enough to accommodate 2 or more legs. Gently remove duck legs from poaching fat and place in jars. Add duck fat until legs are completely covered. Seal and refrigerate.

Leave the legs in the refrigerator for at least a week to allow the full flavor to develop. This is the "aging" process. The legs will keep for 3 months or more in the refrigerator, indefinitely in the freezer.

To cook and serve *confit* of duck: Although one leg per person seems stingy, *confit* is one of life's richest dishes. You might explode if you eat two.

Remove a jar of duck legs from the refrigerator or freezer and place in warm water to soften the duck fat and loosen its hold on the legs. Pop open the lid and—carefully—remove the legs. Save the duck fat for cooking. Wipe off fat still clinging to the skin—gently, so you don't break the delicate skin. Place 8 inches (20 cm) under a broiler, skin side down, for 3 minutes. Turn over, skin side up, and broil until the skin is crisp. Remember, the duck is already cooked. All you are doing is heating it up and crisping the skin. Serve at once.

If you find your *confit* is too salty or too fatty, place legs in a steamer for ten minutes. Then broil, skin side up, for two minutes, or until the skin becomes crisp. Serve with *frites* and broccoli *frizonnes*.

To make Marcel's *confit*: Marcel's chef, Jean-Jacques, speeds up the process by salting and spicing the legs overnight, as above. He wipes them clean, then plops them into duck fat he has brought to a boil in an ovenproof pot. He immediately takes the pot off the heat and puts it, covered, into a 300°F (150°C) oven for 1 ½ to 2 hours. He uses his *confit* for shredded duck salads and pasta dishes. The rich taste is there, but if you are not careful you can overdo the duck, and it will be tough at the edges.

Duck Soup with Omelettes

Preparation time:			
1 hour		Duck carcass, cut up	
	2	carrots, cleaned and roughly chopped	2
Cooking time:	1	onion, cut into quarters	1
6 ½ hours	1	celery stalk	1
Serves: 8	2	bay leaves	2
	4	sprigs fresh thyme, or 2 tsp (10 mL) dried	4
	20	black peppercorns, roasted in the oven for 10 minutes	20
	2 tbsp	water	30 mL
	¼ cup	fresh bread crumbs	60 mL
	4	eggs at room temperature	4
	4 tsp	duck fat	20 mL
	1	onion, minced	1
	2	cloves garlic, minced	2
	¼ cup	parsley, finely chopped	60 mL
	1	leg of duck *confit*, shredded	1
	2 tbsp	Calvados, Armagnac or sherry	30 mL
		Salt and pepper to taste	

Cut the duck carcass into small pieces. Place bones in a roasting pan at 350°F (180°C) for 45 minutes, or until the bones are well browned. Place bones, wings and fat in a large pot; cover with cold water. Add just enough hot water to the roasting pan to loosen the brown bits on the bottom; add to pot. Add carrots, quartered onion, celery stalk, bay leaves, thyme and peppercorns. Bring to a boil, spoon off the scum that rises to the top, lower heat, partially cover, and simmer for 6 hours. Strain, pour into a clean pot and reduce by half. The cooled broth can be stored in the refrigerator for a few days or in the freezer indefinitely.

To make Duck Soup with Omelettes, prepare the omelettes while the stock is reducing. In a bowl, combine water, bread crumbs and eggs and whisk until the eggs foam with air bubbles. Divide mixture in half.

Melt 2 tsp (10 mL) duck fat in a fry pan; add half the minced onion and garlic. Fry until both are golden but not burned. Add half the parsley, then half the egg mixture. Make a circular omelette by frying on one side until browned, then flipping it over and frying the other side for 3 minutes. Remove omelette from heat and reserve. Repeat process with remaining egg, onion, garlic and parsley.

Cut finished omelettes into quarters, slip them into the duck broth and let simmer for 5 minutes. Add shredded duck *confit* and heat for 2 to 3 minutes.

To serve, add Calvados to the broth at the last moment. Put one omelette quarter in each soup bowl; spoon duck broth over omelettes. Add salt and pepper to taste and serve at once.

Broccoli Frizonnes

	Frizonnes (see pp. 72–73)	
3	spears trimmed broccoli per person	3
	Melted butter	

PREPARATION TIME:
5 MINUTES
COOKING TIME:
20 MINUTES

In a fry pan over medium-low heat, fry duck skin in butter until crisp, like bacon. Drain, chop small enough to sprinkle and reserve.

Clean and trim broccoli and steam for 4 minutes. Drain, coat with melted butter, then sprinkle with *frizonnes*. Serve immediately.

Duck à l'orange

PREPARATION TIME:

45 MINUTES

COOKING TIME:

1 HOUR,

45 MINUTES

SERVES: 8

A restaurant can't take an order for duck and expect the guests to sit still for the ninety minutes it takes to roast it. Nor can most kitchens roast twelve ducks before the dinner hour in the hope that twenty-four to forty-eight people will order duck at the same time. A duck might cost eight dollars; the experience could be financially ruinous. Therefore restaurateurs rarely offer a whole roasted duck. They use duckling, a much smaller and quicker-roasting bird, or offer duck halves or quarters, which cook faster still.

However, good restaurateurs can predict approximately how many ducks they will sell on any particular night of the week in any particular month. And if their proven specialty is *duck à l'orange*, it will be even easier.

In this recipe, the basting sauce is made well ahead of time. So is the finishing sauce. A breast of duck will take only thirty minutes to cook.

2	ducks	2
	Salt and pepper	
	Juice from 4 oranges, about 1 ½ cups (375 mL)	
1 tbsp	soy sauce	15 mL
1 tbsp	sugar	15 mL
1	orange	1
⅓ cup	sugar	80 mL
⅓ cup	white wine vinegar	80 mL
2 cups	beef stock	500 mL
⅓ cup	lemon juice	80 mL
3 tbsp	butter	45 mL
2 tbsp	cornstarch	30 mL
2 tsp	water	10 mL
3 tbsp	Grand Marnier	45 mL

Preheat oven to 450°F (230°C). Wash ducks inside and out, sprinkle cavity with salt and pepper, and salt the outside skin. Place in a shallow roasting pan on a rack and roast for 10 minutes. Turn down heat to 350°F (175°C) and roast for 1 hour. Meanwhile, in a saucepan, over medium low, heat orange juice to just below the boiling point. Reduce heat to low and reduce juice to ¼ cup (60 mL), about 40 minutes. (Watch that the orange juice does not boil over—it will the second you look away.) Whisk in soy sauce and 1 tbsp (15 mL) sugar. After the duck has roasted for 1 hour, remove excess fat from the roasting pan and baste duck with half the orange–soy mixture. Roast another 30 to 35 minutes, basting with the rest of the orange–soy mixture occasionally; roast until the juices run clear when the thigh is pricked.

Meanwhile, with a zester or sharp knife, peel off the skin of an orange. You want just the orange outside layer, not the white pith beneath it. Long peelings look most attractive. Squeeze the juice from the orange and reserve. Blanch the zest in boiling water for 2 minutes, then plunge into cold water. Dry and set aside.

In a pot over medium heat, dissolve ⅓ cup (80 mL) sugar in the vinegar and cook until the mixture starts to turn golden. Turn heat to low, carefully stir in beef stock (to avoid splattering) and simmer for 5 minutes. Add orange and lemon juices and simmer for another 5 minutes. Whisk in butter in small bits. In a small bowl, mix cornstarch and water into a smooth paste; add a little of the sauce; then add cornstarch–sauce mixture to the sauce and stir until it thickens. Add Grand Marnier.

When duck is done, remove birds to a heated tray. Skim fat from roasting pan. Strain any nonfatty juices and add to the sauce. Add any leftover basting sauce, too. Place 1 duck quarter on each plate. Divide the orange zest among them, then drizzle with sauce. Serve any remaining sauce in a sauce boat.

Frites

PREPARATION TIME:

20 MINUTES

COOKING TIME:

7 MINUTES

SERVES: 6 TO 8

Frites are thin fries that are so caramel-colored and crisp on the outside and so tender on the inside that when they come to the table all salted and hot, "They go craack!" says Eli Benchitrit, master *frites* maker and the chef-owner of Provence in Toronto, who taught me how to make them.

The perfect *frite*—simple to contemplate, hard to master, mainly because modern man tends to think answers lie in technology. You will be forgiven if you honestly believe you need a deep-frying machine to make *frites*. But *frites* were perfected long before the invention of the deep fryer. All the original *frites* chef did was take an ordinary pot, fill it one-third full with ordinary oil and put it on the stove.* You make thick English chips in a deep fryer, not *frites*. Fryers are designed to hold the oil at a relatively constant temperature. But the secret of *frites* is fluctuating oil temperature. Fry twice, fry fast.

Another secret is movement. When you get into a very hot bathtub, you try to stay as still as possible because, when you move, it seems even hotter and more painful, right? Right. Same thing here. During the second fry, stir the *frites* around in the oil with a slotted spoon once in a while; this crisps the outside at a slightly higher temperature and you get the *craack!*

Use fresh, hard russet potatoes and ordinary vegetable oil.

8	large russet potatoes	8
	Vegetable oil for frying	
	Salt	

Anytime up to 6 hours before you plan to serve them, give your *frites* their first fry. Peel russets and cut into ¼-inch (5 mm) square fries the length of the potato. Fill a 3-quart (3 L) pot one-third full of vegetable oil. Using a candy thermometer, heat oil to 375°F (190°C). Add a third of the frites to the oil. Watch thermometer closely. When temperature drops to 300°F (150°C), immediately remove fries to a baking sheet and let cool. Repeat process twice more for remaining fries.

For the second fry, just before serving, heat oil to 385°F (195°C); add a quarter of the partially cooked fries. (If the temperature drops too quickly, use fewer fries the next batch.) Stir fries around to crisp them. When they are golden brown, about 3 minutes, remove to a sheet or bowl and sprinkle generously with salt. Repeat until all fries are done. If the first batch is too cool by the end of the process, drop the cool fries back into the hot oil for a few seconds to revive them.

*He wasn't French, by the way. "French fries" were invented in Belgium in the 1860s.

Salmon Medici

	Béarnaise Sauce (recipe, p. 40)	
2 cups	fresh fine bread crumbs	500 mL
1 ½ tbsp	dried thyme	20 mL
1 ½ tbsp	dried oregano	20 mL
2 tsp	cayenne pepper	10 mL
2 tsp	salt	10 mL
	Generous grinding of fresh black pepper	
2 lb	filet of salmon, skinned and cut into equal pieces	900 g
2	eggs, beaten with 1 tbsp (15 mL) cold water	2
¼ cup	unsalted butter, and more as needed during cooking	60 mL
28	cherry tomatoes or 1 large tomato	28
	Salt to taste	
	Finely chopped parsley	

PREPARATION TIME:
10 MINUTES
COOKING TIME:
5 MINUTES
SERVES: 4 AS A
MAIN COURSE,
8 AS A FISH COURSE

Make béarnaise sauce and set aside.

Combine bread crumbs, thyme, oregano, cayenne, salt and pepper. Dip salmon pieces in egg mixture, then completely coat with bread crumb mixture. Put slices back in the egg, then once again in the bread crumbs to get a thick coating. Heat butter in a large pan over medium-high heat until it foams. Fry salmon quickly until the crust is golden on both sides, about 2 minutes per side. Remove to a heated plate. In the same pan, swirl in the cherry tomatoes for 45 seconds, just until the skin is coated and the tomatoes are slightly warmed. Remove and salt generously.

Coat the bottom of heated plates with béarnaise sauce, making sure the sauce entirely coats each plate. Arrange salmon filets in the middle of the plates. Ring each filet with an equal number of cherry tomatoes. If cherry tomatoes are out of season, slice a large tomato into ½-inch (1-cm) thick slices. Use 1 slice per plate if the tomato is larger than the salmon. If not, arrange 3 slices in a trillium pattern in the middle of each plate; coat with sauce and put the salmon on top. Dust everything, including the plate edges, with finely chopped parsley. Serve immediately.

Poached Salmon Marcel Prévost

PREPARATION TIME:
45 MINUTES
COOKING TIME:
25 TO 30 MINUTES
SERVES: 6

Great restaurateurs know their guests eat with their eyes first, their noses second and their mouths last. This dish is spectacular to look at: poached salmon sits on a bed of creamy spinach, drizzled with a white wine sauce, topped with a single mussel and surrounded (like a picture frame on the plate) by eight or nine more mussels, each napped inside its shell with the sauce. The nose is subtly aroused by the aroma of the sea creatures, the tang of the wine sauce and a sour squeeze of lemon. As for the taste? Everything on one plate. Marie-Antoine Carême, the architect of French cuisine, would not dismiss the scene.

You can make the spinach well before service and reheat it. Poaching the salmon and steaming the mussels are virtually foolproof. To get you out of the kitchen, an hour before your guests arrive assemble the wine and aromatic vegetable ingredients in the casserole (for the salmon) and steaming pot (for the mussels). When the poaching is done, cook the mussels and reduce the sauce at the same time. Both will take five minutes. Assemble and serve.

A restaurant will prepoach the salmon and finish it in the oven for the time it takes to steam the mussels and reduce the wine and cream. You can, too, of course, but it is unnecessary because it will only take thirty seconds to slip the salmon into the wine, dot with butter, cover with waxed paper or parchment paper, slip it into the oven and set the timer. Your guests will wait for it. If they don't, they don't deserve to be your guests.

1 ½ lb	salmon filet	680 g
2 cups	dry white wine	500 mL
¼ cup	roughly chopped shallots	60 mL
40	black peppercorns	40
4	bay leaves	4
2	cloves garlic, crushed	2
1 ½ tbsp	butter	20 mL
1 ½ cups	whipping cream	375 mL
	Salt to taste	
1 cup	white wine	250 mL
1	carrot, roughly chopped	1
¼ cup	rock or kosher salt	60 mL
8	cloves	8
2 lb	cultured mussels,* cleaned and bearded	900 g
	Creamed spinach (recipe, p. 186)	

*You should get about 18 mussels to a kilo, or 9 mussels to a pound. Cultured mussels are farmed on ropes or, in the case of some Southern Californian mussels, on the pilings of ocean oil rigs. Cultured mussels are easy to clean. When eaten like this, they taste just like the wild ones.

Preheat oven to 350°F (175°C).

Skin salmon and cut into 6 equal portions. Place in a casserole just large enough to accommodate the fish. Add wine, shallots, peppercorns, bay leaves and garlic. The liquid must cover the salmon; if it doesn't, top it up with more wine. Dot each portion of salmon with butter; place a piece of waxed paper or parchment paper tightly over fish. The paper should be in contact with the fish, like a second skin. Bake for 20 minutes. Remove fish with slotted spoon to a hot plate. Strain half the cooking liquid into a small pot. Return the fish to the casserole with the remaining cooking liquid to keep the fish warm and moist. Reduce liquid in pot over high heat to about ¼ cup (60 mL), about 7 minutes. Add whipping cream and reduce to a silky sauce, about 5 minutes.

As the salmon is about to come out of the oven, bring wine, carrot, salt and cloves to a boil. Throw in mussels, cover and steam for 5 minutes, or until all the shells open. Throw out any mussels that don't open.

To assemble: In the middle of each heated dinner plate, make a bed of heated creamed spinach only slightly larger than the salmon pieces. Place a piece of salmon on top of the spinach. Nap both with sauce. Top with one mussel, nap it with sauce and arrange the remaining mussels around the salmon. Nap each mussel with a drop of sauce, too.

Skate with Black Butter

PREPARATION TIME:
10 MINUTES
COOKING TIME:
15 MINUTES
SERVES: 2

This is a traditional bistro dish, very simple, fascinating (no-bones-about-it safe) to eat the way the flesh peels off the skeleton, awesome in both its presentation and aroma, a classic, absolutely superb, but... it is essential that the skate is fresh. Some people will tell you skate is about the only fish that can be aged, or ripened. It is in many European countries. But this is not to most people's tastes, and few know how to do it here. Fresher is still better.

Skate, ray and shark all have properties in their systems* that turn to ammonia if they are not processed quickly and well after being caught, if they're stored poorly, if they're not fresh or if they're not frozen quickly. Because skate is a flat fish, it is difficult to process, and the processing is often botched. If anything, this underlines the importance of finding a good fish retailer. Retailers who know how to buy skate and shark are worth their weight in caviar. If you go to a restaurant and order shark or skate, and you smell (or even worse, taste) ammonia, send it back to the kitchen. You won't like it no matter how much black butter and capers are on it, and you shouldn't have to pay for it. Tell them to bring you something else and put the black butter (without the capers) on broccoli or whatever happens to be the vegetable du jour.

I have probably grossed you out, and now you have no intention of trying skate. So I might as well get it all out of my system since you are already put off.

Imagine a shark run over by a steamroller. With a poisonous barb, it's a ray; without one, it's a skate. If you are wary about fish bones, fear not the skate—it does not have a bone in its body. The skeleton of a skate is all cartilage, the soft stuff you blow out playing tennis or running from the police. In fact, some dictionaries call a skate a "fishlike vertebrate." You have to believe in dinosaurs.

A well-trained chef knows a fresh skate by its slime. The fish's skin exudes a slimy substance for at least ten hours after death. To test the claim that the fish was just caught, killed and put on ice, the sharp chef will wipe the skin clean and watch to see if it gets slimy again. Chances are it won't, unless the sharp chef lives in a fishing village.

*Actually, for cocktail party chatter with someone you don't especially like, they all have urea in their blood, which turns to ammonia quickly if the fish are not bled as soon as they are caught. I believe in being truthful, but if I talked about this straight out in the recipe you'd never try it, and that would be a great pity because it is wonderful. Tastes like chicken. Honest. And while I'm on the subject, try snow shark; it *really* tastes like chicken. As of August 1994, experimental fisheries were being established on the west coast of Canada for the commercial fishing of this species. Its real name is six gill shark, because all other sharks (except the seven gill) have five gills. Snow shark makes trendy mako look like bad canned tuna. Okay, now you know, take a big black ink marker and cross this out so you won't be faced with gory details again. And, hey, enjoy.

Now the good news. Skate are abundant in polar and temperate waters. This means cold. Cold is good. And clean. And it means growing quite slowly so it develops a fine taste and fresh aroma that the fast-growing fish and seafood of tropical waters cannot. A skate has class—it feasts on shrimp, snails and clams. It all adds up to a meal Europeans have long known to be fabulous. That's why it is in this book.

If you buy skate from a good monger, he or she will have skinned it. If not, ask. If the monger won't skin the skate, find another monger. If you're stuck, take the wings and put them into a pan of salted water, bring to a boil, reduce heat and poach for three minutes. Remove, cook and peel off skin. Then proceed with the recipe.

4 cups	cold water	1 L
5 tbsp	vinegar	75 mL
1 ½ tsp	salt	7 mL
½	carrot, sliced	½
½	small onion, sliced	½
½ tsp	whole black peppercorns, about 30 small ones, lightly smashed with a mallet	2 mL
	Bouquet garni (1 sprig parsley, 1 bay leaf, 1 sprig thyme, 1 ½ inch [4 cm] piece of celery, tied up together with string or in a piece of cheesecloth)	
2	skate wings	2
	Black butter (recipe, p. 41)	
2 tbsp	capers, rinsed and dried	30 mL
¼ cup	chopped parsley	60 mL

Preheat oven to 200°F (95°C). Place 2 plates in oven to warm.

In a pan just large enough to accommodate the skate wings, combine water, vinegar, salt, carrot, onion, peppercorns and bouquet garni. Bring to a gentle boil. This is standard vinegar court bouillon for skate. Substitute white wine for the vinegar and add ½ cup (125 mL) cold water, and you get the usual court bouillon for poaching or baking other fish.

You may find a tough, white membrane on one side of the skate. Cut the edge of it away from the flesh at a corner and peel it off. Wash wing under cold running water, then slide skate wings into the court bouillon. Turn heat down. When bouillon returns to a bubbling simmer, poach skate for 10 minutes, from time to time skimming off any scum or foam. Carefully remove the fish to a plate and place on the open oven door to allow the fish to dry for about 2 minutes. (You can help by gently patting it dry with a paper towel.)

One minute before serving, heat black butter. Add capers. Place skate on the warmed plates. Sprinkle parsley over skate and pour on hot black butter. Serve immediately. Perfect *frites* go beautifully with skate.

Skate Meunière

<table>
<tr><td>PREPARATION TIME:</td><td>2</td><td>wings of a small skate</td><td>2</td></tr>
<tr><td>10 MINUTES</td><td>4 cups</td><td>cold water</td><td>1 L</td></tr>
<tr><td>COOKING TIME:</td><td>5 tbsp</td><td>vinegar</td><td>75 mL</td></tr>
<tr><td>10 MINUTES</td><td>1 ½ tsp</td><td>salt</td><td>7 mL</td></tr>
<tr><td>SERVES: 2 AS AN</td><td>½</td><td>carrot, sliced</td><td>½</td></tr>
<tr><td>APPETIZER OR A</td><td>½</td><td>small onion, sliced</td><td>½</td></tr>
<tr><td>SMALL FISH COURSE</td><td>½ tsp</td><td>whole black peppercorns,
lightly smashed with a mallet
Bouquet garni (1 sprig parsley, 1 bay leaf,
1 sprig thyme, 1 ½ inch [4 cm] piece of celery,
tied up together with string or in a piece of
cheesecloth)</td><td>2 mL</td></tr>
<tr><td></td><td>½ cup</td><td>flour</td><td>125 mL</td></tr>
<tr><td></td><td>2 tsp</td><td>salt</td><td>10 mL</td></tr>
<tr><td></td><td>2 tsp</td><td>freshly ground black pepper</td><td>10 mL</td></tr>
<tr><td></td><td>5 tbsp</td><td>unsalted butter</td><td>75 ml</td></tr>
<tr><td></td><td>24</td><td>capers</td><td>24</td></tr>
<tr><td></td><td>1 tbsp</td><td>lemon juice</td><td>15 mL</td></tr>
<tr><td></td><td>2 tbsp</td><td>freshly chopped parsley
Black butter (recipe, p. 41)</td><td>30 mL</td></tr>
</table>

Have the fishmonger skin the skate wings. In a pan just large enough to accommodate the skate wings, combine water, vinegar, salt, carrot, onion, peppercorns and bouquet garni. Bring to a gentle boil. Add skate wings and poach for 5 minutes. Remove, cool and pat dry. Combine flour, salt and pepper. Melt 4 tbsp (60 mL) of the butter in a fry pan over medium-high heat until it foams. Dredge skate wings in flour and fry in butter on both sides until golden brown. Remove to heated serving plates. Add remaining butter and capers; swirl around until butter browns and capers smell like roasted hazelnuts. Add lemon juice. Spread chopped parsley over cooked wings; pour hot black butter over them. The hot butter should make the parsley fry right on top of the skate. Serve immediately.

Hot Cherries Eldorado

The mark of a good restaurant is that it is tuned to the seasons. The North American sweet cherry season is notoriously short, between two and four weeks in mid-summer. Washington State and several areas of Europe produce dried cherries, which restaurants rehydrate. They are very expensive, but not available to you and me. Their flavor is even more intense than that of fresh cherries, and they can be rehydrated in cognac or wine to achieve heights that even the scientists tinkering with an infinite shelf life for tomatoes have not dreamed of. Since the season is so short, take advantage of it. With this recipe, you get not only my version of a wonderful classic dessert, but also the ingredients for many more delicacies for other seasons. By the way, if you use Marsala wine instead of brandy in the sabayon, you get the Italian dessert zabaglione.

PREPARATION TIME: 20 MINUTES
COOKING TIME: 40 MINUTES
ASSEMBLY: 5 MINUTES
SERVES: 4

2 lb	cherries	900 g
	Vanilla syrup (recipe follows)	
	Sabayon (recipe follows)	
8	mint leaves for garnish	8

Pit cherries. Place in vanilla syrup for 1 minute only, until they are coated and hot. Remove and divide among 8 wineglasses. Top with sabayon. Garnish with 1 mint leaf per glass. Serve immediately.

Vanilla syrup

2 cups	water	500 mL
2 cups	sugar	500 mL
1 tsp	vanilla extract	5 mL

Combine ingredients in a saucepan. Bring to a low boil, then cook until the liquid thickens into a syrup. Timing is not crucial, but the syrup should not be too thick.

Sabayon

4	eggs	4
½ cup	icing sugar	125 mL
¼ cup	brandy	60 mL

Separate eggs. Beat yolks with sugar until the mixture becomes light in color and creamy, about 2 minutes with an electric beater. In a double boiler over simmering water—or on a low burner with the eyes of a hawk—whisk mixture until it becomes foamy. Add brandy and continue whisking until the mixture begins to thicken; its volume will increase by half. Remove from heat. Beat egg whites until they peak. Fold in. Set aside. (This can be prepared several hours ahead of time and kept in the refrigerator.)

Apple Clafouti

PREPARATION TIME:
15 MINUTES
COOKING TIME:
40 MINUTES
SERVES: 4

The beauty of this simple, luscious dessert is you can use any fruit in season or several at one time, but you can get apples any time. This version was given me by Chef Fabien Siebert, of Marcel's Bistro and Le Saint Tropez restaurants in Toronto.

2 tbsp	butter	30 mL
¼ cup	sugar, plus 15 mL (1 tbsp) for dusting	60 mL
4	apples, peeled, cored and quartered	4
1 tsp	rum	5 mL
2	eggs	2
1 cup	milk	250 mL
1 tsp	vanilla extract	5 mL

Lightly grease a baking pan with butter and dust with just enough sugar to cover the buttered surface, about 1 tbsp (15 mL). Preheat oven to 350°F (175°C).

In a sauté pan, melt butter and sauté apples for 3 minutes. Add the remaining 2 tbsp (30 mL) sugar, mix well and sauté for another 2 minutes. Remove the apples to the baking pan. Deglaze the sauté pan with rum and add it to the apples. Mix eggs, remaining sugar, milk and vanilla. Pour over apples. Bake for 40 minutes.

Serve cold or lukewarm with your favorite ice cream.

Peach Pear Tart

1	8-inch (20 cm) pie pastry shell (recipe follows)	1	
2	ripe pears	2	
2 tbsp	brown sugar	30 mL	
2 tbsp	orange liqueur	30 mL	
3 tbsp	cornstarch	45 mL	
¾ cup	white sugar	180 mL	
⅓ cup	orange juice	80 mL	
	Juice of ½ lemon		
¼ tsp	grated lemon rind	1 mL	
¼ tsp	grated orange rind	1 mL	
1 tbsp	butter	15 mL	
4	egg yolks, lightly beaten	4	
2	ripe peaches	2	
½ tsp	cinnamon	2 mL	

PREPARATION TIME: 30 MINUTES
COOKING TIME: 45 MINUTES
SERVES: 8

Preheat oven to 325°F (160°C).

Cover the bottom of the pie shell with dried beans to keep the bottom from rising and bake for 10 minutes. Remove from oven; remove beans and allow to cool slightly before filling.

Peel and mash the pears coarsely, sprinkle with brown sugar and splash on orange liqueur. Cover and set aside to allow flavors to meld.

In a double boiler over bubbling water, whisk together the cornstarch, white sugar, orange juice, lemon juice, lemon and orange rinds and butter. Cook for 5 minutes; cover, reduce heat to medium low and cook for 10 minutes undisturbed. Remove from heat and cool. Stir in egg yolks. Reduce heat to low; continue cooking for 2 to 3 minutes. Remove from heat and whisk until heat and steam are released from the mixture.

Drain the pear mixture and line the pie shell with it. Add two-thirds of the lemon–orange mixture. Peel and slice the peaches ½ inch (1 cm) thick; lay slices on top of the pears in an attractive swirl pattern. Gently spoon the remaining lemon–orange filling on top without disturbing the pattern. Sprinkle with cinnamon.

Return pie to oven and bake for 35 to 40 minutes, watching the pie edges carefully to ensure they do not darken too much during the last 5 to 10 minutes of baking.

Serve slightly warm with whipped cream flavored with a pinch of Cointreau, Triple Sec or other orange liqueur or with vanilla ice cream.

Flaky Pie Pastry

PREPARATION TIME:
15 MINUTES
RESTING TIME: 1 HOUR
MAKES: PASTRY FOR
TWO 8-INCH
(20 CM) PIES

You can buy perfectly adequate pie pastry in the frozen-foods section of your supermarket. Or you can make your own quite easily, as long as you remember to chill the mixing bowl and lard for at least five minutes in the freezer or fifteen minutes in the refrigerator. Call me nuts, but I chill the flour, too. The water must be ice cold.

2 cups	all-purpose flour	500 mL
1 tsp	salt	5 mL
⅔ cup	lard	160 mL
5 tbsp	ice water	75 mL
1 tsp	lemon juice	5 mL

In a large, cold mixing bowl, sift together flour and salt. Using a wire pastry blender, blend in half the lard until the flour resembles coarse meal. Blend in the remaining lard, but not as thoroughly. The lumps should be about the size of large peas. Combine water and lemon juice. Sprinkle 2 tbsp (30 mL) over the flour and whisk in with a fork. Sprinkle another 2 tbsp (30 mL) over the flour and whisk in. You only want enough water to hold the dough together. No more. With your hands, squeeze the flour together. If it doesn't hold, add water drop by drop until it does. When it does hold, turn it out onto a very lightly floured board and form it into a ball. Do not knead. Wrap it in heavy plastic wrap, a heavy plastic bag or plastic wrap and aluminum foil, and refrigerate 1 hour to allow the water to penetrate the flour.

Remove from fridge and divide in half. Rewrap one piece and return it to the refrigerator. (It will keep up to 2 weeks in the refrigerator or 6 months in the freezer.) On a lightly floured board, form dough into a ball, flatten it, then with a rolling pin roll it out into a circle 1 inch (2.5 cm) wider than the outer rim of the pie pan. Don't flip it over during the rolling; you don't want more flour in the dough. Carefully roll it over the rolling pin and place it in the pie pan.

Crêpes à la Bones

This was the knockout dessert my wife made in the North American Soffitel French Amateur Cooking Finals.

PREPARATION TIME:
45 MINUTES
COOKING TIME:
30 MINUTES
SERVES: 8

½ cup	sugar	125 mL
5 tbsp	pastry flour	75 mL
½ cup	milk	125 mL
½ cup	whipping cream	125 mL
1 tsp	grated orange zest	5 mL
½ cup	fruit juice (orange, peach or apricot nectar—a combination of juices such as orange, banana and strawberry is especially tasty)	125 mL
8	crêpes (Palacsinta recipe, p. 160)	8
⅓ cup	apricot preserve	80 mL
	Cinnamon	
⅓ cup	sugar	80 mL

In the top of a double boiler, combine sugar and flour. Slowly add the milk, then the cream, constantly whisking until blended and smooth. Add the orange zest and cook for 4 minutes, or until mixture begins to thicken. Slowly whisk in juice. Continue stirring until the custard has a rich thickness.

Preheat oven to 225°F (110°C).

Place 8 buttered ramekins or muffin cups on a baking sheet. Gently stuff a crêpe into each cup. Fill the crêpes with custard and spread 2 tsp (10 mL) of apricot preserves on each. Sprinkle with cinnamon. Bake for 15 to 20 minutes.

Melt sugar in a small, heavy pot (preferably nonstick) over medium-low heat. Stir with a wooden spoon. When sugar begins to melt and becomes amber in color, drizzle in a fine stream over crêpes straight from the hot pot, to make a caramel spiderweb effect.

Crème Brûlée

PREPARATION TIME:
1 DAY
COOKING TIME:
1 HOUR
MAKES: 12 RAMEKINS

Commonly found on dessert menus, crème brûlée is not French, but English. Originally called burned cream, it was renamed at Cambridge University to impress. It is an egg yolk, sugar and cream custard allowed to set for a day, then topped with sugar and run under a broiler until the sugar becomes caramelized. In a restaurant kitchen the custard is made the day before. More important, the sugar is caramelized under a salamander—a gas-fired, free-standing broiler that provides an even, extremely hot heat, which you can never duplicate in your home oven. In the salamander, the sugar caramelizes so quickly the custard below doesn't heat up and curdle. And that is what you want: hot above, cold underneath; crunchy top, smooth custard.

If you have no salamander, there are three solutions.

A common practice in restaurants that do not have salamanders is to make an aluminum-foil mold slightly smaller than the surface of the ramekin. Pour in sugar and broil until the caramel is set. Remove, let cool, peel off the hardened disk and lay it on the custard. No-fail crème brûlée: the custard is never ruined.

The second solution is a bit messy. Place custards topped with uncooked sugar in a deep tray filled to the rim of each ramekin with ice. Then broil. The ice usually keeps the custard from curdling.

The best alternative by far comes from the hardware store. A small propane blowtorch duplicates the consistent, extremely high heat of a salamander and creates a more even crust, as the chef can better control the burn.

Crème brûlée is utterly delicious, and chefs can take the basic recipe and add their own flavors and twists. To wit:

At Chinois on Main in Santa Monica, Wolfgang Puck serves three little pots flavored differently. One night it was mint, lemon and ginger.

Patina in Los Angeles serves the custard mixed with bits of sweet corn under the caramelized crust.

Nicola Silvrio, pastry chef at Toronto's Centro, creates an essence of passion fruit and sugar and adds it after the custard has cooked.

The classic crème brûlée is made by cooking cream with a flavor, such as vanilla, adding it to a mixture of beaten egg yolks and sugar, baking it in ramekins until set, letting it cool overnight in the refrigerator, then caramelizing it with fire before serving.

A far richer version starts by cooking the egg yolks, adding the remaining ingredients and cooking it some more. You don't get this version often these days because too many chefs aren't classically trained, it takes too much labor and therefore money, and today's chefs know they can get away with an inferior product.

This version is made with a near-classic butter cream custard, flavored in three ways and blowtorched.

	Juice of 2 lemons	
2 tbsp	sugar	30 mL
3 cups	whipping cream	750 mL
2 tsp	vanilla extract	10 mL
½ cup	mint leaves	125 mL
9	egg yolks	9
⅔ cup	sugar	160 mL
2 tbsp	sugar	30 mL
6 tbsp	unsalted butter	90 mL
½ cup	brown sugar	125 mL

In a small pot over medium-low heat combine lemon juice and sugar. Stir until sugar dissolves. Reduce to about 2 tbsp (30 mL) golden brown liquid that coats the back of a spoon, about 20 minutes.

Pour 1 cup (250 mL) whipping cream into a small pot. Add the mint leaves; heat over medium heat until the cream begins to boil. Reduce heat to low and cook for 20 minutes. In a second pot, combine the lemon essence and 1 cup (250 mL) of cream, bring to a boil and simmer 20 minutes. In a third pot, combine the vanilla extract and the final cup of cream, heat, simmer and cool.

In a double boiler over boiling water, combine the egg yolks and sugar and beat with an electric mixer until mixture is lemon yellow and thickened. (Chefs claim that the "batter" forms "ribbons" as you beat it; parents say to cook it to the consistency of Elmer's Glue-All.) Pour the egg-yolk mixture into three bowls, dividing evenly. Add the hot mint cream to the egg mixture in the first bowl very slowly, beating all the time. Add the hot lemon cream to the egg mixture in the second bowl equally slowly, beating all the time. Whisk the vanilla cream into the third bowl any old way.

Make the separate custards individually over a simmering double boiler—that is, over low heat. Cook each one for 15 to 20 minutes, stirring occasionally. They are done when they don't drip on your shoes as you taste them, which you will be unable to resist. As soon as each is done, whip in 2 tbsp (30 mL) butter, then pour into four ¼ cup (60 mL) ramekins. Cover and refrigerate overnight.

If you have a very efficient broiler, top each ramekin with ¼ inch (5 mm) sugar and place under an extremely hot broiler for about 2 minutes, or until the sugar turns to caramel.

If you are sensible, however, you'll cover each ramekin with the sugar and then blowtorch the sugar until it is evenly brown and crusty. Just pass the tip of the blue flame over the sugar, painting the sugar with the flame like a watercolorist with a wet brush. Serve. Hot crunch, cool silk below. Perfection.

Chocolate Balls

Truffles, those little balls of bittersweet chocolate, hard on the outside and silky ganache on the inside, are terrific with espresso to finish off a grand bistro meal. They are also a pain in the neck to make. These are Bones's quick versions, which also go perfectly with coffee.

4 oz	sweet white chocolate	115 g
1 tbsp	butter	15 mL
1 tbsp	whipping cream	15 mL
2 tbsp	icing sugar	30 mL
2 tbsp	finely ground almonds	30 mL
2 tbsp	cocoa	30 mL
2 tbsp	unsweetened coconut	30 mL
2 tbsp	cinnamon	30 mL

In a small pot over low heat, melt chocolate. Add butter, whipping cream, icing sugar and almonds, whisking until perfectly smooth. Cool in refrigerator for about 30 minutes, or until hard. Roll 1 tsp (5 mL) chocolate into a ball and roll it in the cocoa; roll the second chocolate ball in the coconut and the third in the cinnamon. Repeat until all chocolate is used. Serve in paper petit four cups.

CHAPTER FIVE

The Trattoria

Trattoria Mia

ANTIPASTI E ZUPPE

Pasta e Fagioli 97
The white bean soup of Italy

Roasted Yellow Pepper Soup 98
With herbed croutons

Focaccia 99
With onion, sweet peppers and sage

Crostini all Casea 103
With roasted red pepper, anchovy
and romano, or gorgonzola and
marinated wild mushrooms

Bruschetta 104
The original, with first cold pressed
extra virgin olive oil and garlic
With tomatoes, basil and Parmesan
With smoked salmon, garlic and oil
With caponata

Polenta 106
With Parmesan and aioli, or wild
mushrooms and gorgonzola

Hot Pear and Gorgonzola Salad 109

PASTA E RISOTTI

Garlic Spaghetti 110
Garlic, Parmesan and pasta

Pasta of the Sea 110
Shrimp and scallops in a shrimp
essence and wine cream sauce

Fettuccine Alfie 112
North American version, with cream,
bacon and Parmesan cheese

Risotto 112
With gorgonzola, salmon or
porcini mushrooms

PIATTO PER SERVIRE I LEGUMI

Wild Mushroom Timbalio 116

CROSTACEI

Lobster Spargalo Grill 118
Fettucine with lobster in brandy
cream sauce

Steamed Mussels 119
In wine, leeks and cream

POLLO

Roasted Chicken 120
With prosciutto, black olives
and sage

*Chicken with Orange Mustard and
Cream Vermouth Sauce 121*

VITELLO E CARNI

Scallopini Limone 122

Veal with Prosciutto 123

Thyme-Roasted Veal Chop 124
With apple brandy sauce

Grilled Pork Chop 125
With a thyme and oregano crust

DOLCE

Brandied Coffee Ricotta 126

Zabaglione 126

Panna Cotta 127

Tiramisu 129

You could get in trouble with this concept, through no fault of your own. Italian cuisine, as interpreted in North America for more than a hundred years, is under attack and all you have come to love in your favorite Italian eatery is being questioned. The new restaurateurs want you to eat "real" Italian, not "Frenchified" or "Continentalized" Italian. What are they talking about?

Take Fettuccine Alfredo, one of the most common Italian dishes—fettuccine in a creamy Parmesan bath with ground pepper. Sublime. Slippery. Wonderful. A typical recipe would have you sauté some garlic until translucent (or not), add chicken stock and reduce it (or not) and cream, then the cooked fettuccine, into which you would grate fresh Parmesan and bubble it down until it is thick and sticks slightly to the noodles. It would be delicious and fattening— and it would have nothing to do with the real Fettuccine Alfredo, which is noodles, butter and *parmigiano reggiano*, period. No cream, no garlic, no broth. The dish is usually Frenchified because in North America you cannot buy traditional Italian butter (cultured, unsalted butter with a very low water content), Parmesan (it is specially made for the restaurant) or noodles (made from local durum semolina flour).

The "Continental" style was first challenged in the 1970s, largely by a few brave New York restaurateurs who were tired of checked tablecloths, straw-basket Chianti bottles and candles. Tony May, now owner of San Domenico, presided over a rare festival of Italian cuisine at the Rainbow Room, and it became a hit. Since then, real Italian cuisine has been warmly embraced, although its Frenchification continues.

I will not play into the purist camp here. I will allow Mr. May to prepare eel as a mark of pure Italian cuisine, but I will not venture to do so, nor will I ask you to, either.

True Italian cuisine is as diverse as French or Chinese. The south and north are as different as night and day. And everywhere in between has its own style, culture, products and tradition.

To be able to deliver purity is a luxury that few in the restaurant business can afford. Restaurants survive by catering to the tastes of regulars, who usually come from the neighborhood. If the regulars don't like anchovies, the restaurateur can't use them, which makes it impossible to be true to many authentic trattoria recipes.

It is easy, however, to create a trattoria with the atmosphere of just about any Italian restaurant in just about any house. All you need is a love of good food and the ability to share it unconditionally.

In 1968, I had the privilege of having lunch on the slopes of Mount Vesuvius with one of the vintners of Lacrima Christi. Some lunch. It started with a huge bowl of spaghetti and wine from the private cellar—a bottle per person. Impressive. I leaned back in my chair, stuffed to the gills; another bottle of heavenly vintage was offered, accepted and drunk. My stomach was blissfully settled by the excellent wine, and as I struggled to say thank you for the wonderful repast, out came a huge bowl of mussels. And another bottle.

Lunch was seven courses, six bottles, more than five hours. After lunch, I went back to the hotel in Sorrento, where my friends were eating dinner. "I'll wait out on the balcony," I said, and promptly fell asleep. I woke up at midnight, crawled to my room and slept until dawn.

In creating the trattoria menu, I chose recipes that should be shared. They reflect atmosphere more than authenticity. The dishes are Italian, of course, but they are Italian as interpreted in several different restaurants, which means Italian cuisine touched by ingredients, cooking techniques and tastes common to the regions in which those restaurants thrive. Many were inspired by the west coast, and that is reflected in, for instance, roasted peppers. Others have Canadian touches (lobster, smoked salmon). All will give your home trattoria that feeling of unconditional hospitality.

Pasta e Fagioli

If a soup dish can be trendy, *Pasta e Fagioli* is it. Over the past few years, this peasant, thick-as-stew soup has popped up on menus and food pages everywhere. The Greeks make a very similar winter soup they call *fasolatha*, and in one form or another it can be found all around the Mediterranean. Some versions add tomatoes. I don't. Some use navy beans, and most call for cannellini (white kidney) beans. I use the canned ones. At Joe DiMaggio Wet Paint Café, a Toronto restaurant owned by a distant relative of the baseball great, the chef adds sherry. So do I.

Pancetta is thick Italian bacon that is cured but not smoked. It is usually packaged as a roll of meat and is critical to the taste of this dish.

PREPARATION TIME:
40 MINUTES
COOKING TIME:
45 MINUTES
SERVES: 8

2 tbsp	olive oil	30 mL
5 oz	pancetta, thinly sliced then finely chopped	140 g
2 ½ cups	roughly chopped onions, about 2 large onions	625 mL
1 cup	roughly chopped celery	250 mL
¾ cup	sliced carrots	180 mL
4	cloves garlic, finely chopped	4
16 oz	can white kidney beans	500 mL
1 cup	chicken stock	250 mL
1 tsp	Tabasco sauce	5 mL
¼ cup	dry sherry	60 mL
1 cup	cooked elbow macaroni	250 mL
	Salt and pepper to taste	

In a large pot, heat oil over medium heat and sauté pancetta for 2 minutes. Add onion, celery, carrots and garlic and sauté, stirring, until onions are limp, about 5 minutes. Add beans and their liquid, chicken stock, Tabasco and sherry; turn down heat and simmer for 20 minutes. Add pasta and cook a further 10 minutes. Taste and adjust salt and pepper.

Serve in heated bowls with chunks of crusty Italian bread.

Roasted Yellow Pepper Soup

PREPARATION TIME:
45 MINUTES
COOKING TIME:
45 MINUTES
SERVES: 4

And while we're on the subject of bean soups …

Roasting peppers in small quantities is easier if you cut them into small, flat pieces, set them in one layer on a baking sheet skin side up, and broil them in the oven. Chefs don't do it this way because they roast so many at a time. It would take longer to trim them than to have someone throw whole, unseeded, uncut peppers under the broiler and turn them when required. Time means money. And if the defining mark of a good chef is an ability to buy well, it is almost equally an ability to save money and contribute to the profit.

3	sweet yellow peppers	3
2 tbsp	olive oil	30 mL
⅓ cup	roughly sliced carrots	80 mL
⅓ cup	roughly chopped onions	80 mL
⅓ cup	roughly chopped celery	80 mL
2	cloves garlic, minced	2
2 cups	chicken stock	500 mL
½ cup	white kidney beans	125 mL
¾ cup	whipping cream	180 mL
	Salt and pepper to taste	
	Herbed croutons (recipe follows)	

Set oven to broil.

Cut peppers in half lengthwise, grab the seed pods and rip them out. Discard any remaining seeds. Cut peppers lengthwise into quarters; cut out white membranes. Turn pepper pieces skin side up and flatten with pressure from your palm. Place on a baking sheet, skin side up, and broil until the skins turn completely black. Place blistered peppers in a paper bag, close the top and let stand until cool, about 20 minutes. Remove from bag, peel off and discard charred skin and roughly chop peppers. Reserve.

In a heavy pot, heat olive oil over medium heat. Add carrots, onions, celery and garlic and sauté until all the vegetables are limp. Add chicken stock and beans, lower heat and simmer for 30 minutes. Cool mixture.

In a food processor, purée vegetable-stock mixture and the roasted peppers. Blend in whipping cream. Add salt and pepper to taste.

At this point, the soup can be refrigerated for 2 days and reheated just before serving.

Heat soup, pour into heated bowls, top with herbed croutons and serve.

Herbed Croutons

4	slices Italian white bread, ½ inch (1 cm) thick	4
2 tbsp	extra-virgin olive oil, more if required	30 mL
1 tbsp	dried rosemary	15 mL

Preheat oven to 250°F (120°C).

Cut the crust from the bread. Coat both sides of the bread slices with oil. With a rolling pin, crush dried rosemary leaves to a powder and sprinkle evenly over the bread slices. Cut bread into 1 inch (2.5 cm) cubes, spread on a baking sheet and bake for 1 hour, or until the croutons are golden and toasted through.

Focaccia, Crostini, Bruschetta

Walk into many a trattoria and these will be brought to the table just to make you feel at home. They are simple and wondrous: a herb-scented flat bread, sometimes crispy, sometimes chewy; little toasts, some thick, some thin, brushed with oil and topped with antipasto; and a thick hunk of Italian garlic bread, often topped with oil, fresh tomato and basil.

Onion, Sweet Pepper and Sage Focaccia

PREPARATION TIME:
3 HOURS
COOKING TIME:
20 MINUTES
MAKES: 2 BREADS

Valentino in Santa Monica serves all sorts of focaccia, the flat, aromatic bread of Italy. Several years ago the chef created one topped with eggplant, onions and peppers and served it with a sage oil.

By combining onions and sweet peppers on one focaccia, I am encroaching on Neopolitan pizza territory. Been there. Done that. Don't care.

To seed a raw pepper, cut it lengthwise. The seeds will be clustered at one end. Grab them with your fingers and rip them out all in one clump. Skinning is easy: quarter the pepper, cut out the membranes (white bits), flatten it with the palm of your hand and cut straight along the flat. (The tough skin of a pepper is not easily digestible, which is why you want it off.) If you cut an unpeeled pepper, place the skin side down on the cutting board to make the job easy.

1 tsp	active dry yeast (half a packet)	5 mL
1 tsp	sugar	5 mL
1 ½ cups	lukewarm water	375 mL
1	sweet red pepper (or yellow or green)	1
¼ tsp	olive oil	1 mL
6 cups	all-purpose flour	1.4 L
2 tsp	salt	10 mL
2 tbsp	olive oil	30 mL
1	small onion	1
24	fresh sage leaves (small and tender)	24
2 tbsp	extra-virgin olive oil	30 mL
	Freshly ground salt	

Dissolve the yeast and sugar in ¼ cup (60 mL) of the lukewarm water and let it rest for 10 minutes until it foams. Take a fork and whisk it down a bit, then let it proof another 5 minutes.

Meanwhile, coat the skin of the pepper with ¼ tsp (1 mL) olive oil and broil 6 inches (15 cm) from the heat source until the skin is charred and blackened all over. Put pepper in a paper bag, scrunch up the top and let cool about 20 minutes.

Sift flour and salt together in a large bowl. Make a well in the center and pour in yeast and 2 tbsp (30 mL) olive oil. With your fingers (guess what western chefs have discovered? Chopsticks add "finger" control without being fingers), start folding the flour into the yeast. Add water to the well as the liquids soak up the flour. When the flour is sticky, pull it out and set it on a floured counter. Knead for 10 minutes. Form dough into a ball, plop it back in the bowl, make a cross on the top with a knife, cover it loosely with a damp tea towel, put the bowl in a warm place where the cat won't get it and let it rise for 1 hour. If the yeast is working it will rise considerably.

Meanwhile, take the pepper from the bag. Wipe off blackened skin with your hands and discard. Cut pepper in half pole-to-pole, remove seeds, quarter the pepper and cut into very fine matchsticks. Set aside. Slice onion on the round as thinly as you can; you should be able to see through the slices. Take the stems off the sage leaves.

After the dough has risen, punch it down and roll it out on the floured countertop until it is about ½ inch (1 cm) thick. Oil 2 cookie sheets or pizza pans, divide the dough in half and spread dough out corner to corner, if you are using cookie sheets, or in large rounds, if you are using pizza pans. Stab the surface all over with a fork to let the steam escape during cooking. Cover with damp tea towels and let dough rise for another 30 minutes.

Preheat oven to 425°F (220°C).

Paint both breads generously with the extra-virgin olive oil (not first cold pressed—the fine properties of cold-pressed oil are destroyed when baked). Distribute the peppers, onions and sage leaves on the two breads. Don't let them overlap, so each bite will give a different experience. Finally, give each bread a good grind of salt. (Table salt is far too fine. If it's all you have, forget it. Coarse sea salt is okay, as long as it isn't the size of road salt, which would break your teeth.)

Place breads in the oven and bake for 20 minutes. If your oven is like most people's, the temperature is not accurate. After 20 minutes, check it. If it doesn't appear done in the middle but is golden on top, turn the temperature down 50°F (10°C) and continue cooking another 5 minutes or so.

Serve, as at Valentino, with a bottle of first cold-pressed, extra-virgin Tuscany oil for dipping the ripped focaccia.

Crostini

PREPARATION TIME:
1 DAY
PLUS 50 MINUTES
SERVES: 8

I don't like canned anchovies except in Caesar salad, where I can't taste them, and in very small doses on pizza, where I can, often too distinctly. Delicate they aren't. But being a masochist, I tried a variation on Valentino's crostini, little toasts topped with buffalo mozzarella, red pepper and anchovies.

Buffalo mozzarella is no relative of the mozzarella made on this continent. For starters it's made with water buffalo milk and, let's face it, there are few water buffalo roaming the range. Besides, like all great commodities, it has a season, and a good chef stays in season. I wasn't, so I used a stronger, slightly crumbly imported Romano cheese, sliced very thin. It's so good that I have no intention of trying this with buffalo mozzarella.

Try it with a perfect gin martini: a cap of French vermouth sloshed over two ice cubes and then immediately poured out, cubes and all. Pour 2 oz (60 mL) Tanqueray into the frosted, vermouth-tinged glass, float a drop of ice water on top, add an olive or a twist and have the class to sip rather than slurp. I've never mastered the sip.

1	loaf Italian white bread	1
¼ cup	olive oil	60 mL
1	red pepper, roasted, seeded, peeled and cut into very thin julienne strips	1
2	anchovy filets	2
12 oz	fresh Romano cheese	340 g
24	leaves flat leaf parsley for garnish	24

The day before, preheat oven to 250°F (125°C).

From the loaf, cut 12 slices, each about ¼ inch (5 mm) thick. Stack them. Slice off the round corners and the bottom crust. Slice off as much of the top crust as you can without destroying the whole damn thing. Cut the slices in half vertically. You should now have 24 small pieces of bread that look like they can be small slices of toast. If you don't, try again—you should still have about half a loaf of bread left. This is just making Italian Melba toast, and how hard can making toast be, for heaven's sake? Forget it—make whatever shape of toast you want.

Place the bread slices on a cookie sheet. Thoroughly brush them with olive oil (don't waste the extra-virgin) and bake until golden brown, about 1 hour. Let cool, wrap loosely in tin foil and set aside for the next day.

To serve, cut Romano into 24 slices and place 1 on each toast. Cut anchovy filets into 24 squares and place on top of the cheese. Cross 3 roasted red pepper strips on top. Garnish each piece of toast with a parsley leaf and serve.

Crostini all Casea

24	crostini	24
¼ cup	first cold pressed extra-virgin olive oil	60 mL
	Salt	
12 oz	Gorgonzola cheese	340 g
	Pepper	
	Mushrooms in oil and parsley (recipe below)	

Make the crostini, the "little toasts," as in recipe above. Paint each toast with more olive oil, sprinkle with salt, top with Gorgonzola, grind on some pepper, then top with a dollop of Mushrooms in Oil and Parsley.

Mushrooms in Oil and Parsley

¼ cup	extra-virgin olive oil	60 mL
¼ lb	fresh porcini mushrooms	115 g
	(or hydrated dried porcini)*	
2	cloves garlic, finely chopped	2
¼ cup	balsamic vinegar	60 mL
	Salt and freshly ground pepper	
2 tbsp	chopped fresh Italian parsley	30 mL

Put oil in a small fry pan or saucepan over medium heat, add porcini and garlic and fry until golden but not browned. Add balsamic vinegar, turn heat down and cook until all the mushroom juices have evaporated, about 4 minutes. Remove from heat. Add a generous grinding of pepper and a dash of salt. Add parsley and stir it in quickly. Taste. Adjust seasoning. Transfer to a bowl, cover and cool. Makes an excellent antipasto, as well.

*Porcini have a wild taste. If you can't find any fresh porcini, use any mushroom other than white button supermarket mushrooms—shiitake, oyster or portobello, the latter of which is a North American commercially produced porcini. Even a brown cultivated mushroom is better. If you can find dried porcini mushrooms, use them, or dried boletus, chanterelles, morels or those dried mushrooms simply labeled "European." Soak dried mushrooms in 1 cup (250 mL) warm water for 30 minutes. Remove the mushrooms and use in the recipe. Keep the mushroom water. Soak a paper coffee filter in water and pour the mushroom liquid through to strain out grit. The mushroom water is full of flavor to add to soups, gravies or sauces.

Bruschetta, the Original

When the olives are ready in Tuscany, they are handpicked, then crushed by huge granite stones that do not heat up with the pressure. (Heat would spoil the oil.) The mush is laid out on mats, and the green peppery oil is pressed out. That is first cold pressed olive oil; it has an acidity of less than one percent, which also makes it extra-virgin.

Fresh bread is toasted, garlic is rubbed over the crusty surface, and that first cold pressed oil is liberally poured over the bread. A sprinkle of salt. Some wine. Heaven. That's *bruschetta*.

Bruschetta, Tomatoes, Basil and Parmesan

The *bruschetta* that has taken root in North American restaurants is one with basil and tomatoes. Usually the basil isn't fresh and the tomatoes are not in season. A disaster.

2	large ripe tomatoes, peeled, seeded and diced	2
1 cup	chopped fresh basil (1 large bunch)	250 mL
	Salt and pepper	
4	large slices Italian bread	4
4	cloves garlic, peeled	4
¼ cup	freshly grated Parmesan	60 mL

In a bowl combine the tomatoes, basil; add salt and pepper to taste. Toast the bread on 1 side; while still hot, rub garlic all over crusty surface. Cut slices in half to make 8 pieces. Top with tomato mixture and sprinkle with Parmesan. Arrange *bruschetta* on a large plate and let your guests fight amongst themselves.

Bruschetta with Smoked Salmon, Garlic and Oil

Now we're getting fancy. Make the little toasts in the crostini recipe and rub with garlic. Then top with a slice of smoked salmon or lox or some smoked salmon mousse.

Caponata

Caponata is a Sicilian salad that has been turned into an all-purpose condiment in North American restaurants. Serve it as a cold summer salad, side dish or as a fabulous relish for leftover cold beef or lamb. Or use it as the restaurants do, as a bruschetta topping, an hors d'oeuvre stuffing (as below) or a pasta sauce (just add pasta, a little olive oil and parmesan).

1	large eggplant	1
2 tbsp	olive oil	30 mL
¼ cup	chopped onion	60 mL
2 tbsp	chopped celery	30 mL
2	tomatoes, peeled and seeded, about 1 lb (450 g)	2
¼ cup	balsamic vinegar	60 mL
1 tbsp	brown sugar	15 mL
1 tbsp	capers	15 mL
2	anchovy filets, soaked, julienned	2
6	black Italian olives, thinly grated or sliced	6
	Salt and pepper to taste	

Grill the eggplant over coals until the skin has blistered all over. Cool, remove skin and slice in half, then scoop out as many seeds as you can and chop roasted flesh. (If you don't have a barbecue, broil the eggplant.)

Put the olive oil in a large pan over medium heat and sauté the onion and celery until both are limp. Add all the other ingredients, including the eggplant, and simmer over low heat for 30 minutes. Adjust salt and pepper to taste. Spoon into a sterilized glass jar and refrigerate. It can be used immediately but improves with age. It lasts for weeks in the refrigerator and a year in the freezer.

Prosciutto and Caponata

Dab 1 tsp (5 mL) caponata on a slice of prosciutto, roll it up, douse with a little lemon juice and serve as an hors d'oeuvre.

Colman Andrews, a Los Angeles food writer and the author of Catalan Cuisine, *describes a very efficient way of seeding, peeling and chopping a tomato. All you need is one of those four-sided tin graters with the large grating holes. Cut the tomato in half "along the equator," as Andrews says. Squeeze the seeds out into the garbage; then simply grate the tomato. The skin won't grate through. Instant concassée. The old-fashioned method—cutting a cross on the underside of the tomato, opposite the stem, plunging the tomato in boiling water for ten seconds, then draining it under cold water so the skin peels off easily, is better if you are peeling dozens of tomatoes. But for one or two, as in this recipe, Andrews's method is faster and easier.*

Polenta with Parmesan

PREPARATION TIME:
5 MINUTES
COOKING TIME:
20 MINUTES
SERVES: 8

Polenta, a northern Italian specialty, is cornmeal cooked in salted water, stirred until your hand cramps up and your arm falls off. Luckily, you can now buy ready-made polenta in tubes weighing more than two pounds. If you can't find any, an Italian supermarket will have the coarse cornmeal you need to make your own. (You will then be able to form it into any shape you want by simply choosing the dish.)

These recipes are based on slices of round, store-bought polenta. The mushroom and Gorgonzola recipe is a vegetable accompaniment to a roast dish, so the recipe calls for small rounds of polenta to fit the plate. But the recipe could make an antipasto or first course in place of pasta or risotto. I have also made polenta in 8 inch (20 cm) circles, ½ inch (1 cm) thick, and barbecued them, then topped them with mushrooms and Gorgonzola. Cut into wedges for a cocktail gathering; the Gorgonzola helps it stand up to a martini or a cheap Scotch on the rocks.

You can fry, broil or—best of all—cook cooled (that is, solid) polenta over coals. (Frying polenta tends to spit oil all over the kitchen.) Polenta is also a delicacy in its original, hot form. Centro, a grill and wine bar in Toronto owned by Franco Prevedello, cooks polenta in beef broth, pours it over cool mascarpone cheese and tops it with shaved white truffles from Piedmont. This is serious treatment for humble cornmeal.

24	polenta squares or rounds, 1 inch (2.5 cm) across and ½ inch (1 cm) thick	24
24	slices good Parmesan, about the same size as the polenta slices	24
	Aioli (recipe, p. 107)	
	Italian parsley for garnish	

Broil polenta slices on both sides until golden (not brown). Place a slice of Parmesan on top of each and put under the broiler until the cheese turns golden. Remove from oven, put a dab of aioli in the center of each, top with a sprig of parsley and serve.

Polenta

1 tbsp	salt	15 mL	**COOKING TIME:**
6 cups	water	1.4 L	35 MINUTES
2 cups	cornmeal	500 mL	MAKES: 2 LB (1 KG)

Add salt to water, bring to a boil; reduce heat to a simmer. Slowly pour in the cornmeal, stirring constantly with a big, strong wooden spoon for 30 minutes, or until the cornmeal is as thick as Portland cement; it will pull away from the side of the pot, and you will curse the local Italian supermarket for not having ready-made polenta at any price.

Spread the hot polenta on two large greased baking sheets and let cool. Note: you will have to work quickly because polenta sets quickly. Spread it with a knife or spoon dipped in water, or use your hands. When it has cooled you can cut it to whatever size or shape you want with a knife or cookie cutter.

Aioli

This is a garlic mayonnaise that can be used as a killer vegetable dip or a sauce, or spoon it into soup as you would *pistou*.

PREPARATION TIME:
5 MINUTES
MAKES: 1 CUP
(250 mL)

1	slice bread	1
2 tbsp	milk	30 mL
3	cloves garlic	3
1	egg yolk	1
¼ tsp	salt	1 mL
½ cup	olive oil	125 mL
	Juice of ¼ lemon	
	Chicken stock (optional)	

Cut off crusts, rip bread into small pieces and soak in milk for 5 minutes. Squeeze out excess milk. In a mini-chop or food processor, purée (or as close to it as you can) bread, garlic, egg yolk and salt. Pulsing in a mini-chop or pouring through the food chute of a food processor, add olive oil to make an emulsion. Stir in lemon juice. Add more lemon to taste. If mayonnaise is too thick, add chicken stock to thin.

Polenta with Wild Mushrooms and Gorgonzola

PREPARATION TIME:
10 MINUTES
COOKING TIME:
10 MINUTES
SERVES: 4

John Barrett of Café Nola in Philadelphia grills polenta and tops it with shiitake mushrooms and crumbled Stilton. This variation calls for portobello mushrooms and Gorgonzola, but you can use any "wild" mushroom and any creamy blue cheese. This is a simple and strikingly delicious accompaniment to a strong main dish. The tamer the blue cheese, the tamer the result, but it will still be striking.

½ cup	chopped portobello mushrooms	125 mL
1 tbsp	butter	15 mL
4	slices polenta, ½ inch (1 cm) thick	4
1 oz	Gorgonzola	30 g

Over medium heat, sauté mushrooms in butter for 5 minutes. Reserve mushrooms.

On a hot barbecue, grill polenta on one side until golden, about 5 minutes depending upon the polenta. Don't let it burn. Flip polenta over, top with mushrooms and then cheese, and cook until bottom is crisp and cheese has melted into the mushrooms on top. Keep hot until service.

Hot Pear and Gorgonzola Salad

The idea for this salad came from seven words in *Gourmet* magazine, the May 1994 issue, page 64, about Jody Adams, the chef of Caffè M, part of the larger Italian restaurant Michael's in Cambridge, Massachusetts. "... Spinach salad with roasted pears and Gorgonzola." Seven words to set the taste buds tingling.

This recipe is for two, but you can multiply the ingredients for any number of guests. The type of pear doesn't matter (purists disagree) as long as it's firm and not quite ripe, so the oven heat doesn't finish it off. A Bosc pear is good, but I've used Bartletts, too (purists disagree strongly!).

PREPARATION TIME:
5 MINUTES
COOKING TIME:
1 HOUR
SERVES: 2

½ cup	red wine	125 mL
2 tsp	brown sugar	10 mL
1	pear, whole, peeled with the stem left on	1
	Various lettuces (radicchio, red leaf or Bibb)	
2 oz	Gorgonzola or cambozola, chopped into marble-size nuggets	60 g
4 tsp	first cold pressed extra-virgin Tuscan olive oil	20 mL
2 tsp	balsamic vinegar	10 mL
	Pepper	

Preheat oven to 350°F (175°C).

In a small ovenproof dish, mix the wine and sugar. Add the pear, coat it thoroughly and bake for 1 hour, basting and turning frequently.

Meanwhile, wash and dry lettuces and rip into bite-size pieces. Set aside a third of the Gorgonzola to garnish.

Just before serving, mix the lettuces with the oil and vinegar, pepper and remaining Gorgonzola. Divide between 2 plates or bowls. Take pear from the oven by the stem. Cut ¼-inch (5 mm) slices and top each plate. Top the hot pears with reserved Gorgonzola and serve immediately.

Balsamic vinegar is a fabulously aromatic and wonderful-tasting vinegar used extensively these days in almost all cuisines. The best is aged for decades, and is as thick as molasses. Your wallet has to be as thick to buy it. Luckily, good, cheaper versions are available. In the event you can't find it, Claude Troisgros, son of Pierre of Roanne, France, the three-star Michelin chef of nouvelle cuisine and owner of C.T. Restaurant in New York City, suggests substituting red wine vinegar mixed with soy sauce.

Garlic Spaghetti

PREPARATION TIME:
1 HOUR
COOKING TIME:
1 MINUTE
SERVES: 4 AS A SIDE
DISH

I know, I know, pasta is supposed to be a course unto itself. Well, sometimes it can be a side dish, if the pasta is this simple and this delicious—the victory of flavor over unnecessary preparation.

8	cloves garlic, peeled, roughly chopped	8
2 tbsp	finely chopped onion	30 mL
½	tomato, roughly chopped	½
¼ cup	olive oil	60 mL
	Spaghetti for 4	
	Freshly grated Parmesan cheese (*parmigiano reggiano*)	
	Fresh ground black pepper	

Combine garlic, onion, tomato and oil in a small pot over low heat and let the flavors infuse for 1 hour. Strain oil through a sieve and discard lumps.

Just before service, boil pasta in a large amount of salted water for 3 minutes (if fresh pasta) or 10 to 12 minutes (if dried). Drain. Toss with just enough garlic oil to coat the noodles and enough Parmesan to coat the oil-slicked noodles. Serve extra Parmesan on the side, and offer freshly ground black pepper to your guests.

Pasta of the Sea

PREPARATION TIME:
20 MINUTES
COOKING TIME:
50 MINUTES
SERVES: 8 AS AN
APPETIZER, 4 AS A
MAIN COURSE

As a seasoned restaurant critic (which is to say well fed and fat), I take exception to menus in restaurants, especially Italian restaurants, that call shrimp or prawns "scampi." Langoustines are scampi; shrimp and prawns are shrimp and prawns. Of all shellfish, I love langoustine—also known as Dublin Bay Prawn or Norwegian lobster—best, but shrimp and prawns are creatures too lovely to pass off as something else. (I also love scallops, raw or cooked.)

1 lb	large, fresh shrimp—about 16	450 g
1	celery stick 3 inches (8 cm) long, coarsely chopped	1
1	carrot stick 3 inches (8 cm) long, coarsely chopped	1
1	small onion, whole	1
2	bay leaves	2
2	sprigs parsley	2

¾ cup	white wine or dry vermouth	180 mL
1 tbsp	white wine vinegar	15 mL
	Water	
2 tbsp	butter	30 mL
2 tsp	olive oil	10 mL
3 tbsp	finely chopped onion	45 mL
2	cloves garlic, minced	2
1 lb	sea scallops	450 g
	Pasta (any kind, but spirals hold the sauce well)	
2 cups	whipping cream	500 mL
2	drops vanilla (optional)	2
4	sprigs parsley for garnish	4

Peel shrimp and put shells in a small pot. Add celery, carrot, whole onion, bay leaves, parsley, wine and vinegar and enough water, if necessary, to cover shells. Bring to a boil, lower heat immediately and simmer for 30 minutes. Strain and reserve this shrimp stock.

Over medium heat in a large, high-sided frying pan or a large pot, melt butter and oil together. Add chopped onion and garlic and sauté until onion is soft, about 5 minutes. (Don't let garlic brown.) Add peeled shrimp and scallops and sauté for 2 minutes, just until the shrimp start to curl and the scallops begin to turn milky in color. Remove shrimp and scallops and reserve. Add shrimp stock and reduce over medium-high heat until only ¼ cup (60 mL) remains.

Meanwhile, in a large pot three-quarters filled with boiling salted water, cook pasta until it is *al dente*. (Pasta continues to cook in the sauce.) Drain pasta and add to pot with shrimp essence. Add cream and vanilla and cook until the sauce begins to thicken, about 4 minutes. Add shrimp and scallops and cook another 1 minute until the sauce thickens some more—it should be creamy, not gluey—and the shrimp and scallops are warmed through. Divide among 8 plates or bowls and garnish with sprigs of parsley.

Fettuccine Alfie

PREPARATION TIME:
15 MINUTES
COOKING TIME:
10 MINUTES
SERVES: 8

Everyone has a North American version of fettuccine Alfredo, none of them close to the original. This is mine. It is not close, either. It borrows a trick from Jean-François Casari who, when executive chef of the King Edward Hotel in Toronto, made a lobster ravioli appetizer with truffle oil. It was the touch of vanilla in the sauce that brought out the truffle aroma and the sweetness of the lobster.

2	rashers bacon, cut into ½-inch (1 cm) cubes	2
	Fettuccine for 8	
2	egg yolks	2
2 cups	whipping cream	500 mL
1 ¼ cups	grated *parmigiano reggiano*	300 mL
½	capful vanilla	½
1 tsp	salt	5 mL
	Generous grinding of pepper (white looks best)	
	Parsley as garnish	

In a large, high-sided pan or pot over medium-low heat, fry bacon until crisp. At the same time, in a large pot of salted boiling water, cook noodles until *al dente* (about 8 to 10 minutes). Drain noodles and add to cooked bacon. Swirl noodles so they are coated with bacon fat.

Beat egg yolks into cream. Add ¼ cup (60 mL) of the cheese, vanilla, salt and pepper. Pour over noodles, mix well, raise heat to medium and cook until the sauce is silky smooth and slightly thickened. Divide among heated plates and garnish with parsley. Offer remaining Parmesan on the side to your guests.

Risotto

I became hooked on risotto thanks to Toronto restaurateur Charles Grieco and his chefs at La Scala. For three or four very hot nights in July 1988, Grieco invited me into his kitchen to cook risotto—but not before giving me a thorough history and detailed instructions on the way the Venetians make this sophisticated dish of creamy aromatic rice full of infused flavor, in which each kernel pops with the slightest pressure of your teeth, and if you close your eyes and breathe in, you can smell the Po Valley of Lombardy.

Among shining examples of how simple foodstuffs can be turned into universal obsessions, pasta and risotto are two of the brightest. My first risotto experience was Gorgonzola risotto, followed by risotto with porcini mushrooms. That's the beauty of it—you can add just about anything to a risotto to make it your signature dish, which is what restaurants kill to have—something that everyone talks about, associates with the restaurant and makes customers come back for more. Risotto is arborio rice lightly fried in oil and onions (*soffritto*), then simmered in broth (*brodo*) and flavored with almost anything (*condimenti*).

A few years ago Manhattan restaurateur Tony May was serving an entrée risotto with butter, *parmigiano reggiano* and beef glaze for $21 in his restaurant, San Domenico. Alfredo's, The Original Of Rome (in Manhattan) was serving a risotto with mascarpone and spinach. Keith Frogett of Scaramouche in Toronto combined chicken and quail stocks for a risotto topped with half a grilled quail. And Sara Moulton, chef in the executive dining room of *Gourmet* magazine, made pumpkin risotto.

Arborio rice, the longest of the Italian short-grained rices (superfino), is crucial to risotto. (Other superfino short-grained rices such as *Roma* and *Carnaroli* can also be used but are not widely available.) Arborio rice absorbs vast quantities of liquids without the outer skin breaking, so it has a firm texture (*al dente*), which is the dish's signature. You don't want your rice turning to mush. In Milan, risotto is dryer. In Venice, it is creamier—and it is this risotto I prefer. You'll never mistake it for flavored Uncle Ben's.

The other point about risotto is the time it takes to make: it must be stirred constantly for twenty-five minutes. This is why restaurants charge $21 for a plate of flavored rice—you're paying for half an hour of a cook's time to stir a single dish. Or at least they will tell you that, and in theory it is true. More often than not, however, restaurants do what owner Larry Forgione and chef Richard D'Orazi, at An American Place in New York City, do: cook large quantities of risotto until it is three-quarters done in advance, then spread it on a sheet to cool. They finish cooking it as needed. And no one is going to argue with the results those two chefs produce.

Buy the best rice you can. Make your own chicken stock and heat it to simmering before adding the rice. Buy *parmigiano reggiano*, use unsalted butter, and extra-virgin olive oil. Depending upon the recipe, buy good Gorgonzola (while pricy, it is one of the greatest blue cheeses in the world) and the best porcini mushrooms. Mushrooms are nothing but flavor, so you might as well get the best, as great restaurants do. Serve the risotto in bowls heated at 200°F (93°C) for twenty minutes.

Charles Grieco wrote me a note to prepare me for my work at La Scala. In it he said, "The constant stirring required should be anticipated and approached with an expectation and a joy that will help to reach one of the world's truly magnificent gastronomic heights." Risotto recipes generally call for ½ cup (125 mL) good white Italian wine. I suggest after you've removed this quantity from a well-chilled bottle, there will be more than ample left to sip while you work. Beats whistling, right?

Risotto al Gorgonzola

PREPARATION TIME:	2 tbsp	unsalted butter	30 mL
5 MINUTES	1 tbsp	olive oil	15 mL
COOKING TIME:	⅓ cup	finely minced onion	80 mL
30 MINUTES	1 ½ cups	unwashed arborio rice	375 mL
SERVES: 4	½ cup	white wine (or dry Italian white vermouth, or chicken stock)	125 mL
	5 cups	chicken stock, simmering hot	1.2 L
	4 oz	Gorgonzola, cut in small pieces	115 g
	1 tbsp	half-and-half cream	15 mL
	1 tbsp	chopped Italian parsley	15 mL
	¼ cup	freshly grated *parmigiano reggiano*	60 mL
	4	sprigs Italian parsley for garnish	4
		Freshly ground pepper	
		Salt	

Step One: In a large, wide pan or pot, melt butter and oil over medium heat; sauté minced onion until transparent (don't let it brown). Add rice, and with a wooden spatula or large wooden spoon, stir the rice in the oil and onions for 1 minute, tops, making sure you coat every rice kernel. (The hot oil sets the starch and heats the kernels up.) Add wine and stir until all the wine is incorporated into the rice. Add ½ cup (125 mL) of the simmering stock and slowly stir it in.

Now, here's the art of risotto—the stirring. You want the liquid to be absorbed by the kernels without breaking the outer coating. So you stir in a slow, deliberate pattern, passing the wooden spoon slowly, lovingly across every square inch of the pan's bottom so the rice doesn't stick. After about 2 minutes at a rolling simmer, you will find that as you pass the wooden spoon or spatula across the bottom of the pan, the rice parts like the Red Sea for Moses and then flows back. When almost all the stock has been absorbed, add another ½ cup (125 mL) of simmering stock. Stir again until the Red Sea does its thing again.

Keep stirring, adding stock, stirring, adding stock, stirring, adding stock for about 18 minutes. The last time, add only ¼ cup (60 mL) of the stock. The rice should be plump. Taste. The texture should be yielding at first and just a tad resistant in the middle. That's *al dente*. Add the last ¼ cup (60 mL) of the stock, stir it in and take the pan off the heat.

Step Two: Now that the rice is pretty well set, you don't have to be as gentle. Whip in the Gorgonzola until it is all melted (save out a few bits for garnish); add the cream, parsley and *parmigiano reggiano*. Divide among heated soup bowls. Garnish each with a small piece of Gorgonzola and a sprig of parsley. Offer pepper and salt to those who dare.

Risotto al Salmone

Now that you know the basics of risotto making, all that's left are variations.

2 tbsp	butter	30 mL
1 tbsp	olive oil	15 mL
⅓ cup	finely minced onions	80 mL
1 ½ cups	arborio rice	375 mL
½ cup	white wine (or vermouth or chicken stock)	125 mL
5 cups	chicken stock	1.2 L
4 oz	smoked salmon, chopped	100 g
3 tbsp	lemon juice	45 mL
1 tbsp	half-and-half cream	15 mL
4	small slices smoked salmon for garnish	4
1 tbsp	chopped watercress or Italian parsley	15 mL

Complete Step One (above). Taste to make sure the rice is *al dente*. If it's not, add boiling water to get it there. Remove from heat; then add smoked salmon, lemon juice and cream. Divide among 4 heated soup bowls and garnish with a slice of smoked salmon and chopped watercress or Italian parsley.

Risotto Porcini

For most of the year, you will find only dried porcini mushrooms. That's okay. For every ¾ oz (20 g) of dried porcini mushrooms, add 1 cup (250 mL) boiling water and soak for 30 minutes. Luckily, that's the exact quantity necessary for this recipe. Coincidental, eh? Strain liquid and reserve—it contains much of the mushroom's flavor—for use in the recipe below.

1 cup	water brought to a boil	250 mL
¾ oz	dried porcini mushrooms	20 g
2 tbsp	butter	30 mL
1 tbsp	olive oil	15 mL
⅓ cup	finely minced onions	80 mL
1 ½ cups	arborio rice	375 mL
½ cup	white wine (or dry white vermouth or chicken stock)	125 mL
5 cups	chicken stock	1.2 L
2 tbsp	butter	30 mL
⅓ cup	Parmesan cheese	80 mL
¼ cup	chopped parsley	60 mL
4	sprigs parsley as garnish	4

In a bowl, pour boiling water over dried porcini mushrooms and let soak for 30 minutes. Strain liquid through a fine sieve or a paper coffee filter soaked with water. Reserve liquid. Coarsely chop mushrooms and set aside.

As in Step One (p. 114), sauté the minced onions in the butter and oil; add rice and stir for 1 minute. Add the wine, the porcini mushroom liquid and the mushrooms. When the liquid is almost completely absorbed, add the first ½ cup (125 mL) of the chicken stock. Continue Step One, above. When rice is done, whip in the butter, cheese and parsley, serve in heated bowls and garnish with parsley sprigs.

Wild Mushroom Timbalio

PREPARATION TIME:
45 MINUTES
COOKING TIME:
25 MINUTES
SERVES: 4

1 oz	dried porcini mushrooms	30 g
½ cup	boiling water	125 mL
4 tsp	butter	20 mL
1 tbsp	minced shallot	15 mL
½ cup	finely minced portobello mushrooms	125 mL
1 tbsp	dry sherry	15 mL

	Pinch nutmeg	
	Pinch salt	
	Grind of black pepper	
2 tbsp	finely diced red pepper	30 mL
2 tbsp	finely diced orange or yellow pepper	30 mL
3	eggs at room temperature	3
1 cup	whipping cream	250 mL
2 tbsp	grated Parmesan	30 mL

Soak dried porcini mushrooms in boiling water for 30 minutes. Strain. (Keep liquid and freeze it for sauces and soups.) Wash mushrooms to remove any grit. Chop finely. Reserve.

In a pan over medium-low heat, melt 1 tbsp (15 mL) of the butter and sauté minced shallot until soft, about 5 minutes. Add portobello mushrooms and cook for another 5 minutes. Add sherry, nutmeg, salt and pepper and cook until the liquid evaporates and the mixture is fairly dry, another 5 minutes. Remove from heat.

Generously butter four small (⅓ cup or 80 mL) ramekins. Arrange diced red pepper on one-third of the bottom of each ramekin. Fill in the center of each ramekin with minced porcini; add the leftover porcini to the cooked mushroom mixture. Cover the remaining third of the ramekin with diced orange pepper. The idea is to make three different-color stripes on the bottom, which will be the top when you unmold it. Don't worry if they overlap inside, as long as the bottom is clearly defined. You can do all this in advance.

Preheat oven to 325°F (160°C).

In a bowl, beat eggs. Add cream, Parmesan and the mushroom mixture. Mix well. Carefully divide cream mixture among the ramekins, pouring it in slowly so as not to disturb the patterns on the bottom. Place ramekins in a casserole just large enough to hold them, pour warm water halfway up the sides and bake for 30 minutes to set the custard. When a toothpick comes out cleanly from the center, they're done.

Take a knife, dip it in hot water and carefully run it around the inside edge of a ramekin. Place a small plate on top, invert, tap the bottom and jiggle the custard out. Use a spatula to transfer the custard to a warmed dinner plate. This custard makes an excellent main course vegetable.

Lobster Spargalo Grill

PREPARATION TIME:
15 MINUTES
COOKING TIME:
35 MINUTES
SERVES: 8 AS A FIRST
COURSE

Cynthia Wine, who succeeded me as restaurant critic for the *Toronto Star*, reviewed a place called Spargalo Grill & Wine Bar in Toronto. She wrote in March '94: ". . . the waiter tells us that the house pride is the lobster pasta prepared for two. A 1 ¼ to 1 ½ lb (560 to 680 g) lobster is halved and steamed in white wine, then released from its shell and diced. The white wine is blended with brandy, tomato sauce and cream, the sauce and lobster (tomalley too) are tossed with fresh fettucine. The dish costs $24 . . ." At the time lobster prices were running at $10.99 a pound (Cdn.), which meant the lobster alone was $16.50 making the menu price an extraordinary treat. But in addition, it sounded wonderful, so I went right out and created what I imagined the dish would be like without ever going to Spargalo myself. I know, I know. Shame on me.

1 tbsp	butter	15 mL
¼ cup	finely chopped shallots	60 mL
20	black peppercorns	20
2 cups	white wine	500 mL
2	bay leaves	2
2	sprigs parsley	2
1 ½ lb	lobster, live	680 g
2 tbsp	tomato paste	30 mL
2	tomatoes, seeded, peeled and diced	2
2 oz	brandy	60 mL
1 cup	whipping cream	250 mL
	Fettucine for four	
¼ cup	chopped parsley for garnish	60 mL

In a large pot or steamer over medium heat, sauté the shallots in butter until translucent and soft. Add peppercorns, wine, bay leaves and parsley. Bring to a boil. Drop in lobster, cover and steam for 10 minutes. Remove lobster, set aside to cool. To the lobster broth, add tomato paste, tomatoes, brandy and cream. Gently allow to reduce until creamy and thickened, about 20 minutes. Remove bay leaves and as many peppercorns as you can see.

Remove lobster meat from the shell and cut into slices. Bring a large pot of salted water to a boil and cook fettucine. Drain thoroughly. Toss with sauce. Add lobsters, toss again, divide among four plates for a main course, six to eight as an appetizer or first course. Dust dish with parsley and serve.

Mussels in Wine and Cream

Mussels latch onto each other (or poles, rocks or anything else) with their beards —the scruffy, hemplike tentacles that extend from inside the shell. The beards are inedible, and they leave gluelike spots on other mussel shells. Scrub the spots and pull out any beards you can see. (Mussels withdraw the beards if they see you coming, the cunning bivalves!) Cultured mussels are farmed and grown in the ocean on strings in North America or on twigs laced between stakes in England and France. They are cleaner and more consistently mild-tasting. I prefer them because they are more easily cleaned and bearded, a time-consuming and tedious chore. Except for this recipe, I wouldn't bother.

PREPARATION TIME: 30 MINUTES
COOKING TIME: 15 MINUTES
SERVES: 8 AS A FIRST COURSE, 4 AS A MAIN COURSE

2 ½ lb	mussels	1.15 kg
1	red pepper	1
2 tbsp	olive oil	30 mL
1	leek, white part only, julienned	1
1	large carrot, peeled and julienned	1
5	cloves garlic, finely minced	5
1 cup	white wine, preferably Italian	250 mL
1 cup	whipping cream	250 mL
3	sprigs thyme, or 2 tsp (10 mL) dried	3
1 tbsp	finely chopped Italian parsley	15 mL
	Fresh Italian bread	

Preheat oven to 150°F (65°C) and heat 8 large soup bowls.

Scrub and beard the mussels. Set them aside.

Roast the pepper under the broiler or over the gas flame on the stove until its skin is evenly blackened. Drop it into a paper bag, scrunch the top closed and let the pepper steam. When it is cool enough to handle, rub off the skin, cut the pepper open, seed it and cut into julienne strips.

In a pot large enough to hold all the mussels, combine the oil, leek, carrot and garlic; sweat vegetables over medium-low heat until the leeks are soft and the carrots partially cooked, about 5 minutes. Add wine, cream, roasted red pepper, thyme and parsley. Bring to a boil. Add mussels, cover and cook for 5 minutes, or until all the shells have opened. (Discard any mussels that refuse to open their shells. They are bad for you.) Remove mussels. Boil cooking liquid down until it thickens slightly, about 5 minutes. Divide mussels evenly among the soup bowls and set each bowl on a large dinner plate. When sauce has thickened, divide it and the vegetables in it among the bowls.

Serve with large hunks of bread to soak up the soup, with crisp Italian white wine and with plenty of serviettes.

Roasted Chicken with Prosciutto, Black Olives and Sage

PREPARATION TIME:
10 MINUTES
COOKING TIME:
1 ½ HOURS
SERVES: 2

Raw olives are unbearably bitter, which is why they have to be cured before we mortals will eat them. Even then they are an acquired taste, which is the polite way my mother told us it was all right not to eat something. (She also called such things as lobster and alcohol acquired tastes, so we wouldn't bankrupt the family or get plastered before it was socially acceptable. Didn't work, of course.)

Here's an example of how chefs cook food in advance. The high heat at the beginning of this recipe kills any bacteria and sears the chicken skin slightly to begin the crisping process. The slow roasting that follows keeps the bird moist without toughening it. This gives chefs leeway—if the chicken is in the oven a little longer than planned, it won't affect the flavor, texture or moisture to any great degree. (Fast roasting needs constant attention.) If you are entertaining and want to serve the guests when they want to eat, as happens in a restaurant, you need that leeway. Put the bird in ninety minutes before you want to eat, and let it go. No muss. No fuss. And exotic-tasting.

To double the recipe, use a whole chicken. That way it serves four.

2 tbsp	chopped fresh sage	30 mL
2	pitted Italian black olives, finely chopped	2
2	large chicken breasts, skin on (or legs and thighs, skin on)	2
1	thin slice prosciutto, about ½ oz (12 g) or enough to cover the meat under the skin Olive oil	1

Preheat oven to 400°F (200°C).

Mix sage and chopped olives. Gently lift skin from chicken and stuff olive mixture evenly under the skin. Arrange the prosciutto slice between the skin and the stuffing so the skin doesn't discolor too much during cooking. Fold skin down again, brush with olive oil, place on a roasting pan, skin side up, and place in the oven. Immediately turn the oven down to 200°F (100°C) and roast for 90 minutes. Do not open the oven door for the first 85 of those minutes. Just before service, broil for a few seconds if the skin needs crisping.

Chicken with Orange Mustard Cream Vermouth Sauce

1	roasting chicken, air-chilled	1	
	Salt and pepper		
10	whole garlic cloves, unpeeled	10	
4	sprigs fresh thyme	4	
4	sprigs fresh oregano	4	
1 tbsp	finely chopped shallots	15 mL	
1 tbsp	butter	15 mL	
¼ cup	dry white Italian vermouth	60 mL	
¼ cup	freshly squeezed orange juice	60 mL	
¼ cup	whipping cream	60 mL	
2 tbsp	prepared Dijon mustard	30 mL	
	Salt and pepper to taste		

PREPARATION TIME:
15 MINUTES
COOKING TIME:
1½ HOURS
SERVES: 4

Preheat oven to 400°F (200°C).

Wipe chicken clean inside and out with a damp cloth. Salt and pepper the cavity. Stuff garlic, thyme and oregano into the chicken. Salt and pepper the outside. Place in a shallow pan and roast for 40 minutes. Turn heat down to 325°F (160°C) and cook for another 40 minutes or until the juices from the thigh run clear. Remove from oven and let stand with a foil tent covering bird for 10 minutes. Quarter and place on heated plates.

Start making sauce 15 minutes before the chicken has finished roasting. In a small pot, sweat shallots in butter over medium-low heat until they are soft. Increase heat, add vermouth and reduce by half, about 3 to 4 minutes. Add orange juice, cream and mustard, and cook until sauce thickens slightly. Adjust salt and pepper. Pour over chicken quarters and serve.

Scallopini Limone

	Juice of 2 lemons	
2 tbsp	unsalted butter	30 mL
	Oil for deep frying	
1 cup	tightly packed Italian parsley sprigs, stems removed	250 mL
1 cup	rice flour	250 mL
¼ cup	oregano	60 mL
2 tsp	salt	10 mL
1 tbsp	pepper	15 mL
2 tbsp	olive oil	30 mL
8	veal scallopini, flattened to ¼ inch (5 mm)	8
¼ cup	dry white Italian wine	60 mL
5 tbsp	butter	75 mL

Put lemon juice in a small pan and reduce over medium heat until it is a syrup. Remove from heat and whisk in 1 tbsp (15 mL) of the butter. Set aside. This is more lemon butter than you will need, but it is difficult to make it in smaller quantities. (For other recipes that use lemon butter, see the index.)

Heat frying oil to 375°F (190°C). Fry parsley until crisp, about 30 seconds. Remove, drain and set aside.

Heat oven to 250°F (120°C).

Combine flour, oregano, salt and pepper. Heat olive oil and remaining butter in a fry pan over medium-high heat until very hot and almost smoking. Dredge scallopini in flour mixture and fry in batches until brown on both sides (1 minute tops). Remove to a heated plate and keep warm. Replenish butter and oil as necessary to fry 8 scallopini.

Pour off excess oil from pan, add wine, and with a wooden spoon stir in all the brown bits on the bottom. Reduce wine until liquid is almost gone. Add 5 tbsp (75 mL) butter and stir for 30 seconds. Remove from heat and whisk in 1 tsp (5 mL) of the lemon butter.

Plate scallopini. Sprinkle the fried parsley in a thin line down the center of each scallopini. Pour sauce over parsley. Serve immediately.

Veal with Prosciutto

4	veal scallops	4	
1 tbsp	olive oil	15 mL	
6 oz	prosciutto, very thinly sliced	170 g	
½ cup	flour	125 mL	
1 tsp	salt	5 mL	
	Black pepper		
1 tsp	dried oregano	5 mL	
1	clove garlic, finely minced	1	
1	shallot, finely minced	1	
½ cup	white wine	125 mL	
1 tbsp	Marsala wine	15 mL	
¼ cup	freshly grated Parmesan	60 mL	

PREPARATION TIME: 10 MINUTES
COOKING TIME: 10 MINUTES
SERVES: 4

With a mallet or the bottom of a heavy pan, pound veal scallops so they are no more than ⅛ inch (3 mm) thick. Cut each into 3 equal pieces. Set aside.

Over medium heat in a large skillet, heat oil and fry prosciutto until it turns darker and crisps up, 3 to 5 minutes. Drain prosciutto well on paper towels and keep warm.

Combine flour, salt, pepper and oregano. Dredge veal in seasoned flour. In the prosciutto skillet, fry scallops for 1 minute on each side. Add oil to the skillet as necessary. Remove cooked veal to paper towels.

Fry garlic and shallot in the skillet for 1 minute. Add wine and Marsala and reduce by half. Return veal to skillet and cook another 2 minutes.

Divide the veal scallops among 4 plates, overlapping the scallops in a fan shape. Dust veal with Parmesan cheese. Pour skillet juices over veal. Top with prosciutto.

Thyme-Roasted Veal Chop with Apple Brandy Sauce

PREPARATION TIME:
40 MINUTES
COOKING TIME:
20 MINUTES
SERVES: 4

Pretty fancy name, typical of restaurants, for a very simple dish using the last of the fresh thyme before the frost gets it. I had no compunction using this much fresh thyme—the frost was upon us; the garden was still full of herbs. The result was spectacular.

Choosing the veal chop is the important bit. If you have any doubt about the tenderness of the meat, pound the chop thin with a mallet. Many fine Italian restaurants do this to produce what appears to be massive veal scallopini on the bone. It's very impressive on the plate and always tender. If you pound it, make sure you grill or barbecue it at a higher heat for a much shorter period.

4	apples (Granny Smiths work well)	4
2 tbsp	butter	30 mL
	Black pepper, freshly ground	
4	veal chops, about 1 ¼ inches (3 cm) thick	4
48	sprigs fresh thyme	48
⅓ cup	brandy	80 mL
	Trussing string	
½ cup	whipping cream	125 mL
	Salt and pepper to taste	
	Thyme for garnish	

Cut apples into similarly shaped ½-inch (1 cm) slices. Melt butter in a large fry pan; lay apple slices in pan, not overlapping, and cook until the undersides caramelize, about 20 minutes depending upon the sugar content of the apples. Flip and caramelize the other sides. (You can do this in advance and set the apples aside until the final assembly.)

Pepper the veal chops on both sides. Lay 6 sprigs of thyme on each chop and flip over onto trussing string. Lay the remaining 6 sprigs on the chops. Tie the sprigs to the chops, using as many loops as necessary, but try not to squeeze the chops out of shape.

Heat a barbecue with a lid to medium heat, put the chops on, close the lid and cook for 10 minutes. Turn chops over and cook for another 10 minutes.

Heat apple slices in frying pan; pour in brandy and light with a match. Toss apples in flaming brandy until flames die. Add cream and reduce until the sauce is creamy and thickened slightly. Taste and adjust for salt and pepper.

Remove thyme sprigs and string from chops. Spoon sauce onto 4 heated plates, place 1 chop on each sauce pool and top with fresh sprigs of thyme. Serve immediately.

Grilled Pork Chop with a Thyme and Oregano Crust

This is a variation on the Thyme-Roasted Veal Chop. (I was experimenting with pork because it is so much cheaper than veal.) Whack it thin, just as you would a suspicious veal chop, to ensure tenderness. Grill it for much less time than an unwhacked chop.

PREPARATION TIME:
10 MINUTES
COOKING TIME:
10 MINUTES
SERVES: 2

2	pork rib chops, 1 inch (2.5 cm) thick	2
½ cup	firmly packed fresh thyme leaves (no stems)	125 mL
¼ cup	firmly packed fresh oregano leaves	60 mL
¼ tsp	salt	1 mL
	Freshly ground black pepper	
5 tsp	olive oil	25 mL

If necessary, pound each chop on either side of the bone with a mallet to reduce thickness.

In a food processor, blend thyme leaves, oregano leaves, salt, black pepper and 3 tsp (15 mL) of the olive oil until the mixture forms a rough but spreadable paste. (Add the remaining 2 tsp [10 mL] olive oil only if necessary.) Spread paste on both sides of the chops.

The idea here is to create a crust of herbs without overcooking the meat. On a barbecue, sear both sides of the chops over high heat to char the herbs, then finish over low coals to cook meat through.

If you are cooking indoors, sear both sides of the chops in a white-hot cast-iron fry pan, then transfer the fry pan to a 350°F (175°C) oven for 10 minutes. Serve as is or with sage butter.

Brandied Coffee Ricotta

PREPARATION TIME:

5 MINUTES

SERVES: 6

The Italians love cheese, so it should not surprise anyone that the hottest Italian dessert of the 1980s was tiramisu, which uses rum and mascarpone cheese, a delightful cream cheese.

The Italians also love coffee—strong coffee. I am grateful for this. I woke up one morning in a hotel room on the Lido with ferrets gnawing through my brain, looking for traces of the well of wine and grappa I had been forced to consume the night before by overly friendly Venetians. As the Lido is an island, you must take a ferry to Venice. Ferries tend to operate on water. Water is not as solid as concrete. Vicious ferrets flee to the stomach when on water.

Luckily, the ferry employed a tidy young man who, with a bemused expression, made me some mud. I even drank the sludge at the bottom. It was like being pumped with oxygen and Pepto-Bismol. I survived, although the owners of the glass factory I visited that morning would not let me walk the narrow aisles of their retail outlet.

This dessert pays tribute to the three great Italian pastimes: cheese, coffee and liqueur.

1 lb	ricotta cheese	450 g
¼ cup	sugar	60 mL
2 tsp	instant coffee	10 mL
¼ cup	cognac, brandy, rum or grappa	60 mL
	Grated chocolate	

With a wire whip, whisk together ricotta and sugar. Whisk in coffee and brandy. Divide among six wineglasses and refrigerate several hours or overnight. Sprinkle grated chocolate over top just before serving.

Zabaglione

This is sabayon (see recipe p. 86) made with sweet Italian Marsala wine. Clean fresh berries in season, put them in wineglasses and drizzle the zabaglione over them.

Panna Cotta

The Italian dessert course is not a triumph of diversity in North America. Apart from fine gelati (notably Gelato Fresco, the impeccable ices made in Toronto by Hart Melvin, who studied gelato-making in Italy), zabaglione and tiramisu, Italian desserts have not captured the public imagination. *Panna cotta*, however, is on the way. It's very easy to make and can be personalized in any number of ways, which is why any number of chefs will be attracted to it. Basically, *panna cotta* is cream infused with flavor, usually vanilla, and set with gelatin. After it is unmolded, it can be drizzled with caramel sauce, chocolate, berries, fruit purées, coffee, nuts —just about anything that comes to mind. (More on that at the end of the recipe.)

So, before restaurant critics and food writers hail it as the Second Coming and shortly thereafter declare it passé, develop your own signature *panna cotta*. Or go to a dim sum restaurant and nab some Yep Jup Go from the dessert trolley. The Cantonese make it with coconut milk and egg whites. Italian restaurant chefs in North America are experimenting on the basic recipe by using various strengths of cream and milk, buttermilk, and combinations of milks and cream. And the French, no strangers to copying the Italians, make it with "almond milk" and call it blancmange. At Stars in San Francisco, pastry chef Emily Luchetti's blancmange is served with raspberries and raspberry sauce. Nothing new under the sun, but delicious any way you spoon it.

PREPARATION TIME:
25 MINUTES
SETTING TIME:
6 HOURS
SERVES: 8 TO 12,
DEPENDING UPON
SIZE OF RAMEKINS

3 cups	half-and-half cream	750 mL
1	vanilla bean, 2 ½ inches (6 cm) long	1
⅓ cup	sugar	80 mL
1 ½	packets gelatin	1 ½
1 cup	boiling water	250 mL
½ cup	sugar	125 mL
1 cup	frozen strawberries with their liquid	250 mL
½ tsp	vanilla extract	2 mL
2 tbsp	butter	30 mL
1 tsp	orange liqueur	5 mL
1 cup	fresh strawberries for garnish	250 mL
¼ cup	shaved bitter chocolate	60 mL

Heat cream and vanilla bean until cream shimmers; reduce heat and simmer 10 minutes. Add sugar and dissolve completely. In a separate bowl, dissolve gelatin in ¼ cup (60 mL) of the boiling water and let sit one minute. Add another ¼ cup (60 mL) boiling water. Then add gelatin mixture to cream. Pour into ramekins and let set in the refrigerator for 6 hours.

In a heavy saucepan over medium-low heat, melt sugar, stirring with a wooden spoon. Add remaining ½ cup (125 mL) boiling water, a spoonful at a time at first. (Be careful—it may splatter.) Stir until the sauce becomes syrupy. Stir in strawberries, vanilla extract, butter and orange liqueur. Simmer for 20 minutes, or until liquid is slightly syrupy. Remove from heat, let cool slightly, then purée in a food processor until smooth. This strawberry-caramel sauce can be made ahead of time, kept at room temperature and heated just before service.

To unmold *panna cotta*, place ramekins in a hot water bath three-quarters of the way up the sides for 5 seconds at most (or it will melt). Invert ramekin on a plate, give the ramekin a quick twist, and the *panna cotta* should fall out. Or run a sharp knife around the edge, invert, then tap on top.

Surround the *panna cotta* with fresh berries. Drizzle hot caramel sauce over the *panna cotta* and the berries, and sprinkle chocolate over all. Serve.

At San Domenico in New York, *panna cotta* is served with a balsamic-vinegar and strawberry sauce. Al Forno tops it with a bitter-chocolate sauce. Gramercy Tavern uses caramel, oranges, ground praline and pomegranate kernels. You get the idea.

Tiramisu

It was the dessert of the 1980s, but like most great dishes, very simple. Dunk biscuits in coffee and booze and top with Italian cream cheese whipped with egg yolks and sugar.

PREPARATION TIME:
   15 MINUTES
STANDING TIME:
   AT LEAST 2 HOURS
SERVES: 4

And, as with all great dishes, the ingredients are key. Mascarpone is an Italian cream cheese with the texture of Devon cream. It's mainly a dessert cheese, although it is also terrific as a pasta sauce. (Sauté a chopped onion and eight strips of roughly chopped bacon, or the equivalent in prosciutto, in half a cup of butter. Boil enough fusilli pasta for four, drain, add it to the onions and bacon, then whip in twelve ounces of mascarpone. Serve with grated Parmesan and freshly ground black pepper. Fast and fabulous.)

Buy the imported stuff, not the cheese made here, and don't try to use Torta Gorgonzola mascarpone in dessert recipes. It is a pungent blend of Gorgonzola and mascarpone used mainly as an hors d'oeuvre cheese (it is sometimes even spread on a celery stick), although eaten with grapes it makes a dessert worthy of Nero.

The biscuits can be light lady fingers, but try to find *biscotti*, the hard-as-rocks Italian biscuits that come in a variety of flavors. Use any booze you want; rum is usual, but sweet Marsala wine is popular, too. Try Frangelico or Tia Maria—anything that makes it yours.

6	*biscotti* or lady fingers	6
3 tsp	orange liqueur	15 mL
3 tsp	rum	15 mL
2 tbsp	espresso, or ¼ cup (60 mL) regular coffee gently reduced by half	30 mL
2 tbsp	icing sugar	30 mL
2	eggs, separated	2
8 oz	mascarpone cheese	250 g
4 oz	bittersweet or milk chocolate, coarsely grated or chopped	125 g

Place biscuits in a bowl. In a cup, combine 2 tsp (10 mL) orange liqueur, 2 tsp (10 mL) rum and the coffee. Pour over biscuits and set aside.

With an electric beater, blend sugar and egg yolks until they turn lemon yellow. Beat in remaining liqueur and rum, then mascarpone. In a separate bowl, beat egg whites until stiff, then fold them into the mascarpone.

Whether you make individual desserts in separate bowls or one large one, the principle is the same: lay half the soaked biscuits on the bottom, add a layer of mascarpone mixture, half the chocolate, a second layer of biscuits, mascarpone and chocolate. Cover and refrigerate at least 2 hours before serving.

CHAPTER SIX

The Greek Ouzeri

Ouzeri Metaxa

OUR MEZEDES

Saganaki 142
Minted and brandy-flamed fried cheese

Zucchini Fritters 134
Fried with mint and feta cheese

Tyropittakia 143
Baked phyllo pastry stuffed with shrimp, garlic, capers, oregano and
shallots, or Kalamata olives flavoured with orange zest and mint

Eggplant in Tomatoes with Feta 146

Roast Lamb with Lemon-Egg Gravy 135

Lamb Shish Kebabs 136

Moussaka 140

Ground Beef Dollars 145
Greek hamburger

Skordalia 146
Potato garlic sauce

House-Brick Lemon Game Hen 144

Feta-Stuffed Quail 136

Deep-Fried Calamari 138

Hot Shrimp Cocktail 139

Baklava 147

Most North American bars offer their patrons peanuts, trail mix or pretzels. That this has been going on for a couple of hundred years only demonstrates the barkeepers' lack of imagination and disregard for the creature comforts of customers.

In Greece they have bars, too, called *ouzeris*. They are named after the national drink, ouzo, which turns milky in water and your body into an unstoppable dancing machine if you drink too much of it.

Greece is the cradle of civilization, which is why we have trail mix and they have fried calamari that melts in your mouth, shish kebab of lamb marinated for three days and grilled over charcoal just long enough to take your breath away. We have peanuts and they have shrimp bathed in brandy, wrapped in tomatoes and capped with soft, hot, fragrant cheese. We have pretzels and they have fat wads of hard cheese fried with mint, delicate little mahogany quails stuffed with wild mushrooms and Feta, and moussaka topped with a silky aromatic nutmeg béchamel.

I'm not talking posh here, like the Palio bar off Broadway, which serves wonderful noshes, or the piano bar at Centro in Toronto, which serves equally wonderful bits and bites. The *ouzeri* has always been a blue-collar bar, where the men meet after work to sip their favorite ouzo from a possible stock of more than a hundred brands made in the country, each subtly different, or suck back a Heineken, Amstel or Lowenbrau beer, brewed in Greece—and cheap. But in recent years, the *ouzeris* of Athens have been invaded by ladies who lunch, business suits and snobs who pride themselves on knowing a good thing even when they're the last to see it. Extensive wine lists and linen tablecloths are invading. The prices have gone up, too, but with them, the quality and breadth of nibbles.

Unlike in Spain, where appetizers or *tapas* are nibbled with sherry before dinner, the Athenians nosh a half dozen or more *mezedes* and call it a meal. And what a meal. *Mezedes* run the gamut from salads to sweets. They can be ordered from a menu, or they might come around on trays from the kitchen like dim sum.

If nothing else, *ouzeri* fare banishes the myth that Greek food is blandness swimming in olive oil. (Canada has won two Culinary Olympics in the past twenty years, but the country is probably associated with overcooked roast beef sandwiches on tasteless white bread drowning in canned gravy.) New Zealand

and Australia ship only their *least* fatty lamb to Greece, because the Greeks demand the leanest lamb in the world.

And all that oil? It is as good as the Italian or French olive oils. After all, the olive was first cultivated in Crete or Syria. (Take your pick, historians can't decide.) The olive has been in Greece since pre-Homeric days, so it shouldn't surprise anyone that after five thousand years they know more about how to eat olives and cook with olive oil than North American critics who have spent two hundred years in bars eating peanuts, trail mix and pretzels.

Zucchini and Feta Mint Fritters

PREPARATION TIME:
1 HOUR
AND 5 MINUTES
COOKING TIME:
5 MINUTES
SERVES: 8 AS A
SMALL APPETIZER

Feta cheese is the fresh, white, crumbly, salty, sharp-tasting cheese that you find in a Greek salad. Buy genuine Greek Feta, not the domestic product. Greek Feta is made from goat's milk or a combination of goat's and sheep's milk. It is stored in brine to keep it moist, so make sure it is displayed in brine at the market. Buy it in quantities you can use immediately. If it must be stored in the refrigerator without brine, wrap it tightly in plastic but remove the plastic wrap an hour before use to let it breathe.

2	zucchini, peeled and grated	2
1 tsp	salt	5 mL
	Oil for deep frying	
½ lb	Greek Feta cheese, grated	225 g
1	egg, beaten	1
	Pepper to taste	
¼ tsp	salt	1 mL
½ cup	fine, dry bread crumbs	125 mL
8	whole mint leaves, for garnish	8

Combine the grated zucchini and salt in a colander, sieve or bowl and let the zucchini sweat out water for 1 hour. Gather up zucchini in a tea towel and squeeze out remaining water. You can do this a day or two beforehand. Store the zucchini in a glass jar with a tight lid or in plastic wrap, and refrigerate.

Heat at least 3 inches (8 cm) of oil in a deep pot to 350°F (175°C).

In a bowl, combine the zucchini, Feta cheese, egg, pepper and salt. Place bread crumbs on a plate. With two soupspoons, form eggs of the zucchini, drop in the bread crumbs and roll until coated. With your hands, form the egg shapes into balls and drop into the hot oil. Fry until golden, about 2 minutes. Remove with a slotted spoon to paper towels to drain. Serve 3 per person on a small bread and butter plate; garnish with a mint leaf.

Lamb with Lemon-Egg Gravy

Square One in San Francisco serves lamb with a reduced lamb stock flavored with a lemon–egg mixture in which asparagus, garlic, mint and lots of onions have been cooked. This is a simplified version, because I'd rather have the asparagus on the side with boiled baby parsley potatoes.

PREPARATION TIME:
30 MINUTES
COOKING TIME:
1 ½ HOURS
SERVES: 8

¼ cup	chopped fresh mint leaves	60 mL
4	cloves garlic cut into slivers	4
5 lb	leg of lamb	2.25 kg

SAUCE:

2 tbsp	flour	30 mL
2 cups	lamb or chicken stock	500 mL
3 tbsp	butter	45 mL
2	egg yolks	2
¼ cup	freshly squeezed lemon juice	60 mL
2 tbsp	fresh mint leaves	30 mL
	Salt and pepper to taste	
8	whole mint leaves, for garnish	8

Preheat oven to 350°F (175°C). In a bowl, combine the mint and garlic slivers so the mint adheres to the garlic. With the tip of a knife, all over the leg of lamb, make slits ½ inch (1 cm) deep and just long enough to accommodate the garlic slivers. Insert the mint-covered garlic slices into the lamb. Roast for 1 ½ hours (for medium rare), remove from oven and cover with foil to keep warm while you make the sauce.

Pour off all but 2 tbsp (30 mL) of fat from the roasting pan. On the stove-top over medium heat, whisk flour into fat and cook for 5 minutes, stirring constantly, to cook the flour. Whisk in stock and scrape up all the brown bits. When thickened, pour into a medium saucepan and whisk in butter. Remove from heat.

In a bowl, whisk together the egg yolks and lemon juice. Add 1 tbsp (15 mL) of gravy to the lemon mixture and whisk in. Continue whisking in gravy by the tablespoon until the volume doubles. Then pour lemon mixture into gravy. Add mint leaves and adjust salt and pepper to taste. Serve in a gravy boat at the table.

Carve lamb into medallion-size pieces—3-inch (8 cm) rounds, each ½ inch (1 cm) thick, or the equivalent in irregular slices. In the center of 8 side plates, pool lemon-gravy sauce; arrange 3 medallions in a slightly overlapping flower pattern on top of the sauce. Place 1 mint leaf in the middle of the arrangement and serve immediately.

Shish Kebabs

PREPARATION TIME:
2 DAYS
COOKING TIME:
10 MINUTES
SERVES: 8

½ cup	olive oil	125 mL
2 tsp	ground cumin	10 mL
1 tbsp	dried oregano	15 mL
3	bay leaves, crushed, ground, pounded or chopped finely	3
2 lb	lamb leg or loin, cut into 1-inch (2.5 cm) cubes	900 g
2	medium tomatoes, peeled, seeded and chopped	2
6	cloves garlic, flattened	6
¼ cup	port wine	60 mL
3 tbsp	red wine vinegar	45 mL
	Salt and freshly ground pepper	
24	bamboo skewers 6 inches (15 cm) long	24

Combine olive oil, cumin, oregano, bay leaves and lamb cubes in a glass bowl, cover and refrigerate for 24 hours. Add tomato, garlic, port and vinegar, salt and pepper, cover and refrigerate for another 24 hours.

Soak bamboo skewers in water for 2 hours. Thread lamb onto skewers and sear over very hot coals for 5 minutes tops, or broil until meat is brown on all sides but medium rare inside—yes, mother, pink. Serve 3 to a person with ouzo, sherry or wine.

Feta-Stuffed Quail

PREPARATION TIME:
15 MINUTES
COOKING TIME:
20 MINUTES
SERVES: 8

Quail are tiny birds with a bad reputation for being dry in taste and texture, fussy to eat and generally an upper-class-twit affectation. True enough, given how most people cook them. In this recipe, the little birds are stuffed with Feta cheese and oregano, which keeps them moist and gives them a tart taste and aroma. They are also glazed with maple syrup, which gives them a sweet-tart whack, which goes perfectly with almost anything you drink with this meal.

If you can't find quail, which any Italian, Portuguese or Greek supermarket has fresh or in the freezer, buy four Rock Cornish game hens, small baby chickens or eight pigeons.

Now, I am Canadian from way back. And I hate it when people from other countries—especially chefs at the Culinary Olympics—think maple syrup is a Canadian cooking staple, like cream to the French and olive oil to the Italians. It isn't. It's too expensive and too sweet except to pour over pancakes (griddle cakes to Americans; fat, ill-mannered crêpes to the French). In fact, maple syrup does not belong in cooking at all... except in this recipe.

4	scallions, sliced, including 1 inch (2.5 cm) of the green	4
6 oz	Feta cheese	170 g
1 tbsp	pepper	15 mL
1	ripe tomato, peeled, seeded and chopped	1
½ cup	finely chopped portobello, shiitake or porcini mushrooms or ½ cup (125 mL) finely chopped button mushrooms sautéed in 1 tbsp (15 mL) unsalted butter and 1 tsp (5 mL) Worcestershire sauce	125 mL
2 tsp	dried oregano, or 2 tbsp (30 mL) fresh, chopped	10 mL
8	quail	8
¼ cup	maple syrup	60 mL
	Salt	
	Zest of one orange, blanched in boiling water for 30 seconds then plunged into cold water	

Preheat oven to 350°F (175°C).

In a bowl, combine scallions, Feta, pepper, tomato, mushrooms and oregano. Wash and dry quail inside and out. Stuff with Feta–mushroom mixture. (You'll be surprised at how much stuffing these little guys can take.) With a pastry brush, paint the quail with maple syrup. Dust with salt. Roast for 20 minutes. Serve hot with blanched orange zest scattered on each bird. Provide a fork and a sharp steak knife (for convenience, not for toughness), many serviettes and ouzo, sherry or a chilled crisp white wine.

Deep-Fried Calamari

PREPARATION TIME:
5 MINUTES
COOKING TIME:
5 MINUTES
SERVES: 4

As a restaurant critic, I used to have great fun describing restaurant disasters—for example, overcooked calamari. It became "a Goodyear product," a term coined by my then rival at the *Globe and Mail*, Joanne Kates. (That did not, of course, stop me from using it.) You have to fry calamari fast, for only thirty seconds after they hit the fat, which means lots of oil in a deep pot so the heat will hold. And you can't overcrowd the pot.

1 cup	very fine cornmeal	250 mL
1 cup	all-purpose flour	250 mL
2 tbsp	dried oregano	30 mL
2 tsp	salt	10 mL
	Vegetable or corn oil for deep frying, at least 6 inches (15 cm) deep	
1 lb	squid, cleaned, body cut into thin rounds	450 g
	Salt to taste	
	Lemon wedges	

Combine cornmeal, flour, salt and oregano. Heat oil to 375°F (190°C). Dip batches of squid in flour mixture and then in hot oil for 30 seconds or until the squid is golden brown. Remove and drain on paper towels. Salt. Serve with fresh lemon wedges.

Hot Shrimp Cocktail

24	raw jumbo shrimp	24
¼ cup	brandy	60 mL
1 cup	finely minced onions	250 mL
2 tbsp	olive oil	30 mL
4	cloves garlic, finely minced	4
2	large tomatoes, peeled, seeded and chopped	2
1 tbsp	dried oregano	15 mL
¼ cup	chopped fresh parsley	60 mL
6	drops Tabasco or other hot sauce (optional)	6
	Salt and pepper to taste	
½ lb	Feta cheese, crumbled	225 g

PREPARATION TIME:
15 MINUTES
COOKING TIME:
20 MINUTES
SERVES: 8

Peel and de-vein shrimp. Place brandy and shrimp in a small pot over medium heat. As brandy warms, ignite it with a match and swirl the pot around until the flames die out. Continue to heat shrimp until they just begin to curl. Remove from pot immediately. Reserve any leftover brandy.

Over medium-high heat in a larger pot, sauté onions in the olive oil until limp; add garlic and sauté until the onions are slightly browned. Add tomatoes, oregano, parsley, leftover cooking brandy and Tabasco. Simmer for 5 minutes, or until sauce is fairly thick. Add salt and freshly ground pepper to taste, but remember that Feta is fairly salty.

In each of 8 ramekins or small ovenproof dishes, put 3 shrimp. Divide the sauce among the ramekins; crumble Feta cheese over top.

The dish can be made to this point and refrigerated for several hours.

Preheat oven to 375°F (190°C). Bake ramekins for 10 minutes. Serve with fork and fresh bread.

Moussaka

PREPARATION TIME:

2 HOURS

COOKING TIME:

30 MINUTES

SERVES: 12

Moussaka can be made with any ground meat (and often is, in North American restaurants, for reasons of profit and consumer taste). I prefer ground lamb. It is usually made in large batches and served as a main course. You can make one moussaka in a large ovenproof bowl rather than the dozens of ramekin portions I suggest here for an *ouzeri* tasting. In either case, serve with an elixir of your choice.

1 ½ lb	ground lamb or ground beef	680 g
1 tbsp	olive oil	15 mL
3	medium onions, finely chopped	3
1	garlic bulb (yes, a whole bulb, not just a clove)	1
8	plum tomatoes, peeled and diced, about 2 cups (500 mL)	8
¼ tsp	ground cinnamon	1 mL
¼ tsp	ground allspice	1 mL
3	bay leaves	3
3	cloves	3
1 cup	lamb stock or beef stock	250 mL
½ cup	red wine	125 mL
	Salt and pepper to taste	
1	eggplant, peeled	1
1 tbsp	salt	15 mL
2 tbsp	butter	30 mL
2 tbsp	flour	30 mL
1 cup	milk	250 mL
¼ tsp	nutmeg	1 mL
	Pinch salt	
½ cup	freshly grated Parmesan cheese	125 mL

In a large pot over medium-low heat, gently cook ground meat in olive oil. With a slotted spoon, transfer cooked meat to a colander or sieve and strain off excess fat. To the same large pot, with 2 tbsp (30 mL) of the leftover fat and juices, add the chopped onions. Increase heat and cook until onions brown, stirring occasionally. While onions cook, slice garlic bulb in half, around the equator, to expose the garlic cloves. Return meat to the pot and add garlic, tomatoes, cinnamon, allspice, bay leaves, cloves, stock and wine. Bring to a gentle boil and simmer for 1 hour. Taste and adjust for salt and pepper.

Cut eggplant into ¼-inch (5 mm) slices and into pieces that will fit the bottom of 12 ramekins. Put slices in a sieve or colander over a pot or a bowl, lightly salt the slices and let them sweat out the water for 30 minutes. Place slices in the bottom of 12 ramekins, or use them to line one large ovenproof dish.

Melt butter in a saucepan, add flour, stir with a wooden spoon or whisk and cook for 5 minutes. Slowly whisk in milk, nutmeg and a pinch of salt. The béchamel should be the consistency of mashed potatoes.

From the meat pot, discard the garlic. Divide the meat among the ramekins and spoon over the eggplant; add another layer of eggplant, then a generous amount of béchamel, and cover the top with grated Parmesan cheese.

Without the béchamel and cheese, moussaka can be frozen for up to 3 months or kept in the refrigerator for several days. The day it is to be served, make the béchamel, top ramekins with cheese and bake at 350°F (175°C) until the cheese browns and the moussaka is hot throughout, about 30 minutes from the refrigerator, 1 hour from the freezer. If you are making a large batch in one dish, bake for 50 minutes from the refrigerator, 90 minutes from the freezer. Put under broiler for a few seconds if cheese needs browning after the 30 minutes.

Saganaki

PREPARATION TIME:
5 MINUTES
COOKING TIME:
6 MINUTES
SERVES: 8

You've heard of a quarter-pounder with cheese? This is nearly a quarter-pounder *of* cheese—fried cheese with a flaming presentation that is a fabulous *ouzeri* staple. Simple, crispy, crunchy. Even the aroma off the plate melds with the ouzo. The Greeks use a cheese called *halmoumi*, a white goat's milk cheese from Cyprus, often made with mint. Or they use *Kefaloityri*, an aged, yellow, hard sheep's milk cheese. Now, assuming you can't find these in the supermarket right there beside the Kraft slices, use an old Cheddar, or, even better, *parmigiano reggiano*.

¼ cup	flour	60 mL
2 tbsp	ground black pepper	30 mL
8	pieces hard, old Cheddar, 3 inches (8 cm) by ¾ inch (2 cm), about 3 oz (75 g) each slice	8
2 tbsp	Metaxa (Greek brandy)	30 mL
¼ cup	oil for frying	60 mL
	Juice of fresh lemon	
8	large fresh mint leaves	8

Combine flour and pepper. Coat the cheese with flour by pushing each piece down hard on the flour until the flour adheres to it.

In a small pot over low heat, warm the brandy.

In a fry pan, heat oil until it smokes. Fry cheese 90 seconds on one side, then flip. (Be careful, the "skin" may want to come off. Don't let it.) Fry another 90 seconds. Remove to small plates. Light heated brandy with a match and, in front of guests, pour flaming brandy over cheese. When flames die, squeeze over a generous amount of lemon juice, top with a fresh mint leaf and serve with a knife and fork—and a glass of ouzo, of course.

Tyropittakia

These flaky pastries are made with phyllo (also spelled filo), a very thin, fragile pastry best purchased frozen from the supermarket. You'll get about twenty-four sheets in a package, each usually about a foot square. Take a sheet of phyllo and lay it out on a greased surface; paint the sheet with melted butter and lay another sheet on top. Paint that sheet with butter, lay the third sheet on top and paint it with butter. Cut the square into three long rectangles. Place 1 tbsp (15 mL) filling right at the bottom, dead center.

For a triangle, fold the strip like an envelope (or like the flag at a government funeral), corner to corner, all the way up.

For a roll, simply fold in both long sides about a quarter of the way into the center all the way up; then roll up from the filling end.

The roll method allows you to fit more on a cookie sheet than the typical Greek triangle form. In either case, place the stuffed phyllo pastries seam side down on a baking sheet. Bake at 375°F (190°C) until the pastry is golden and crisp, about 20 minutes.

Here are a few stuffings that go beautifully with liquorous elixirs.

Shrimp-Caper Tyropittakia

½ lb	cooked, peeled and cleaned shrimp	250 g	**PREPARATION TIME:**
2 tsp	pickled capers (about 50 small ones)	10 mL	30 MINUTES
1	clove garlic	1	**COOKING TIME:**
2 tsp	chopped shallot	10 mL	20 MINUTES
1 tbsp	chopped celery	15 mL	**MAKES:** 24, OR
	Salt		3 PER PERSON
2 tsp	dried oregano	10 mL	FOR 8 GUESTS
1	package phyllo pastry	1	

In a blender or small food processor, blend shrimp, capers, garlic, shallot, celery, salt and oregano. Proceed with the *tyropittakia* phyllo pastry directions above.

Kalamata Olive Tyropittakia

PREPARATION TIME:
30 MINUTES
COOKING TIME:
20 MINUTES
MAKES: 24

1 cup	pitted kalamata olives,* finely chopped	250 mL
¼ cup	finely chopped onion	60 mL
¼ cup	finely chopped fresh mint leaves	60 mL
1 tsp	orange zest, chopped fine	5 mL
1 tbsp	dried oregano	15 mL
1 tsp	ouzo	5 mL
1	package phyllo pastry	1

In a blender or food processor, or by hand, combine olives, onion, mint, zest, oregano and ouzo. Makes 1 cup (250 mL) of paste. Proceed with instructions for *tyropittakia* on p. 143.

House-Brick Lemon Game Hen

PREPARATION TIME:
30 MINUTES
MARINATION TIME:
4 TO 24 HOURS
COOKING TIME:
20 MINUTES
SERVES: 2

1	Rock Cornish game hen	1
¼ cup	lemon juice	60 mL
¼ cup + 1 tbsp	olive oil	60 mL + 15 mL
2 tbsp	dried oregano	30 mL
2	cloves garlic, finely chopped	2
½ tsp	salt	2 mL
2 tbsp	butter	30 mL
3	clean house bricks, preferably glazed	3
	Mint leaves or parsley for garnish	

Cut out the backbone and wishbone of the hen with kitchen scissors or a knife. Spread out hen and whack it with the heel of your hand until it lies as flat as road kill. Looks like a tobacco leaf now, doesn't it? It's supposed to. The dish is known throughout the Middle East and the former Soviet Union as Chicken Tebaka or Chicken Tebak.

Combine lemon juice, ¼ cup (60 mL) of the olive oil, oregano, garlic and salt in a bowl. Put game hen in the bowl, thoroughly coat bird with marinade, cover and refrigerate at least 4 hours, preferably overnight. Remove hen and drain, but don't wipe.

In a large fry pan, preferably nonstick, melt butter and remaining 1 tbsp (15 mL) oil over medium heat. Place game hen in pan, bones down, and weigh

*Pit an olive as you would peel a garlic clove: place under the flat side of a chef's knife blade and punch down with your hand to squish it. The pit slides out easily.

down with bricks to keep the bird flat. (Okay, okay, you can use anything really heavy, like a fry pan that covers the meat weighed down with bricks or rocks, or your stupid overweight tomcat, if he'll stay put. I use a cast-iron pan with a water-filled pot in it.) After 10 minutes, flip the hen over and weigh it down again, cooking until the skin is crisp and a deep mahogany brown, about 7 minutes— or until the cat can't stand the heat any more. Be careful when you are handling the hen, as the skin will tend to stick to the surface of the pan. Present the cooked game hen on 1 plate, garnished with mint leaves or Italian broadleaf parsley. At the table, slice down the middle and transfer to 2 smaller plates.

Ground Beef Dollars with Potato Garlic Sauce

½ lb	medium ground beef	225 g
½ lb	onions, grated, about 3 medium	225 g
¼ cup	fresh bread crumbs	60 mL
1	egg	1
2 tbsp	brandy	30 mL
2 tbsp	freshly chopped basil	30 mL
2 tbsp	finely chopped fresh dill	30 mL
1 tsp	salt	5 mL
1 tsp	cinnamon	5 mL
	Freshly ground pepper	
	Oil for frying	
1 cup	flour	250 mL
	Skordalia (recipe below)	
	Fresh dill, for garnish	

PREPARATION TIME:
10 MINUTES
COOKING TIME:
20 MINUTES
MAKES: 40
MEDALLIONS,
5 EACH
FOR 8 PEOPLE

Preheat oven to 200°F (95°C).

In a large bowl, combine beef, onions, bread crumbs, egg, brandy, herbs, salt, cinnamon and pepper. Heat oil to 375°F (190°C). Pour flour onto a plate. Take 2 tsp (10 mL) of the beef mixture and drop it into the flour; coat all sides. Roll into a small ball, then flatten to the size of a dollar coin. Repeat with the remaining beef mixture. Fry in batches until golden, about 1 minute. Drain and keep warm in oven. Serve 5 per guest around a small pool of the *skordalia* for dipping; garnish with fresh dill.

Skordalia (Potato Garlic Sauce)

PREPARATION TIME:

20 MINUTES

PROCESSING TIME:

2 MINUTES

MAKES: 2 CUPS

This is the Greek version of *aioli*—thicker, starchier, but no less garlicky or good. It is also used as a dip for vegetables such as broccoli, celery sticks and cauliflower. It's great on fish, as well. Place any extra sauce in a glass jar and refrigerate for three days or freeze for up to six months.

3	medium potatoes, about ½ lb (225 g)	3
½ cup	water	125 mL
8	cloves garlic, minced	8
1 tsp	salt	5 mL
½ cup	olive oil	125 mL
¼ cup	white wine vinegar	60 mL

Peel potatoes and boil until soft. In a food processor, blend potatoes, water, garlic and salt until smooth, about 1 minute. In a slow, steady stream, blend in oil, about another minute. Blend in vinegar. Pour into a bowl and let sit for a few hours to build up a wallop.

Eggplant in Tomatoes with Feta

PREPARATION TIME:

40 MINUTES

COOKING TIME:

20 MINUTES

SERVES: 6 AS

OUZERI SNACKS,

4 AS A VEGETABLE

SIDE DISH

3 tbsp	butter	45 mL
1 cup	finely chopped onions	250 mL
3	cloves garlic, minced	3
2 cups	peeled, diced eggplant	500 mL
2	large tomatoes, peeled, seeded and diced, about 1 cup (250 mL)	2
2 tbsp	tomato paste	30 mL
1 tsp	dried oregano	5 mL
½ tsp	salt	2 mL
½ lb	Feta cheese, for topping	225 g

In a pot over medium heat, melt butter and sauté onions and garlic for 5 minutes. Add eggplant and sauté until eggplant softens, about 5 more minutes. Stir in tomatoes, tomato paste, oregano and salt. Reduce heat to low and simmer for 30 minutes.

Preheat oven to 350°F (175°C).

Divide mixture among 6 ramekins or 2 larger ovenproof bowls; top with a generous layer of Feta and bake for 20 minutes, or until the Feta melts and starts to brown.

Baklava

½ cup	honey	125 mL	**PREPARATION TIME:**
¼ cup	orange juice	60 mL	45 MINUTES
	Juice of ½ large lemon		**COOKING TIME:**
1 tbsp	Triple Sec liqueur	15 mL	25 MINUTES
1 cup	finely chopped walnuts	250 mL	**SERVES: 8**
½ cup	finely chopped almonds	125 mL	
2 tbsp	brown sugar	30 mL	
1 tsp	ground cinnamon	5 mL	
1 tsp	ground cloves	5 mL	
2	pinches allspice	2	
1 cup	unsalted butter, melted	250 mL	
20	sheets phyllo pastry	20	

In a small saucepan over medium heat, combine honey, orange juice, lemon juice and Triple Sec. Simmer about 20 minutes until mixture has the consistency of a sticky glaze. In a bowl, combine the walnuts, almonds, brown sugar, cinnamon, ground cloves and allspice.

On a large greased baking sheet, 11 by 15 inches (30 cm by 40 cm), spread one layer of phyllo. Brush it well with melted butter, being careful to reach all the corners. Sprinkle nut mixture over one half; then fold it over to make a package. Take a second sheet of phyllo, butter it, sprinkle half with the nut mixture, fold it over and place it on top of the first package. Repeat until you have used all the phyllo, stacking the packages to make a thick pastry.

With a sharp knife, cut diagonal slits into the top of the pastry to make a diamond pattern.

Preheat oven to 350°F (175°C). Bake 20 to 25 minutes, or until golden brown.

Remove from oven, recut the diagonals and drizzle the honey syrup over the pastry. You may have to warm the syrup to get it running once again. Let cool. Serve.

CHAPTER SEVEN

The Hungarian Csarda

Budapest Csarda

Körözött 152
A fresh ewe's cheese spread

Cabbage Rolls 153
Baked in hock broth, rich with smoked pork sausages

Catfish, Hungarian Style 154
Spiced with paprika, fried in bacon fat

Schnitzel 155
Onion marinated, breaded and fried veal cutlets

Roast Chicken Paprikas 156
An oven-baked version, with paprika gravy

Galushka 157
Plump fresh pasta dumplings

Cucumber Salad 157

Goulash 158
More properly known as gulyas soup, served with csipetke

Plum Pastry 159
A light pastry of plums and walnuts

Palacsinta 160
Hungarian crêpes served with apricot, walnut, or mascarpone and
cocoa filling, or layered with chestnut stuffing

Hans Bueschkens, of Windsor, Ontario, was once the president of the World Association of Cooks Societies, the organization that helps coordinate the Culinary Olympics—possibly the least understood and most widely mocked competition in the world—held every four years in Frankfurt. Bueschkens notes that, from 1896, when the Culinary Olympics began, up to the early 1950s, virtually every winning team, including the French, was either Hungarian or led by a Hungarian.

The popular perception of Hungarian cuisine is greasy schnitzel and over-done liver swimming on an ocean of bacon fat and duck drippings, shoals of potatoes fried in lard and a red tide of paprika—the stuff that adds color to deviled eggs, but virtually no flavor. Yet the finest foie gras in the world is produced in Hungary. A few years ago some French producers were caught buying the Hungarian product and selling it as their own. Oh, the scandal! Oh, the shame!

The Hungarian soil and climate produce superb fruit, especially apricots, peaches and melons. The grapes produce wonderful wines, such as *Tokayi Aszú*. The taste of their sturgeon, carp and certain species of pike are unheard of anywhere else. Wild boar, duck, pheasant and quail are abundant. Suckling piglets are a well-fed specialty …

And, of course, Hungary grows a specific type of red pepper that produces paprika, the national spice, which is both aromatic and distinctly tasty. Nowhere else is this pepper grown, dried and pulverized, then classified from the highest, special or *kulonleges*, grade to the seventh and lowest, hot or *eros*. This is not the paprika you find in most supermarkets, which is why these recipes call for Hungarian paprika, a worthy substitute for cayenne pepper and sometimes hot chilies.

The best paprika comes from the region of Kalocsaj. Sweet and tangy in flavor, rich in pepper smell, it should be bought in small quantities and stored in airtight containers. Hungarian paprika is not always hot, but when it is, it produces a gradual warmth that never blisters or grabs the back of your throat. Hungarian paprika is essential in the following recipes. No substitutes. Use a mild, medium or hot version—whatever you like. I prefer hot paprika, and the following recipes were tested with it.

Three other ingredients dominate Hungarian cooking: sweet bell peppers, green or yellow, onions and sour cream. Traditionally, Hungarians skim the top off sour milk, which produces a taste unlike that of our processed sour cream. Our version is acceptable, but combining it half and half with whipping cream will lighten the taste and lessen the sourness.

Hungarian cuisine has been uniquely influenced over time. The first nomadic tribes, the Magyars, came from Asia; then a Hungarian king married an Italian, who brought her kitchen with her. The Turks invaded in the sixteenth century and ruled the country for a hundred and fifty years. Restaurants were flourishing in Hungary by the late nineteenth century, and the expertise of Hungary's chefs was predominant by the time the Culinary Olympics began in 1896.

Yes, Hungarian fare is heavier than California Spa cuisine. It does use lard, the best being pork fat rendered by frying rather than steaming. But you can substitute butter or vegetable oil, if you like. Remember, however, that the flavor is in the fat. You are trying to create delicious restaurant fare. Live a little. Invite Richard Simmons over another time.

Now, I might have laughed off Hans Bueschkens's assertions of Hungarian culinary supremacy but for one fact: I am married to a very good cook, a finalist in the annual North American Soffitel Amateur Cooking Finals sponsored by *Le Monde* and Novotel hotels. Marian "Bones" Kingsmill, née Fedak, born in Budapest, is a woman possessed of impeccable tastebuds. As I defer to her in life, so I have deferred to her in this chapter, so that you may experience a Hungarian *csarda* through the ingenuity of a Hungarian.

Körözött

PREPARATION TIME: 5 MINUTES
COOKING TIME: 2 MINUTES
MAKES: 1 CUP

This Hungarian ewe cheese spread rivals any French concoction and has a multiplicity of uses—cocktail spread, veggie dip, filling for crêpes or dessert on its own.

8 oz	ewe cheese, soft ripened, French or similar quality	225 g
¼ lb	unsalted butter	115 g
4	scallions, finely chopped, including half the green portion	4
1	garlic clove, finely chopped	1
2 tsp	Hungarian paprika	10 mL
1 tsp	chopped chives	5 mL
1 tsp	salt	5 mL

Combine all ingredients and refrigerate overnight to allow flavors to meld. Bring to room temperature before serving. Serve with crackers, smoked salmon, on toast with raw veggies, in crêpes or as a garnish for roast chicken.

Cabbage Rolls

Why did the Hungarians stuff the cabbage leaf? Just like the mountain. It was there. The Debreczeni (pronounced "Debra-seine-y") is the king of smoked sausages. Boiled or grilled on the barbecue, it stays juicy, has a wallop of flavor and aroma and shines through strong flavors such as mustard. If you find some in a Hungarian deli, don't balk at the expense. It's well worth it.

PREPARATION TIME:
2 DAYS
COOKING TIME:
90 MINUTES
SERVES: 6

2	smoked pork hocks	2
4	bay leaves	4
6 to 8	whole black peppercorns	6 to 8
1	small onion, whole	1
6	garlic cloves, crushed	6
1	carrot, peeled	1
2	stalks celery	2
1 lb	ground veal	450 g
1 lb	ground beef	450 g
2 cups	cooked rice, allowed to cool	500 mL
1 tsp	Hungarian paprika	5 mL
½ tsp	dried marjoram	2 mL
	Salt and pepper to taste	
1 tsp	dried parsley	5 mL
2	garlic cloves, finely chopped	2
2	medium eggs, beaten	2
4	rashers bacon, finely chopped	4
1	small onion, finely chopped	1
12	large cabbage leaves	12
2	cans sauerkraut, in wine, drained	2
4	Hungarian Debreczeni smoked sausages	4

The day before, put pork hocks, bay leaves, 1 peeled onion, crushed garlic, carrot, black peppercorns and celery in a stock pot. Cover with water, bring to a boil, skim off scum, lower heat and simmer for 2 hours. Remove the pork hocks, discard thick skin, bones and underlying fat of the pork hocks; set aside the meat. Allow the broth to cool overnight, then skim off the fat.

In a large bowl, combine the veal, beef, rice, paprika, marjoram, salt and pepper, parsley, garlic cloves and eggs. Set aside.

In a small frying pan over medium-low heat, gently sauté the bacon and finely chopped onion until the onion is translucent; do not crisp the bacon or brown the onions. Cool and add to the meat–rice mixture. Let stand for 2 hours in fridge so the flavors will meld.

Over a vegetable steamer placed in a large pot, steam the cabbage leaves in small batches for 3 minutes, or until they are pliable. Make a deep, narrow cut to remove the rib of the larger leaves. Cool leaves.

Lay out the cabbage leaves. Put 3 tbsp (45 mL) of the meat mixture on each leaf, fold the sides in and roll up.

Preheat oven to 325°F (160°C).

In the bottom of a large roasting pan, spread two-thirds of the sauerkraut. Gently lay all the cabbage rolls, as well as any unused meat mixture, on top of the sauerkraut. Place pieces of Debreczeni sausage and reserved pork-hock meat around and between the cabbage rolls. Cover all with remaining sauerkraut. Pour on enough hock broth to cover.

Bake cabbage rolls, partially covered, for 1 ½ hours. Replenish the broth as needed, checking every 25 minutes or so.

Serve topped with sour cream, freshly ground pepper and accompanied by a hearty bread. For a change, make extra large cabbage rolls using several leaves for each roll. In each, place a Debreczeni sausage surrounded by the meat mixture.

Catfish, Hungarian Style

PREPARATION TIME:
5 MINUTES
COOKING TIME:
10 MINUTES
SERVES: 4

Hungarians are great fish eaters, and favorites include trout and *fogash*, a type of pike–perch cross found in Lake Balaton. They also love what we are just beginning to enjoy widely—catfish.

½ cup	all-purpose flour	125 mL
1 tsp	salt	5 mL
2 tsp	fresh Hungarian paprika	10 mL
4 to 6	grinds fresh black pepper	4 to 6
4	large fresh catfish fillets	4
2 tbsp	olive oil	30 mL
2 tbsp	butter	30 mL
2 tbsp	bacon fat	30 mL

Combine flour, salt, paprika and pepper. Dredge the fish fillets in the seasoned flour to completely cover.

In a large nonstick saucepan over medium-high heat, combine olive oil, butter and bacon fat. When it sizzles, add fish fillets and cook for 4 to 5 minutes per side. Drain excess fat on paper towels. Serve with rice or pan-fried potatoes and enjoy.

Schnitzel

Schnitzel tastes better at a *csarda* because of the secret ingredient: onions. Marinate the scallopini by layering it with mounds of raw onions for at least a day. The veal will suck up a bit of the flavor, which comes subtly through the breading like a ghost in a snowdrift.

PREPARATION TIME:
12 HOURS OR MORE
COOKING TIME:
10 MINUTES
SERVES: 6

6	veal cutlets, 5 to 7 oz (150 to 200 g) each, pounded evenly to ¼ inch (5 mm) thickness	6
3	large cooking onions, sliced thinly	3
2 cups	fresh bread crumbs	500 mL
½ cup	fresh parsley, finely chopped, loosely packed	125 mL
1 tbsp	dried thyme	15 mL
2 tsp	freshly ground white pepper	10 mL
1 tsp	salt	5 mL
1 cup	flour	250 mL
2	eggs, beaten with 2 tbsp (30 mL) milk	2
	Vegetable oil for frying	
	Lemon wedges	
	Parsley sprigs	

With a mallet or the bottom of a heavy pot, pound cutlets until they are less than ¼ inch (5 mm) thick. On a piece of waxed paper slightly larger than the cutlets, place a mound of onions. Place a cutlet on the onions, top with another layer of onions, then another cutlet, and so on, ending with a layer of onions. Cover with waxed paper, roll in a damp tea towel and refrigerate for 8 to 12 hours.

Combine the bread crumbs, parsley, thyme, pepper, salt and flour. Dredge each cutlet in flour mixture, then eggs, then bread crumb mixture, coating each cutlet thoroughly.

Preheat oven to 200°F (95°C).

Heat a scant ¼ inch (5 mm) vegetable oil in a pan over medium-high heat. When the oil is hot, fry cutlets until golden on both sides, 3 to 5 minutes per side. Remove to a plate, pat with a paper towel and place in the oven to keep warm while you cook the remaining cutlets.

Place each cutlet on a warmed plate, with a lemon wedge on the side. Garnish with a sprig of parsley. Serve with roast potatoes and a green salad or dill pickles.

Roast Chicken Paprikas

PREPARATION TIME:
30 MINUTES
COOKING TIME:
45 MINUTES
SERVES: 6

Paprikas (pronounced pa-pree-cash) is a method of preparing meat and fowl. It is a thick paprika-based gravy that coats the main ingredients. This oven-baked version of the classic Chicken Paprikas lends itself to entertaining, as it requires about 30 minutes of preliminary preparation and low maintenance during schmoozing time with guests.

4 lb	chicken legs, cut into thighs and drumsticks	1.8 kg
2	small onions, puréed	2
5	cloves garlic, crushed	5
2 tbsp	flour	30 mL
1 ½ cups	rich chicken stock*	375 mL
1 tbsp	paprika	15 mL
1 tsp	salt, or to taste	5 mL
1	large sprig fresh rosemary, chopped, or 1 tsp (5 mL) , dried	1
2 tbsp	finely chopped fresh parsley	30 mL
½ cup	shiitake or other wild mushrooms, coarsely chopped	125 mL

Preheat oven to 325°F (160°C).

Remove the visible fat from 4 of the chicken pieces. In a fry pan over low heat, melt the fat. Turn heat up slightly, add the onion and garlic and sauté until the onion is soft and the edges are slightly browned. Remove and reserve. In the same pan over medium heat, brown the chicken pieces on both sides, then place in a shallow baking dish. Remove all but 2 tbsp (30 mL) of the fat from the pan. Over low heat, whisk in the flour and cook for 10 minutes, or until flour turns golden brown. Slowly whisk in the chicken stock to make a thick sauce. Add the onion–garlic mixture; add paprika. Cook for 5 minutes. Pour *paprikas* sauce over the chicken and place in oven for 5 to 10 minutes.

Evenly sprinkle rosemary, parsley and mushrooms over the top of the casserole. Return it to the oven and cook for 30 minutes.

Serve with *galushka* and cucumber salad (recipes below).

*To make a rich stock, reduce an unsalted chicken stock to half its volume.

Galushka (Fresh Pasta Dumplings)

The Hungarian version of fresh pasta

2 cups	flour	500 mL	
1	egg, beaten with a whisk	1	
	Water		
2 tbsp	unsalted butter	30 mL	
2 tbsp	freshly chopped parsley	30 mL	

PREPARATION TIME: 10 MINUTES
COOKING TIME: 10 MINUTES
SERVES: 4

Place the flour in a deep, narrow bowl. Make a well in the middle and add the beaten egg. Gradually add small amounts of water while quickly beating the dough with a wooden spoon. The dough is ready when it is firmly elastic and pulls away cleanly from the wooden spoon.

Bring a large pot of salted water to the boil. Using the tip of a teaspoon, drop pieces of dough the size of large raisins into the boiling water. (The spoon can be dipped into the boiling water to release the dough more easily.) When they rise to the surface of the boiling water, the dumplings are done. Remove them with a slotted spoon and rinse under cold water.

In a pan over medium-low heat, melt butter, add parsley and sauté dumplings gently for 3 or 4 minutes. Serve with Roast Chicken Paprikas.

Cucumber Salad

1	large seedless cucumber, finely sliced	1	
¾ tsp	salt	3 mL	
2 tbsp	white vinegar	30 mL	
¼ cup	water	60 mL	
1 tsp	sugar	5 mL	
	Paprika and chopped parsley for garnish		

PREPARATION TIME: 40 MINUTES
SERVES: 6

Place cucumber slices in a bowl, sprinkle with salt and let stand for 30 minutes. Squeeze salt and juices from cucumber slices. Combine the vinegar, water and sugar. Add to cucumbers and toss. Garnish with paprika and parsley.

Goulash

PREPARATION TIME:

30 MINUTES

COOKING TIME:

1 ½ HOURS

SERVES: 6

This most famous of Hungarian dishes, correctly named *gulyas* soup, not stew, is best made in advance and served reheated with fresh crusty bread, butter and chopped hot Hungarian yellow peppers as a fiery condiment.

5	cloves garlic	5
1	large Spanish onion, finely chopped	1
3 tbsp	bacon fat or lard	45 mL
2 ¼ lb	choice sirloin cut into 1-inch (2.5 cm) cubes	1 kg
¼ cup	flour	60 mL
2 tsp	salt	10 mL
½ tsp	fresh ground black pepper	2.5 mL
2 ½ tsp	paprika	12.5 mL
1	large green pepper, seeded, membranes removed, finely chopped	1
1	large tomato, peeled, seeded and diced	1
4 cups	rich beef stock	1 L
	Csipetke (recipe below)	

With the flat blade of chef's knife, crush—don't smash—the garlic cloves. In a large pot over medium-low heat, sauté the onions and garlic in the bacon fat until golden brown. Remove from pan with slotted spoon. Increase heat to medium. Dredge the meat in flour, shaking off excess flour; place meat in pot and sear on all sides until the meat is slightly browned. Return the onions and garlic to the pot. Add salt, pepper and paprika. Cook another 4 minutes. Add the green pepper, tomato and enough beef stock to cover. Lower heat and simmer for 1 ½ hours, topping up the beef stock as necessary. Add *csipetke* and cook for an additional 5 minutes.

Csipetke

Csipetke—pronounced *chee-pet-keh*—means "little pinches of dough," and they are exactly that.

6 tbsp	flour	90 mL
1	egg	1

Combine the flour and egg to make a thick and pasty dough. Roll it out into thin strips. Pinch off pea-size pieces. Bring a pot of salted water to the boil. Drop in the dough pinches and cook until they rise to the top. Drain. Add to goulash.

Plum Pastry

This pastry can be made with apples or apricots, but it's best with fresh ripe prune plums. If you use apples, slice them very thinly and arrange in double layers on top of the pastry. Brush with butter, for a richer taste, before sprinkling final layer of nut topping.

PREPARATION TIME:
15 MINUTES
COOKING TIME:
50 MINUTES
SERVES: 8

1 ¼ cups	flour	300 mL
½ cup	sugar	125 mL
2 tsp	baking powder	10 mL
½ tsp	baking soda	2.5 mL
¾ cup	butter, at room temperature	180 mL
1	egg	1
1 tsp	vanilla extract	5 mL
2 tbsp	water, maximum	30 mL
½ cup	ground walnuts	125 mL
½ cup	sugar	125 mL
1 tsp	cinnamon	5 mL
1 lb	prune plums, halved, pitted, skins removed	450 g

Preheat oven to 350°F (175°C).

Sift together the flour, sugar, baking powder and baking soda. In a separate bowl, cream together the butter, egg and vanilla extract; thoroughly combine with the dry ingredients. Add a little water, up to 2 tbsp (30 mL), to the mixture and quickly roll out the dough to fit two 8-inch (20 cm) square baking pans. Do not work the dough. Bake for 10 to 15 minutes, or until the pastry top turns golden. Remove pan from oven.

Turn oven down to 325°F (160°C). Mix together walnuts, sugar and cinnamon. Sprinkle half the mixture over the pastry; add the fruit in a layer, and sprinkle the remaining nut mixture on top. Return to oven and bake for 30 to 35 minutes.

Serve warm or cold with whipped cream.

Hungarian Palacsinta
with Three Fillings
For the Palacsinta (crêpes) batter:

PREPARATION TIME:

25 MINUTES

COOKING TIME:

45 MINUTES

SERVES: 8

1 cup	flour	250 mL
1 cup	milk	250 mL
1 tsp	vanilla extract	5 mL
1 tbsp	icing sugar	15 mL
3 tbsp	unsalted butter	45 mL
1 to 2 tbsp	soda water	15 mL to 30 mL

In a blender, mix together flour, milk, vanilla, icing sugar and 15 mL of the butter. Blend until smooth. Add 1 tbsp (15 mL) soda water. Add more if needed—the batter should be quite thin. Over medium-high heat, in a heavy, nonstick, 4-inch or 6-inch (10 cm or 15 cm) skillet or crêpe pan, heat 1 ½ tsp (7 mL) butter until it sizzles and starts to smoke. Pour or ladle ¼ cup (60 mL) of the batter into the center of the pan; lift and swirl the pan around to coat the bottom evenly. Return pan to stove. Cook for 1 minute, flip and cook for slightly less time on the other side. Keep finished crêpes warm on a side plate.

The crêpes should have a holstein-cow pattern of golden brown spots over the surface.

These crêpes are traditionally spread with filling and rolled, or folded like a dinner napkin with two sides in to the center. If you want to get really fancy you can melt a little chocolate across the middle to create a bow-tie effect.

Apricot filling

1 cup	tart apricot jam	250 mL
	Cinnamon to garnish	

Spread jam onto crêpes, fold or roll them up, then sprinkle with cinnamon.

Walnut filling

½ cup	walnut halves	125 mL
½ cup	granulated sugar	125 mL
	Cinnamon to garnish	

Combine walnuts and sugar in a blender until the mixture is quite fine. Spread on crêpes, roll up or fold and sprinkle with cinnamon for garnish.

Mascarpone and Cocoa Filling

1 cup	mascarpone cheese	250 mL
1 tbsp	cocoa powder	15 mL
2 tbsp	icing sugar	30 mL
	Cocoa powder and icing sugar for garnish	

Blend together the mascarpone, cocoa powder and sugar till smooth. Spread on crêpes and dust with cocoa powder and icing sugar.

Hungarian Layered Crêpes with Chestnut Stuffing

20	crêpes	20
15 oz	can chestnut purée	450 mL
¼ cup	icing sugar	60 mL
1 tbsp	rum	15 mL
1 ¼ cup	whipping cream	300 mL
1 tbsp	sugar, or to taste	15 mL

PREPARATION TIME:
45 MINUTES
COOKING TIME:
30 MINUTES
SERVES: 8

Prepare a double batch of crêpe batter.

In a food processor or blender, combine the chestnut purée, icing sugar, rum and ¼ cup (60 mL) whipping cream. Blend until smooth.

Place one crêpe on a large plate; spread with a thin layer of the chestnut filling. Top with a crêpe, spread on another layer of filling, top with a crêpe. Continue until all the crêpes and filling have been used. End with a crêpe.

Whip remaining 1 cup (250 mL) whipping cream with sugar. Smooth over stack of crêpes. Cut and serve as you would a cake.

CHAPTER EIGHT

The British Pub

The King's Folly

Stilton, Celery and Port Soup 166
A universally accepted pairing of gustatory decadence

Steak and Mushroom Pie 167
Because, really, this is the ultimate comfort lunch pie

Fish 'n' Chips 168
With either the King's Folly regular or Rafters' basil tartar

Dover Sole Meunière 171
The Queen of flatfish, served with black butter and fried parsley

Scotland Meets Germany Pasta 172
Smoked salmon that takes Germany by the Kasslers

Scotch Eggs 174
The traditional pork-wrapped hard-boiled eggs

Little Scotch Eggs 175
A little daintier, a little more herbaceous

Grilled Dublin Bay Prawns 176
"Dainty lobster tails" with garlic and Scotch butters

The English get a bad rap from food snobs simply because of such peculiar habits as cold toast and bacon grease for breakfast, cold toast and beer for lunch and peculiarities such as bubble and squeak and bangers and mash. The English also like mushy peas, which makes them certifiable. But ...

Historically, the English were cooking far better than the French before 1770. Auguste Escoffier, while French-born, cooked at the Savoy and Ritz-Carlton hotels in London. Until the revolution, French "cuisine" was confined to the tables of the nobility. Then they lost their heads, and their chefs had a paucity of clients. They had to open restaurants to survive. And survive they did. But until then, the likes of Sir Percy Blakeney (the Scarlet Pimpernel) and his cronies dined far better in London than the revolutionaries did in Paris.

More important in all this, however, modern snobs ignore the fact that some of the world's greatest products are native to the United Kingdom and Ireland—Dublin Bay prawns, Dover sole, Stilton, Scottish smoked salmon and beer. I cannot ignore these.

Stilton, Celery and Port Soup

PREPARATION TIME:
30 MINUTES
COOKING TIME:
1 ½ HOURS
SERVES: 4

This is the Caesar salad of soups. I think everyone loves a Caesar salad, because a good one widens your eyes with every bite, and you remember it fondly in your mind and the sides of your mouth and with every breath. You can feel your stomach enjoying it as much as your taste buds. This soup has the same effect. I don't know if it's the beginning of a meal, a whole meal or dessert, but it is wondrous.

I introduced it to a British restaurant as an occasional special, and it met with great success. The owner, however, was cheap, so I tried cheaper blue cheeses. It worked, but the soup lacked finesse. In the end, the cost difference was insignificant: orders dropped like autumn leaves.

3 tbsp	butter	45 mL
2 cups	roughly chopped cooking onions	500 mL
2 ½ cups	finely chopped celery	625 mL
3 tbsp	flour	45 mL
3 cups	chicken stock	750 mL
	Salt and pepper to taste	
¾ cup	whipping cream	180 mL
½ lb	Stilton cheese	225 g
4 tsp	tawny port	20 mL
	Pinch of nutmeg for garnish	

Over medium-low heat in a large pot, heat butter. Add onions and celery and cook until they are limp but not brown, about 15 minutes. Stir in flour and cook, stirring, until flour turns a light brown, about 10 minutes. Add stock; stir up flour crust on bottom of pan. Bring to a boil. Skim. Simmer 1 hour with a cover half on. Purée soup, then strain through a fine sieve into a clean pot. Adjust salt and pepper to taste.

Divide the soup among 4 ovenproof bowls. To each bowl add 3 tbsp (45 mL) of the cream and 1 ½ oz (40 g) of the crumbled Stilton—just a little more than two level tablespoons or 30 mL. Bake at 400°F (205°C) for 5 minutes, just enough time to melt the cheese. Top with 1 tsp (5 mL) Stilton and 1 tsp (5 mL) port, dust with nutmeg and serve.

Restaurateurs make the soup in large quantities up to the salt-and-pepper point and refrigerate it. You, too, can make it ahead of time to that point, then divide it among 4 ovenproof bowls and refrigerate. Add the Stilton and cream when the soup is cool, so the cream won't spoil and the cheese won't melt. Refrigerate until 30 minutes before service; then pop the soup into the oven at 350°F (175°C) for 30 minutes, top with remaining cheese and port, dust with nutmeg and serve.

Steak and Mushroom Pie

3 tbsp	butter	45 mL	
2 cups	roughly chopped cooking onions	500 mL	
1 cup	roughly chopped shiitake, portobello or oyster mushrooms, about 15	250 mL	
1 ½ lb	chuck steak cut into 1-inch (2.5 cm) squares	680 g	
1 tbsp	flour	15 mL	
1 cup	strong brown stock	250 mL	
2 tbsp	Worcestershire sauce	30 mL	
2	bay leaves	2	
1 tsp	dried thyme	5 mL	
1 tsp	dried rosemary	5 mL	
½ tsp	salt	2 mL	
	Freshly ground pepper		
	Frozen puff pastry		

PREPARATION TIME: 30 MINUTES

COOKING TIME: 3 ½ HOURS

SERVES: 6

Preheat oven to 275°F (135°C).

In a fry pan or pot, heat 2 tbsp (30 mL) of the butter over medium-low heat and sauté onions until soft and transparent. Add mushrooms and cook until the onions turn golden brown. Remove onions and mushrooms to a casserole. Increase heat to medium, add remaining 1 tbsp (15 mL) of the butter to the fry pan and brown beef cubes. If necessary, brown the beef in batches. With the browned beef in the pan, stir in flour and cook for 3 minutes. Remove beef to casserole. Into the fry pan pour the stock, scrape up all the brown bits, then pour the stock into the casserole. Stir in Worcestershire sauce, bay leaves, thyme, rosemary and salt and pepper. Cover the casserole and bake for 2 hours. Remove top and cook for another 1 hour.

The pie can be made ahead of time to this point, and finished in the oven 30 minutes before serving.

Increase oven heat to 300°F (150°C). Divide stew among ovenproof bowls, top each with puff pastry (buy it from the supermarket freezer and follow package directions) and bake for another 30 minutes, or until the pie crust is brown. Or make 1 large dish—simply cover the casserole with puff pastry and bake for 30 minutes.

Fish 'n' Chips

PREPARATION TIME:
5 MINUTES
RESTING TIME:
2 HOURS
COOKING TIME:
5 MINUTES
SERVES: 4 TO 6,
DEPENDING UPON
FISH SIZE

To be authentic, you should really serve this meal in old newspapers, but I suspect you won't.

Halibut is the mildest-tasting fish used in fish and chip shops, apart from sole. Haddock, a member of the cod family, is in the middle, and cod has the strongest taste, although even cod is not all that fishy. Those are the most commonly used fishes in North America, but other species often used in Europe include plaice, flounder, brill, lemon sole, gray sole and turbot, the last of which I can't discuss without worrying about the return of the Spanish Inquisition.

A master fryer will lay the battered fish in the oil, holding one end until the fish puffs and floats on its own. Romantics claim the cook wants the fish to swim again; but in truth the method prevents the fish from falling to the bottom and picking up burned crud before refloating.

Batters differ from one shop to the next: flour, water, egg, salt, maybe a pinch of sugar, that's all it takes. Beer is an age-old substitute for water. Try your favorite brand first, because you might as well drink the leftovers. The English use English beer because it's their regular brand. But you can try stout or porter or perhaps a dark Irish Guinness. Canadian beers are generally sweeter, German beers hoppier.

1 cup	flour	250 mL
1 cup	beer	250 mL
1	egg yolk	1
2 tsp	salt	10 mL
1 tsp	white sugar	5 mL
1 tsp	white pepper	5 mL
2 tbsp	vegetable oil	30 mL
	Oil for deep frying	
8	filets of fish (your choice)	8

In a large bowl, combine flour, beer, egg yolk, salt, sugar, pepper and oil. Cover and let rest for 2 hours.

Heat oil to 375°F (190°C). Dip fish into batter and gently lower each piece into the oil, holding onto one end until the fish floats. Fry until golden and crisp, about 5 minutes. Flip it over halfway through cooking to cook evenly.

Chips

Like *frites* (see p. 78), chips have to be cooked twice, the first time to release the gummy starches, the second time to brown the outside. English chips, of course, are fat logs of potato, mushier in texture than French fries.

Each fish and chip shop fries its chips at its own temperature in its own brand of oil. Sometimes they fry the fish in the same oil at the same temperature as the chips. The oil, naturally, breaks down in a day or two, and this, too, flavors the dish. You can't compete with this, so just make chips the easy way. To wit:

Microwave a fresh hard russet potato; let it cool, then cut it into chips. Fry the chips in a pot ⅓ filled with oil at 375°F (190°C).

When you cut the potato into chips, you will find it sticky with starch, thanks to the microwave. The chips will fry up quickly and beautifully.

Or you can twice fry the chips, as usual. Cut a hard russet potato into chips and fry for 4 minutes, remove, drain and cool. Just before service, fry them again for 4 or 5 minutes, until golden.

Tartar Sauce, Standard Version

What a nutritionally incorrect but delicious sensation is English-style batter-fried fish! Fresh from the hot oil, the crust crunches and crackles as you bite into it, maybe a drop of oozing fat spurts from the flesh and scalds your cheek, and you wince.

PREPARATION TIME:
15 MINUTES
MAKES: 3 CUPS

As good as it is, it's naked without something else, without the nostril-tweaking twang of salt and aged malt vinegar—or tartar sauce. My version of tartar sauce mimics the commercially bought sauces. (I have never been in a fish and chip shop that didn't use commercial tartar sauce.) But purists legitimately will challenge it, because a true *sauce tartare* is a flavored mayonnaise made with hard-boiled egg yolks.

½ cup	mayonnaise (p. 170)	125 mL
2 tsp	lemon juice	10 mL
1 tsp	salt	5 mL
½ tsp	ground white pepper	2 mL
¼ cup	finely minced onions	60 mL
3 tbsp	finely chopped dill pickle	45 mL
3 tbsp	chopped parsley	45 mL

Combine all ingredients thoroughly. Let sit at least 2 hours before serving.

Basil Tartar Sauce

Rafters, in Beaver Creek, Colorado, near Aspen, makes a basil tartar sauce. Why not? Such innovation separates the good from the ugly. Substitute finely chopped basil leaves for the parsley in the recipe above.

Mayonnaise

PREPARATION TIME:
5 MINUTES
MAKES: 375 ML
(1 ½ CUPS)

For some odd reason, mayonnaise is a North American commercial product whose composition and processing have been legislated by politicians. It's true. By law, mayonnaise must have a certain amount of eggs per whatever. Would someone name just one politician who knows anything about food or whose taste can be trusted? Is this an example of a public waste of time? Let's get real: we're talking about something you can make in the comfort of your own home in minutes without the aid of a politician.

I must have made mayonnaise a hundred times. I made it the first time because I was curious, the second time to try to get it right, the next twenty times because I mindlessly bought into the snobbish argument that homemade is better, and the next seventy-eight-plus times because I was too stubborn to admit that, (a), Commercial mayo is more than good enough for most applications, including the tartar sauce in this book, and, (b), even the so-called sweet "salad dressings" such as Miracle Whip by Kraft, which aren't legal mayos, are preferable in things like egg salad sandwiches and my mother's deviled eggs. These things are, after all, a matter of taste. Your taste.

This is a recipe for food processor mayonnaise, should you want to try your hand at it. You can make it by hand, of course, but I suspect your wrists will fall off. Other than repetitive wrist injury syndrome, the difference between the two is that, in the food processor recipe, you use whole eggs, but you use only egg yolks in a hand-whipped one. The principle is the same—egg yolks absorb oil. The yolk of one large egg will absorb between ½ to ¾ cup (125 mL and 180 mL) vegetable or olive oil. Any more oil will ruin it. Make sure the eggs and oil are at room temperature.

2	Grade A large eggs	2
1 tbsp	lemon juice, freshly squeezed	15 mL
2 tsp	Dijon mustard (or other smooth mustard)	10 mL
½ tsp	salt	2 mL
¼ tsp	cayenne pepper	1 mL
1 ½ cups	vegetable oil	375 mL
1 tbsp	boiling water	15 mL

In a food processor, place egg yolks, lemon juice, mustard, salt and cayenne. Process until the eggs turn pale yellow and thick, about 5 seconds. This is important. Before eggs can absorb oil, they must be beaten until they thicken. Now, through the food chute, add oil very slowly, a drop or two at first, then in a slow stream. After you have added 1 cup (250 mL) of oil, you can add it at a faster rate. The oil-pouring process will take only about 1 minute. Add water and process for 2 seconds; the water sets the mayo.

If the mayo is too thick, add chicken stock to thin it out.

Dover Sole Meunière

In the days of the horse and buggy, smart fishermen in Dover, England, acquired fast horse-drawn wagons. When they came into port with a catch of common European sole, they immediately rushed it to the Billingsgate fish market in London. Because their sole arrived so much fresher than other fish from the south coast of England, it was in great demand. Billingsgate fishmongers labeled it "Dover sole" to indicate that it was the freshest and best fish in the market. Free enterprise being what it is, all the other fishmongers began calling their flatfish Dover sole, as well. North Americans take such entrepreneurism farther by calling other types of flatfish sole, when they are not, and by officially naming a Pacific flatfish Dover sole, although it ain't the original.

Until quite recently, you could buy true European Dover sole frozen, but culture is evolving in the colonies, and it is now flown in fresh. It is, however, sold almost exclusively to restaurants and is very expensive.

The most common "sole" in North American shops is either a flounder called gray sole or plaice, also known as dab, sand dab and blackback, but usually sold as "lemon sole" or "French sole." My fish-expert friend, Harm, says frozen Dover sole has nothing on really fresh flounder or plaice in North America, and I think he's right. But I will never forget the first time I had real Dover Sole Meunière, in the early 1970s at the Prospect of Whitby, the oldest pub in London.

PREPARATION TIME:
5 MINUTES
COOKING TIME:
7 MINUTES
SERVES: 2

4 tsp	black butter (recipe, p. 41)	20 mL
¼ cup	flour	60 mL
2 tsp	salt	10 mL
1 tsp	white pepper	5 mL
2	filets of sole	2
2 tbsp	butter	30 mL
¼ cup	stemmed and coarsely chopped parsley	60 mL

Heat dinner plates in the oven at 250°F (120°C).

Make black butter and keep it warm.

Mix flour, salt and pepper. Dredge sole in seasoned flour. Heat fresh butter in fry pan over medium-high flame until it starts to brown. Fry sole on both sides quickly until flour browns. Remove from pan and place on hot plates. Pour off butter, add black butter and heat until hot. Sprinkle parsley on fish; pour hot black butter over all. Serve immediately.

Scotland Meets Germany Pasta

PREPARATION TIME:
10 MINUTES
COOKING TIME:
5 MINUTES
SERVES: 4

The best smoked salmon I have ever had was from Scotland—I ate it and damn near fainted. I have never tasted smoked salmon as good since, even when I've looked for it, which makes me suspicious. But for what it's worth, here's the story: I was told that the salmon was line caught, which means caught by the mouth on a rod and reel, and handled carefully to prevent bruising. It was then cured according to an ancient recipe I do not have. Finally, it was smoked over wood from Scotch whisky barrels, cast aside after a hundred years of producing the Scots' gold that the Queen favors. There you have it. Honestly, could you get a better sell job than that?

Salmon are what they eat and what they swim in. The tastier the salmon's diet, the better the salmon will taste. The colder the water, the purer the food, the better the product. If a salmon swims in very cold water, it develops more fat. More fat, more taste. More fat, more smoke retention, because smoke permeates fat more easily than it permeates flesh, which is denser. The problem with all this is that it assumes all fish were created equal, and that God smokes them with the same tender care worldwide.

Kick the ball, Charlie Brown.

Received wisdom is that Atlantic salmon is superior to Pacific. No one mentions that Atlantic and Pacific salmon are different species (Atlantic salmon is actually a trout), or that Atlantic salmon is commercially farmed in British Columbia. In my experience, some Pacific sockeye salmon, commonly found in cans, makes damn fine smoked salmon in the right hands.

No one from whom you buy smoked salmon can tell you how the salmon was caught or processed, leaving you to believe the outrageous price is proof of quality alone. Of course, price really reflects the ratio of volume of fish smoked to the rent on the processing plant. Smoked salmon is smoked (by whom and how you will never know). Lox is "soaked," or cured, salmon. It is a lot cheaper, but tastes almost the same when cooked or put on a bagel with cream cheese. The texture is different. Side by side, the taste is different. But use your common sense.

If it is good enough for you, it is good enough. Start with lox; when you can afford it, go up to smoked. If you are like the rest of us, you won't have time to go further with something as insignificant. But if you find a salmon smoked over whisky barrels, call me.

Now, surf and turf is an abomination—seafood and meat on the same plate, yuck. So, when Jeff Baker told me that he combined smoked salmon and smoked pork at the Grand Hotel in Stockholm, Sweden, and it was bringing people back time and time again, I laughed. Actually, I just stared, as if he were claiming he could spark a fire by bashing his head against a concrete wall. And then I sneaked home and tried it.

Apart from the fact that this is a fabulous dish and takes five minutes, its three wonderful raw ingredients—smoked salmon, Kassler chops and pasta—provide an opportunity to pontificate, which is why people write books.

A Kassler chop is a German triumph. It is the loin of pork that has been cured, smoked and then roasted—in effect, cooked three times before you buy it to cook again (albeit very briefly). Yet it will be so moist and smoky and tender you can crush it between tongue and palate. (Well, almost. I am occasionally given to exaggeration, or so say my mother and my wife.) And you're North American, trained to eat pork only when it has been cooked to a gray cardboard. You'll balk at a Kassler because it is always pink, like ham. If you ever see a Kassler chop, buy it. Make this recipe. Or simply coat the Kassler with barbecue sauce and grill it, five minutes tops. (It's cooked already. All you are doing is creating a caramelized crust for flavor.)

Finally, pasta. If you are a food person you have probably read a restaurant review something like: "The pasta was fresh, and perfectly *al dente*." More revealing, however, is the review that whines, "The fresh pasta was overcooked. At that price it should have been *al dente*."

Price be damned. You and I know that fresh pasta cannot be cooked *al dente*, that is, with a slight core in the middle to make it chewy, because it has not been dried to create that core. Only dried pasta can end up *al dente*.

Which is better? Which should the home restaurateur use? Make fresh pasta—even if you do it only once. It is a wonderful experience. Pasta, in all its forms and under all its names, is merely flour, water, sometimes eggs, salt and a splash of oil made into a dough. It is rolled out thinly, twisted into shapes, rolled into tubes or cut into ribbons or strings. You can do it in a bowl with a blunt stick. It's easy, delicious and trendy; but it does *not* make for a religious experience. So, once you've made fresh pasta, do what very good restaurants do—buy dried pasta. Buy Italian. Buy expensive—"expensive" isn't expensive, anyway.

	Pasta (fusilli, fettuccine or	
	linguini) for 2	
1 tbsp	unsalted butter	15 mL
2 tbsp	finely chopped onions	30 mL
½ cup	white wine	125 mL
1 cup	whipping cream	250 mL
6 oz	Kassler meat, about ½ lb	170 g
	(225 g) chop before removing the bone,	
	thinly sliced or cubed	
3 oz	smoked salmon or lox	85 g
	Freshly ground black pepper to taste	

In a large pot in plenty of salted water, boil pasta. Fresh pasta needs about 3 minutes. With dried pasta, check after 7 minutes. When you cut a piece in half, a small, barely perceptible dot of white uncooked inside should show.

Meanwhile, in a saucepan or pot large enough to hold both sauce and pasta, melt butter. Add onions and sauté until onions are wilted. Add wine and reduce to a syrup. Add cream and Kassler; cook until sauce is slightly thickened. Add pasta and smoked salmon; cook until the sauce clings to a spoon but is still liquid. Serve with a good grind of pepper.

Scotch Eggs

PREPARATION TIME:
30 MINUTES
COOKING TIME:
10 TO 12 MINUTES
SERVES: 6

In its simplest form, a Scotch egg is a hefty pub meal, a hard-boiled egg packed about with sausage meat, deep fried, cooled and cut lengthwise to expose the layers of sausage, egg white and yolk. (You can, of course, also eat one hot.)

7	medium eggs	7
1 lb	finely ground, mild breakfast sausage meat	450 g
½ cup	fresh bread crumbs	125 mL
½ tsp	cayenne pepper	2 mL
½ tsp	salt	2 mL
¼ tsp	ground sage	1 mL
	Oil for deep frying	
	Chopped parsley for garnish	

Hard-boil 6 of the eggs. Cool, shell and set aside.

In a bowl, thoroughly combine sausage meat, bread crumbs, pepper, salt, sage and the raw egg. Press the sausage meat around the hard-boiled eggs, encasing them entirely.

Heat oil to 300°F (150°C). Fry eggs until they are a dark mahogany brown, about 10 to 12 minutes. Cool, cut lengthwise and dust with chopped parsley—or eat 'em hot.

Little Scotch Eggs

Good as Scotch eggs are, many people find that they sit in the pit of your stomach like a shot put. If a taste of the good life is an adequate substitute for living it fully, you might want to try these miniatures, which I whipped up several years ago to go with an English sampling meal.

PREPARATION TIME:
5 MINUTES
COOKING TIME:
5 MINUTES
SERVES: 4

Quail eggs can be purchased raw in many Portuguese, European and Asian markets. They are small, they hard-boil in about eight minutes—and they're a royal pain to peel without ripping the white away from the yolk. Luckily, quail eggs can also be purchased in cans, hard-boiled and peeled, in the same markets. A can usually costs less than two dollars and contains about thirty hard-boiled eggs packed in water. Rinse them well under running water. The sausage overwhelms any subtle taste advantage of freshly boiled eggs.

½ lb	finely ground English breakfast sausage meat	225 g
1	small egg	1
¼ cup	fresh bread crumbs, rubbed to a fine texture	60 mL
2 tsp	dried parsley	10 mL
1 tsp	dried rosemary, crushed with a rolling pin	5 mL
¼ tsp	salt	1 mL
	Generous grind of freshly ground pepper	
12	hard-boiled quail eggs	12
	Oil for deep frying	
	Paprika for garnish	

Thoroughly combine sausage, egg, bread crumbs, parsley, rosemary, salt and pepper. Oil your hands so the mixture won't stick to them and completely encase the quail eggs in the meat mixture. Heat oil to 325°F (160°C) and fry the eggs until they float to the surface and turn a dark mahogany brown, about 5 minutes. Drain on paper towels.

These can be served hot as a breakfast or side dish, or cold as an hors d'oeuvre. Either way, cut them in half lengthwise; with the tip of a knife, place a tiny mound of hot or sweet paprika in the center of each yolk.

Grilled Dublin Bay Prawns

PREPARATION TIME:
30 MINUTES
COOKING TIME:
5 MINUTES
SERVES: 8

Dublin Bay prawns are neither prawns nor shrimp. They are langoustines, close relatives of the spiny lobster, the ones without claws. They are all tail, the tarts—and the sweetest creatures to feed on the ocean's bottom.

They are also small and have sharp undersides, which makes breaking them apart painful on the fingers. For those reasons, they have been neglected for centuries by almost all but the French, the race that has the patience to clean and cook or clean and squish escargot and sweetbreads.

Many great eating experiences are frustrating. In New Orleans they feast on crawfish, sucking the fat from behind the head with a thwap of the lips that rebounds off the walls. It's fussy and messy, and often requires hours of eating to produce a smile that lasts a lifetime in the back of your mind. Eating Dublin Bay prawns is much more civilized. You use a small fork, a lobster pick or a trussing needle, dip the meat in Scotch butter and try not to slurp. Oh, to be in England …

Look for tiny lobster tails marked scampi, langoustines, langoustes, Dublin Bay prawns or Norwegian lobster. The best grow in cold water, where it takes longer, so flavors develop, flesh is firmer and there is more internal fat. Iceland processes good stuff, if small, about three inches in length. If you can find bigger ones from cold waters, so much the better.

This recipe is essentially that of my university roommate, Glenn Hainey, who got it from his father, Alex Hainey, who has great taste.

6	cloves garlic, crushed and finely chopped	6
½ cup	unsalted butter	125 mL
40	Dublin Bay prawns	40
¼ cup	fine dried bread crumbs	60 mL
2 tbsp	finely chopped parsley	30 mL
8	lemon wedges as garnish	8

In a small pot over low heat, combine the garlic and butter; let steep for at least 30 minutes.

Turn each prawn on its back. With a sharp knife or kitchen scissors, cut down the middle of the underbelly. Using either gloved hands or pliers, spread the shell so the tail flesh is well exposed. Brush the flesh with garlic butter and arrange on a cookie sheet. Broil 6 inches under the heat just until the tails begin to curl, about 2 minutes. Sprinkle each tail with bread crumbs, drizzle with more garlic butter and return to the broiler. Cook until the tails curl right up and the bread crumbs brown, 1 to 3 minutes. Divide among 8 heated plates, sprinkle prawns and plates with parsley, place a wedge of lemon on each plate and serve.

CHAPTER NINE

The Home Steakhouse

The Sizzling Cow Steakhouse

Steaks
(of course)

In addition to our New York Strip, Porterhouse,
Rib Eye, Filet and Chateaubriand Bearnaise Steaks, we are
proud to offer the following:

Roasted Garlic Bread 180

Steak au Poivre 181

Chateaubriand Diane 182

Barberian's Shish Kebab 183

Scotch Lobster 184

Elephant-Garlic-Stuffed Baked Potatoes 185

Creamed Spinach 186

Apple Beignets 187

So, how come your steak doesn't taste as good as a steakhouse steak? The answer is that steakhouses start off with the best marbled and aged beef. Then you have to know how to cut the steaks, when to cut them and how many to cut.

Harry Barberian, owner of Barberian's Steak House in Toronto and my friend and coauthor of "The Bottom Line" in *Foodservice & Hospitality* magazine, calculated that if a chef consistently cuts steaks 1 oz (30 g) heavier than the menu offers, the restaurant will lose between $25,000 and $48,000 a year, depending upon volume and beef price. This won't affect you, the home restaurateur, as long as you realize that meat must be cut perfectly straight-sided to cook evenly. That's the butcher's job. (Reject wedge-shaped steaks.) A porterhouse, for example, is a filet (tenderloin), a sirloin and a strip steak all in one. Each of these steaks cooks differently because of its texture; furthermore, the grains do not match up. A great cutter can minimize the grain differences. Don't ask me how. I haven't a clue. It's magic.

The other thing you should know is that a steak is best if it is cut from the carcass just before cooking. (Harry won't sell a steak if it has been cut the day before.) The chef must figure out how many steaks to cut every day, using guesswork and experience.

Once the steaks have been cut, it's time to season them. However good the beef is, human conceit intervenes, and we throw on some secret blend of spices or marinade. A restaurateur cannot resist making a personal statement. (Harry developed a subtle yet distinct sea salt and spice formula more than thirty-five years ago and still sells jars of it. Most good steakhouses do. If your favorite doesn't, ask the owner if you can buy some.) Some other distinctive tastes evolve accidentally and become famous. Although marinating does *not* tenderize meat, people continue to believe it does. Marinades, however, definitely flavor meat. One restaurateur decided not to buy U.S. Prime beef because it was too expensive. He purchased a lesser cut and marinated it in oil to add fat. To disguise the oil taste, he added garlic to the marinade. Lots of it, too. His customers loved it. Another steakhouse slathers butter over the steak just before serving it. It gives the steak added fat, which gives the meat a smooth, rich taste. It is also unnecessary on a good piece of marbled and aged meat.

Another way to flavor the meat is to cook it over an aromatic fire. Barberian's uses Quebec maple charcoal. Others use a more aromatic hardwood such as mesquite, which creates an extremely hot fire and therefore an intense caramelization on the surface of the meat. It also imparts a distinctive taste through the smoke that rises from the drippings and permeates the meat.

The final things that separate you from the steakhouse steak are the surroundings. The steakhouse atmosphere is dark-paneled walls, pewter, white linen tablecloths and special steak knives. (The pickles and black olives, garlic bread, baked potatoes, big wines, cognac and good coffee can be replicated at home.) Harry's steakhouse has seen more than two million guests in its thirty-five-plus years, and the wait staff have been there about as long. Then, of course, there's Harry. You can't have him, but you can give your guests Harry's warm treatment by being gracious when you have to, outrageous when you can and unfailingly focused on your guests' comfort.

Roasted Garlic Bread

PREPARATION TIME:
10 MINUTES
COOKING TIME:
45 MINUTES
SERVES: 8

The secret of steakhouse garlic bread is butter—more butter than you would need to grease a ten-year-old stuck in a milk chute. The better restaurants use finely chopped fresh garlic mixed into the butter with chopped parsley. The lazy ones, who usually cheat in other ways, as well, use garlic powder, or, worse, garlic salt. You'll know them by the gritty texture.

This recipe has several advantages. First, it uses far less butter. Second, when garlic is baked whole, it becomes mellow. You get a satisfying experience without morning-after clear-the-elevator embarrassment. Really. And third, garlic is good for you, and you should probably eat more of it.

This is also the way to bake garlic for a baked potato stuffing that would cost you a lot of money in Nice and Cannes.

2	whole heads garlic	2
12	sprigs parsley	12
1 tbsp	olive oil	15 mL
	Salt	
	Pepper	
1 cup	butter, softened	250 mL
1	loaf French bread	1

Preheat oven to 350°F (175°C). Coat the garlic and 8 of the parsley sprigs with oil. Salt and pepper garlic and parsley and wrap loosely in aluminum foil. Bake for 45 minutes. Let cool. Discard parsley. Cut garlic buds horizontally and squeeze out the cooked cloves into a bowl. Purée the garlic and add it to the butter. Finely chop remaining parsley and whip it in. Adjust salt and pepper. Let stand for at least 2 hours to develop the taste.

Cut the bread partially through in thick slices, but retain them in a loaf. Butter slices with the garlic spread and bake at 350°F (175°C). A crisp loaf will take about 10 minutes. To get a softer steamed loaf, wrap it in aluminum foil and warm it at 250°F (120°C) for 10 minutes. Or grill individual buttered slices over coals.

Steak au Poivre

Most restaurants make pepper steak by rubbing a New York strip steak with crushed black peppercorns and cooking it over charcoal. But the only charring associated with a true pepper steak is done to the ceiling when you light the brandy. A true pepper steak must be pan-fried, its sauce made of brandy and cream. It's very simple but utterly luscious.

Use fresh whole black peppercorns. Put them on a baking sheet and roast them at 350°F (175°C) for 15 minutes beforehand, and they'll be even better. To crush them, put them between two layers of tea towel or heavy-duty plastic film and pound with a mallet or the bottom of a pot until they are smashed into a grainy mass. Never, ever simply grind pepper in a pepper mill for this dish. I have a heavy metal mallet with tenderizing peaks on one side, which I refuse to use, and a flat surface on the other, which is perfect for pounding schnitzel or peppercorns. (The device is also an amusing answer to my children whining, "We're bored. What are we going to do now?")

PREPARATION TIME:
10 MINUTES
COOKING TIME:
15 MINUTES
SERVES: 2

1 ½ lb	New York strip, Delmonico or	680 g
	sirloin steak, 1 ½ inches (4 cm) thick	
¼ cup	freshly crushed black peppercorns	60 mL
2 tbsp	oil	30 mL
¼ cup	brandy	60 mL
¾ cup	whipping cream	180 mL
	Salt to taste	
2 tbsp	chopped parsley	30 mL

Preheat oven to 200°F (95°C).

Score the edges of the steak fat so the steak does not curl in the pan. Rub cracked pepper into both sides of the steak, then cover both sides with cracked peppercorns. In a large, heavy fry pan over high heat, heat oil. Slap in the steak and fry until the underside is well browned, about 4 minutes. Flip and fry until the first sign of blood seeps through the cooked crust. Take steak out, place on a platter and keep warm in the oven.

Pour brandy into fry pan and light with a match. Swirl the pan around to keep the flames lit as long as possible, usually about 30 seconds. With a wooden spoon, scrape up all the brown bits on the bottom of the pan. Add cream and reduce until it thickens to a sauce, stirring with the wooden spoon occasionally. Salt to taste. Place steaks on 2 plates, pour sauce over the top and garnish with parsley.

Chateaubriand Diane

This is a particularly show-off version of Steak au Poivre, especially if you have a chafing dish. If not, make it romantic—in the kitchen in a cast-iron pan.

PREPARATION TIME:
15 MINUTES
COOKING TIME:
15 MINUTES
SERVES: 2

½ cup	unsalted butter	125 mL
	Chateaubriand or filet mignon, cut into 2 steaks, each 2 inches (5 cm) thick	
½ cup	chopped green onions	125 mL
2 tbsp	Worcestershire sauce	30 mL
1 tbsp	dry mustard	15 mL
	Salt and pepper to taste	
¼ cup	brandy	60 mL
2 tbsp	chopped parsley	30 mL

Preheat oven to 200°F (95°C).

In a chafing dish over the flame, or in a cast-iron fry pan over medium-high, heat butter until it foams. Add steaks and brown on all sides, about 7 minutes total. Remove steaks and keep warm on a platter in the oven. Lower heat to medium. Add onions, Worcestershire sauce and mustard and simmer for 3 minutes. Taste and adjust seasoning with salt and pepper. Return steaks to sauce and cook 2 minutes on 1 side. Turn steaks and cook another 2 minutes, or until meat is as well done as you want it. (After the first turn, when the blood starts to seep out the top, it's medium rare.)

Meanwhile, heat brandy over low heat. When the steaks are done, pour on heated brandy and light it. Whoosh! Transfer steaks to individual heated plates, nap with sauce and garnish with parsley. Serve remaining sauce in a boat on the side.

Barberian's Shish Kebab

¼ cup	red wine	60 mL	
	(Barberian's uses Ontario Pinot Noir)		
¼ cup	tomato juice	60 mL	
¼ cup	olive oil	60 mL	
¼ cup + 2 tbsp	chopped parsley	60 mL + 30 mL	
4	cloves garlic, crushed	4	
1 tsp	dried oregano	5 mL	
¼ tsp	ground black pepper	1 mL	
3	medium yellow onions, quartered	3	
2 lb	lamb, cut into ¼ to ½ inch	900 g	
	(5 mm to 1 cm) cubes		
2	green bell peppers, quartered	2	
2	red bell peppers, quartered	2	
2	firm tomatoes, quartered and seeded	2	
2	large Vidalia (sweet) onions, thinly sliced	2	
	Salt and pepper to taste		
2 tsp	sumac* (or lemon juice to taste)	10 mL	
	Lemon slices for garnish		

PREPARATION TIME:
15 MINUTES
MARINATING TIME:
4 TO 12 HOURS
COOKING TIME:
15 MINUTES
SERVES: 4

In a glass, porcelain or enamel bowl or container, combine wine, tomato juice and olive oil. Stir in ¼ cup (60 mL) parsley, garlic, oregano and pepper. Add onions and lamb, then cover and refrigerate for at least 4 hours, overnight if possible. Remove from refrigerator, add green and red peppers and bring to room temperature, about 2 hours. Ten minutes before assembly, add tomatoes.

In a separate bowl, mix Vidalia onions, remaining parsley, salt, pepper and sumac. Divide among 4 plates.

On 4 large skewers, alternate lamb, yellow onions and red and green peppers. (Keep the tomatoes near the handle end, for slowest cooking.) Grill over charcoal 10 to 15 minutes, turning frequently, until lamb is firm, browned but still slightly pink inside, and the vegetables are roasted.

Serve kebabs on the bed of Vidalia onions with a sprinkling of parsley around the plate rim and lemon slices as garnish.

* Sumac is a Middle Eastern lemon-flavored, red-pepper-looking spice sold in most Middle Eastern groceries.

Scotch Lobster

One day, the culinary devil popped up for a visit and said, "If you open that steak-house, Earl, you must serve lobster." And so it was, although I don't know why. Lobster by itself is a wonder. And I certainly would not object to a feast of steak and lobster if they are separate courses. But together on the same plate?

Boiling lobster is a no-brainer. Bring a large covered pot of water to the boil, thrust in the lobster head first, slap on the lid and time it. Most people boil the hell out of it, as if trying to purify the kill. But the more you cook lobster, the tougher it gets.

- A lobster less than 1 lb (450 g) is called a "canner" and is available only from the Canadian Maritimes. If you get these, boil them for 7 minutes.
- A 1 lb (450 g) lobster is called a "chicken lobster" in Maine, a "chick" in the Maritimes. Boil it for 10 minutes tops.
- A 1 ¼ lb (560 g) lobster is called a "quarter," and you boil it for 10 to 12 minutes.
- A 1 ½ lb (680 g) lobster is called a "half." Boil it for 13 minutes.
- A 2 lb (900 g) lobster should boil for 17 minutes but resist buying one because they usually cost way too much.
- Don't bother buying anything bigger.

Serve one lobster per person, with lobster crackers or nutcrackers, small forks, many serviettes or bibs and individual pots of hot butter. And put a large bowl in the center of the table for the detritus. All this you already know. The butter, however, can make all the difference.

Don't bother with drawn butter, which is clarified butter. Restaurants proudly advertise it on the menu but, in fact, they're making a virtue of necessity. The butter sits on the stovetop keeping warm and clarifies itself. The butter taste is in the butter fat, which is removed during clarification. All you get in drawn butter is the oil. You want taste, not oil.

For each person, you'll need 2 tbsp (30 mL) melted butter, 2 tsp (10 mL) Scotch whisky, and a small bowl. *Stir the whisky into the butter.* That's it—the simple secret to great lobster butter. If, however, you do not partake of alcohol in any form, substitute a goodly squeeze of lemon. Just don't serve the butter by itself.

Elephant-Garlic-Stuffed Potatoes

A good steakhouse knows, roughly, how many baked potatoes it will need at any given hour on any given night. As a result, the sous chef is always putting russet potatoes in the oven so they will be perfectly cooked when needed. That's the secret. Knowing your customers and timing it right.

A poor steakhouse, whose owner doesn't know who is going to show up when, bakes potatoes in an aluminum-foil jacket. This is as stupid as wrapping fish in aluminum foil, putting it over coals and claiming you are barbecuing. What an aluminum-foil wrapping actually does, of course, is steam the tuber. It can sit in the oven, overcooked in its little aluminum steam oven, for a time without going wrinkly or dry, but it is not a baked potato. So, if you don't know when dinner is going to be served, by all means wrap a potato in foil and put it in the oven. But don't buy it wrapped; it will cost you roughly five times the cost of the potato plus the aluminum foil. And half the time, the packager hasn't washed the spud before wrapping it.

By the way, elephant garlic looks just like garlic, except huge. It isn't a member of the garlic family at all, which is why it has the taste but no lingering effects. Ain't nature grand?

PREPARATION TIME:
15 MINUTES
COOKING TIME:
1 HOUR
SERVES: 2

2	russet potatoes	2
1	clove elephant garlic	1
1 tbsp	olive oil	15 mL
1 tbsp	chopped parsley or fresh thyme	15 mL
½ cup	butter	125 mL
1 tsp	salt	5 mL

In a 400°F (200°C) oven, roast potatoes for 1 hour.

Coat elephant garlic with oil and parsley and microwave on half power (5) for 2 minutes. Or coat garlic with oil and parsley, wrap loosely in tin foil and bake with the potatoes for 30 to 40 minutes. Either way, the garlic is cooked when it has turned to mush and can be squeezed out of the skin like toothpaste from a tube. You will still have to chop it up to distribute it evenly in the butter. Let it cool a bit so you don't burn your fingers, squeeze it, chop it up and mix with butter.

Slice the top off the potatoes and scoop out the insides. (Think of a canoe and you'll get the idea.) Whip the insides with the garlic butter and salt, and stuff the lot back into the potato jackets.

Creamed Spinach

PREPARATION TIME:
15 MINUTES
COOKING TIME:
15 MINUTES
SERVES: 4

A staple at the finest steakhouses, this follows the Great Garlic Bread Principle. In other words (to paraphrase A.J. Liebling), it has enough butter to thrombose the Marine Corps.

The trick with spinach is to remove not only the stem but the center vein. Fold the leaf in half lengthwise. Peel the vein running down the middle down and out of the leaf. Say goodbye to bitterness. One big bunch of spinach serves two people.

2	bunches fresh spinach	2
⅓ cup	butter	80 mL
2 tbsp	olive oil	30 mL
¼ cup	finely chopped shallots	60 mL
2	large garlic cloves, finely chopped	2
	Salt and pepper to taste	
¼ cup	whipping cream	60 mL
¼ cup	fresh bread crumbs	60 mL
2 tsp	thyme	10 mL
2 tsp	parsley	10 mL
1 tsp	oregano	5 mL

Stem and vein spinach and wash thoroughly in running water at least twice to remove all sand and grit. (Lord, I hate it when a restaurant doesn't clean spinach and I get that sickening crunch. Hell hath no fury like a restaurant critic with no dental plan.) In a large pot of lightly salted boiling water, cook the spinach 3 minutes, stirring occasionally, until the leaves are wilted and thoroughly reduced in volume. Drain in a sieve, squishing down with the back of a spoon to remove as much water as possible. Set aside to cool.

In a small saucepan over medium heat, put butter and oil. Sauté shallots and garlic until they are soft, about 4 minutes. Do not brown.

Transfer cooled spinach to a cutting board. Chop it lengthwise at ½-inch (1 cm) intervals, then crosswise at ½-inch (1 cm) intervals. Add spinach to saucepan with shallots and garlic; add salt and pepper to taste, mix well, and sauté for another 2 minutes. Add cream and cook for 3 or 4 minutes. Meanwhile, combine the bread crumbs, thyme, parsley and oregano. Mix thoroughly into spinach mixture and cook another minute. Turn heat down to low, cover and keep warm.

Apple Beignets

They sell a ton of these at Barberian's Steak House in Toronto.

PREPARATION TIME:
10 MINUTES
COOKING TIME:
5 MINUTES
SERVES: 8

2 cups	flour	500 mL
1 tsp	sugar	5 mL
	Pinch salt	
2 cups	milk	500 mL
2	eggs	2
1 tsp	vanilla	5 mL
2	large apples	2
	Oil for deep frying	
½ cup	sugar	125 mL
1 tsp	ground cinnamon	5 mL

In a bowl, mix flour, 1 tsp (5 mL) sugar and salt. Whisk in milk, eggs and vanilla. No lumps allowed. Peel and core apples and cut into ¾-inch (2 cm) crescents. Heat oil to 360°F (180°C). Dip apple slices in batter and fry to a golden brown. Combine sugar and ground cinnamon. Serve 2 or 3 apple slices per person, lightly dusted with cinnamon sugar. (You might not need all the cinnamon sugar.)

CHAPTER TEN

The Crabshack

The Old Chesapeake Bay Crabshack

THE OYSTERS

Oysters Rockefeller 192
New Orleans baked oysters covered
with Pernod-flavored spinach

Oysters Windsor 193
Oysters with bacon and eggs,
because the combination is a natural

*Fried Oysters with Black
Lemon Butter 194*
Rolled in cayenne-spiced
cornmeal, fried and served
with the butter sauce

Oyster Stew 194
The traditional stew in sherry and
ginger cream broth

Scalloped Oysters 195
A casserole of bacon and oysters

Panned and Roasted Oysters 196
Shiitake mushrooms and oysters on
toast with Hollandaise sauce

THE CRABS

Buttermilk Soft-Shell Crabs 196
Buttermilk seasoned, fried
and served with onion *confit*
and sautéed pecans

Crab Sandwiches 198
Crab with shrimp, onions,
celery, capers, kalamata olives
and red peppers

Crab Cakes 199
Two versions: Classic with a
dash of curry, and mint and oyster
sauce scented

Crab Royal 200
A casserole of wild mushrooms
and crab flavored with brandy,
wine and mustard

Red Deviled Crab 201
Casserole of crab with a
spicy red sauce

Years ago I went out with a woman who told me straight-faced that both she and her mother went completely off their heads if they mixed gin and seafood, especially oysters. Right. Then one night we had martinis before going to visit friends. They served seafood. Sure enough, Cass blew a gasket and berated my very existence over dinner. Yes, some of her comments were valid, but that's beside the point. She had become Mrs. Hyde. It was frightening.

Years later, after she had introduced me to my wife, thus getting rid of me in a mutually acceptable manner, Bones and I were visiting friends in Florida. I had a martini and oysters Rockefeller. Twenty minutes later, I had a major public breakdown because the restaurant served whipped butter. Now, this is not proof positive that a restaurateur who serves whipped butter is in the same league as, say, Charles Manson, although that night I was sure of it. But take this as a warning: avoid gin with seafood. If you can't, avoid firearms.

Almost every cookbook author and food writer will tell you there is considerable debate on whether the oyster should be cooked in some fashion or eaten fresh and raw with, perhaps, a hit of lemon juice. What a colossal waste of time. Granted the late M.F.K. Fisher and the equally late James Beard waxed eloquent on the merits of both positions; indeed, perhaps they invented the putative disputation. If such an unlikely debate took place, however, the participants should be ashamed of themselves. They would have been better off debating the merits of whipped butter.

Truth is, you eat raw oysters to show off. You eat cooked oysters because they taste good.

Oysters Rockefeller

PREPARATION TIME:
20 MINUTES
COOKING TIME:
5 MINUTES
SERVES: 4

3 tbsp	butter	45 mL
2 tbsp	chopped shallots	30 mL
2 tbsp	chopped celery	30 mL
1 tbsp	finely chopped fresh thyme	15 mL
3 tbsp	dried bread crumbs	45 mL
3 tbsp	Pernod or ouzo	45 mL
½ cup	butter	125 mL
2 tbsp	Worcestershire sauce	30 mL
8 oz	spinach, cleaned, stemmed and chopped finely	225 g
	Rock salt or pickling salt	
12	oysters	12

In a small pot over medium heat, melt the 3 tbsp (45 mL) butter; sauté shallots and celery until translucent and soft. Add thyme and cook 1 minute. Add bread crumbs, Pernod, the ½ cup (125 mL) butter and Worcestershire sauce; remove from heat. Cool. Finely chop spinach by hand, or chop in a food processor for a few seconds. Add to sauce. Set aside.

Heat oven to 400°F (200°C).

Fill as many aluminum pie pans or roasting pans as needed to hold the oysters with ¼ inch (5 mm) of salt, to stabilize oyster shells. Place in oven for 15 minutes to heat salt.

Clean and shuck oysters, strain liquor and add to spinach sauce mixture. Wash out the bottom shells and place an oyster in each. Place shells on hot salt in pans and spoon 1 tbsp (15 mL) of the spinach mixture over each. Bake for 5 minutes, or until the mixture is bubbling and the oysters are heated through. Serve 3 oysters per person on plates covered with rock salt to stabilize shells.

Oysters Windsor

I named this dish after the first city in Ontario to open a legal casino. Well, it's sort of a casino. You can't smoke at the tables, and for a time it seemed you wouldn't be able to drink there, either. And dice games are forbidden. So, it's a sort-of casino where you can lose your shirt, but not decadently. James Bond would have died laughing.

This recipe is a sort-of Oysters Casino, hence the name. Mine has a touch of egg in it—seems to me bacon and eggs are a natural. You might even consider this for a first-class bed and breakfast operation.

PREPARATION TIME: 20 MINUTES
COOKING TIME: 10 MINUTES
SERVES: 4

12	oysters	12
	Rock salt	
3	strips bacon	3
¼ cup	finely chopped red pepper	60 mL
¼ cup	finely chopped English parsley	60 mL
¼ cup	finely chopped onion	60 mL
¼ cup	butter	60 mL
2 tbsp	lemon juice	30 mL
2 tbsp	dried bread crumbs	30 mL
1	egg	1
	Salt to taste	

Shuck oysters, clean bottom shells and set up pans with rock salt, as in Oysters Rockefeller, above.

Fry bacon until it's limp and fat is translucent. Cut each strip into quarters. Set aside.

Preheat oven to 400°F (200°C).

Combine remaining ingredients in a bowl. Place an oyster in each shell, cover with 1 tbsp (15 mL) of the sauce mixture and place a piece of bacon on top. Bake for 10 minutes, or until the bacon has crisped up.

Fried Oysters
with Black Lemon Butter

PREPARATION TIME:	40	oysters	40
20 MINUTES	1 cup	butter	250 mL
COOKING TIME:		Juice of 1 lemon	
10 MINUTES	1 cup	cornmeal	250 mL
SERVES: 8	4 ½ tsp	cayenne	22 mL
	1 tsp	salt	5 mL
		Oil for deep frying	

Shuck oysters. Put butter in a small pot over low heat and cook very slowly until the butter turns amber or caramel brown and exudes a nutty aroma, about 30 to 45 minutes. Stir in lemon juice.

Combine cornmeal, pepper and salt. Coat each oyster thoroughly with seasoned cornmeal and deep fry at 375°F (190°C) until golden brown, about 3 minutes total. Divide oysters among 8 plates, sprinkle with black lemon butter and serve.

Oyster Stew

PREPARATION TIME: 15 MINUTES

COOKING TIME: 2 MINUTES

SERVES: 2

To be honest, this is being a bit stingy with the oysters per person, but in reality it is the oyster liquor you need for the stew's flavor. By all means, if you have the means, double the number of oysters. To make sure the liquor doesn't have grit in it, use a paper coffee filter. Soak it in water first, then drain the liquor through it; you may need as many as four filters to do the job on two dozen oysters. You must soak the filters in water first or they will simply soak up the precious flavor before allowing the liquid through.

12	oysters	12
3 tbsp	butter	45 mL
3 tbsp	finely minced onion	45 mL
1 tsp	grated fresh ginger	5 mL
1 tsp	celery salt	5 mL
	Dash each of Worcestershire and Tabasco sauces	
¼ cup	milk	60 mL
¾ cup	whipping cream	180 mL
2 tsp	sherry	10 mL
2 tsp	minced parsley, for garnish	10 mL

Shuck the oysters and reserve the liquor. If there is less than 125 mL (½ cup), top up with clam juice, available at fish stores either canned or frozen. If you don't have clam juice, forget it. It's not a big deal. Sorry, that's how chefs think, too. In a heavy saucepan over medium-low heat, melt butter and sauté onion and ginger until the onion is soft and slightly golden. Add oysters, oyster liquor, celery salt, Worcestershire and Tabasco; poach oysters until their edges curl, 1 to 2 minutes. Remove oysters with a slotted spoon and divide between 2 heated soup bowls. To the saucepan add milk and cream and heat just until the edges bubble—don't let it boil. Pour cream mixture over the oysters. Add sherry to each bowl, top with chopped parsley and serve with crackers.

Scalloped Oysters

12	oysters	12	**PREPARATION TIME:**
2	strips bacon	2	30 MINUTES
3 tbsp	butter	45 mL	**COOKING TIME:**
3 tbsp	finely chopped onion, about half a small onion	45 mL	15 MINUTES
1 cup	fresh bread cubes, cut into ½-inch (1 cm) cubes	250 mL	**SERVES: 2**
2 tbsp	finely chopped parsley	30 mL	
1 tbsp	finely minced fresh thyme	15 mL	
1 tsp	dried tarragon	5 mL	
¼ tsp	ground nutmeg	1 mL	
1 tsp	celery salt	5 mL	
½ tsp	cayenne pepper, or 1 tsp (5 mL) hot Hungarian paprika (optional)*	2 mL	
2 tsp	lemon juice	10 mL	
2 tbsp	whipping cream	30 mL	

Shuck the oysters and set aside. Preheat oven to 375°F (190°C).

Dice bacon. In a heavy pan over medium-low heat, melt 1 tbsp (15 mL) of the butter and sauté bacon, onion and fresh bread cubes until the bacon is almost crisp and the bread is fried.

Add parsley, thyme, tarragon, nutmeg, celery salt, cayenne, lemon juice and cream, and mix well. Remove from heat.

Grease two ovenproof bowls. Layer half the bread mixture on the bottom, add 6 oysters and top with the remaining bread mixture. Dot tops with remaining butter. Bake for 15 minutes. Serve immediately.

*If your cayenne or paprika is fresh, this is a real whack of heat. Adjust according to your taste.

Panned and Roasted Oysters

PREPARATION TIME:	24	oysters	24
20 MINUTES	4	slices French bread, each 1 inch (2.5 cm)	4
COOKING TIME:		thick, buttered on both sides	
10 MINUTES	1 tbsp	butter	15 mL
SERVES: 4 AS A	½ cup	roughly chopped shiitake mushrooms	125 mL
STARTER COURSE,		Cayenne pepper to taste (optional)	
8 AS A COCKTAIL		Hollandaise Sauce (p. 67)	
APPETIZER		Parsley, minced, as a garnish	

Shuck oysters. Preheat oven to 375°F (190°C).

Fry buttered bread rounds over medium-low heat until both sides are golden and crisp. Remove to a cookie sheet. In the same pan, melt butter and sauté mushrooms for 2 minutes. Divide among the bread rounds. Place 6 oysters on each round. Sprinkle with cayenne pepper. Bake in the middle of the oven for 10 minutes.

As a starter course, place a bread round on a small heated butter plate; as a cocktail appetizer, cut rounds in half and arrange on a heated platter. Spoon Hollandaise over oysters and sprinkle with parsley.

Buttermilk Soft-Shell Crabs

PREPARATION TIME:
1 HOUR
COOKING TIME:
5 MINUTES
SERVES: 6 AS AN
APPETIZER,
2 AS A MAIN COURSE

Female crabs have frustrating lives: they can't get it on unless they get their hard shells off. So they do. And then fishermen catch them while they are one-hundred-percent edible, soft shell and all. The softest and the most sought-after are called Velvets.

The restaurant Valentino in Santa Monica places soft-shell crabs on onion *confit*. Gerry Klaskala at the Buckhead Diner in Atlanta makes a soft-shell crab salad by dipping the tasty devils in buttermilk and seasoned flour and frying them. He serves them with greens in a vinaigrette with a dill-shallot mayonnaise on the side. Cooking teacher Nathalie Dupree suggests preparing them with pecans. I couldn't decide whose version was better so I combined all three on the principle that you can't get too much of a good thing.

1 cup	goose or duck fat (lard works, but the taste isn't as good)	250 mL
2	medium onions, sliced in ¼-inch (5 mm) thick rings	2
6	cloves garlic, peeled	6
3 tbsp	butter	45 mL
¼ cup	pecans	60 mL
6	soft-shell crabs, cleaned	6
1 cup	buttermilk	250 mL
1 cup	flour	250 mL
2 tsp	salt	10 mL
2 tsp	ground black pepper	10 mL
¼ cup	skinned and blanched almonds	60 mL

First, make the onion and garlic *confit*. In a small pot over low heat, heat fat to no more than 175°F (80°C). Add onions and garlic and poach for 1 hour. Drain onions and garlic thoroughly, getting as much fat off the surface as possible. Set them aside.

In a small pan, melt 1 tbsp (15 mL) of the butter and sauté pecans slowly for 10 minutes, or until they are toasted. Remove, drain well and reserve.

Put soft-shell crabs in buttermilk for 10 minutes. Combine flour, salt and pepper. Remove crabs from buttermilk, thoroughly coat them with seasoned flour, dip them back into buttermilk, then back into the flour. Heat remaining 2 tbsp (30 mL) butter in a large fry pan over medium-high heat. Sauté 2 or 3 crabs in butter until crisp on each side. Drain cooked crabs on paper towels, then remove to a heated plate. Repeat with remaining crabs.

In the center of each plate, mound some *confit*. Make sure each plate gets a garlic clove. Place a single fried crab on the *confit* for an appetizer, and top with pecans and almonds. (For a main course, top the *confit* with 3 crabs, then top with pecans and almonds.)

Crab Sandwiches

Some kinds of seafood are fine when purchased in cans. Crab is one of them.

¼ lb	canned crab meat, picked over to remove cartilage	110 g
¼ cup	cooked salad shrimp	60 mL
3 tbsp	finely chopped onion	45 mL
3 tbsp	finely chopped celery	45 mL
1 tbsp	finely chopped hot red pepper, or sweet red pepper with 2 dashes of Tabasco	15 mL
4	kalamata olives, pitted and chopped fine	4
1 tsp	finely chopped capers	5 mL
	Dash Worcestershire sauce	
	Squeeze of lemon	
	Mayonnaise to bind	
	Salt to taste	
	Bread, hot-dog rolls or soft buns	
	Leaf lettuce	

Combine crab, shrimp, onion, celery, red pepper, olives, capers, Worcestershire sauce and lemon. Add just enough mayonnaise to bind the mixture, salt it to taste, place on buttered bread or toast, top with lettuce and eat.

Crab Cakes I

½ lb	crab meat, flaked and cartilage removed	225 g
3 tbsp	finely chopped scallions	45 mL
2 tbsp	finely chopped hot red pepper,	30 mL
	or sweet pepper with several dashes of Tabasco	
2 tbsp	finely chopped parsley	30 mL
½ tsp	celery salt	2 mL
	Freshly ground pepper	
½ tsp	Worcestershire sauce	2 mL
1	small egg, beaten	1
1 tbsp	curry powder	15 mL
	Dry bread crumbs to coat	
¼ cup	butter	60 mL

PREPARATION TIME: 10 MINUTES
COOKING TIME: 8 MINUTES
SERVES: 2

Combine all ingredients except bread crumbs and butter. Gently form into patties the size of hockey pucks; coat in bread crumbs. In a large fry pan over medium heat, melt butter and gently place cakes in pan. Fry until golden on both sides.

Crab Cakes II

1 cup	crab meat, flaked and cartilage removed	250 mL
2 tsp	oyster sauce or soy sauce	10 mL
2 tbsp	cornstarch	30 mL
1 tbsp	finely minced fresh mint leaves or chives	15 mL
1	egg	1
	Bread crumbs	
¼ cup	butter	60 mL

PREPARATION TIME: 5 MINUTES
COOKING TIME: 8 MINUTES
SERVES: 4

Combine the first 5 ingredients, form into hockey-puck-size patties, dredge in bread crumbs and fry in butter over medium heat in a large fry pan until golden on both sides.

Crab Royal

PREPARATION TIME:
20 MINUTES
COOKING TIME:
20 MINUTES
SERVES: 4 AS AN
APPETIZER,
2 AS A MAIN COURSE

Both this dish and deviled crab can be made ahead of time, refrigerated, then slipped into the oven for five to ten minutes to heat through.

This variation on Crab Imperial is more rich than most.

3 tbsp	butter	45 mL
2	slices white bread, cut into small cubes	2
¼ cup	chopped shiitake or other wild mushrooms	60 mL
¼ cup	finely chopped onions	60 mL
¼ cup	finely chopped green bell pepper	60 mL
1 tbsp	flour	15 mL
1	egg yolk	1
½ cup	whipping cream	125 mL
¼ cup	white wine	60 mL
1 tbsp	brandy	15 mL
2 tsp	prepared Dijon mustard	10 mL
1 tsp	Worcestershire sauce	5 mL
1 tsp	curry powder	5 mL
	Drop vanilla	
½ lb	crab meat, flaked and cartilage removed	225 g

In a fry pan over low heat, melt 1 tbsp (15 mL) of the butter. Toast bread cubes in the butter until slightly golden.

In a medium-size pot over medium heat, melt remaining butter and sauté mushrooms, onions and pepper until soft. Stir in flour and cook for 3 minutes.

Whip egg yolk into the cream, then add the wine, brandy, mustard, Worcestershire sauce, curry powder and vanilla. Add to vegetables in pot and stir until sauce thickens. If it becomes too thick, add milk to thin it. Remove from heat, mix in crab meat.

Preheat oven to 400°F (200°C).

Pour mixture into 4 small ramekins if an appetizer, or 2 large ovenproof bowls if a main course, top with bread cubes, and bake for 20 minutes. Serve immediately.

Red Deviled Crab

The devil wears red and comes from a hot climate, right? So why isn't anything deviled, from crab to eggs, red and hot? I have remedied this culinary faux pas.

PREPARATION TIME:
20 MINUTES
COOKING TIME:
20 MINUTES
SERVES: 8 AS AN
APPETIZER,
4 AS A MAIN COURSE

2 tbsp	butter	30 mL
¼ cup	finely chopped onions	60 mL
¼ cup	finely chopped celery	60 mL
2 tbsp	flour	30 mL
1 cup	milk	250 mL
⅓ cup	whipping cream	75 mL
2 tbsp	tomato paste	30 mL
2 tbsp	sherry	30 mL
1 tsp	cayenne pepper or	5 mL
	hot Hungarian paprika	
½ tsp	lemon juice	2 mL
3	dashes Worcestershire sauce	3
	Pinch nutmeg	
1 lb	crab meat, flaked and picked over	450 g
¼ cup	bread crumbs	60 mL

Preheat oven to 400°F (200°C).

In a pot over medium heat, melt butter. Sauté onions and celery in the butter until the vegetables are limp but not browned. Stir in flour and cook for 3 minutes. Add milk slowly, then add cream and whisk until the sauce thickens and bubbles. Add tomato paste, sherry, cayenne, lemon juice, Worcestershire sauce, nutmeg and crab. Pour into ovenproof bowls or ramekins, top with bread crumbs and bake for 15 to 20 minutes, or until the bread crumbs are brown and the mixture bubbles. Serve with chilled Russian vodka straight up.

CHAPTER ELEVEN

The Backroad Barbecue Shack and Adobe

The GYCAT
(GET YOUR CHOPS AROUND THIS)
Backroad BBQ

Dinner #1 206
Fall-off-the-bone tender juicy pork ribs rubbed and smoked
in the backyard at least 3 hours.

Dinner #2 208
Melt-in-the-mouth beef brisket rubbed hard and cooked
softly for at least 8 hours.

We serve 'em with…
Hush puppies 211
Pork stuffed onions 212
Grilled oyster mushrooms 213
Mopping up sauces

Also

Larry Morse's Quesadillas 214
served with:
Monterey Jack and jalapeños
Monterey Jack and *salsa cruda*
Seared beef and BBQ sauce
Grilled pineapple, cheddar and black beans
Lobster in garlic butter
Crab, cheese, tomatoes, onions, jalapeños

Corn Tortillas 216

Flour Tortillas 217

Chili, Texas Style 218
No beans in this here cumin-spiked chili

Pozole 220
The famous Mexican pork stew

Caesar Salad 222
Yup, the original is from Tijuana

Some of the great restaurant names in the United States are on barbecue joints: Maurice's Piggy Park in Columbia, South Carolina, and Stick To Your Ribs in Long Island City, New York, not to mention Jake and Earl's Dixie Barbecue in Cambridge, Massachusetts, Henry's Hi Life Bar-BQ in San Jose, and Curtis' All American Ninth Wonder of the World Bar-BQ in Vermont. The names may lack a certain élan, but don't think the restaurants are not serious about barbecue. If you do, you're courtin' trouble.

When it comes down to it, barbecue is a matter of equipment, hardwood and personal taste. Cooking time is measured in hours—eight or more—and the result is always smoky, tender and juicy.

Barbecue really is smoking over low heat. We are talking brisket, shoulder pork roasts, small spare ribs and large beef ribs—cuts that are tough. But the best barbecue joints use the best meat. So should you.

One big decision is whether you want to season the meat before smoking it on the backyard barbecue. (If you had a real barbecue, probably made from a fifty-five-gallon drum, you wouldn't need me.) You can rub spices on it (dry rub) or soak it and baste it while cooking (marinate), or do nothing (heaven forbid).

The other decision is what to serve with it. Here I part company with most barbecue fiends. The last thing I want is a plate of heavy beans, which is what many shacks serve. A little slaw is good; with ribs, I like buns and hush puppies. Barbecue is no place for *frites*. If you want fried potatoes, go for English chips.

Barbecue can and should be personalized. If you have juniper berries growing in your backyard, crush them and add them to the dry rub of your choice. If you happen to have beehives, add honey to a basting sauce, and it will be yours forever.

Barbecued Pork Ribs

PREPARATION TIME:

20 MINUTES

COOKING TIME:

3 HOURS

SERVES: 4 MODERATELY

HUNGRY FOLKS OR 2

SERIOUS RIB EATERS

People keep telling me that the secret of tender pork back or spare ribs is to par-boil them. Even a few restaurateurs. Even an executive of a popular chicken and ribs chain. Yet these are the same people who are grateful that humans have evolved to the point they no longer boil the nutrition, color and flavor out of peas. Go figure.

I asked Denise Meehan, owner of the Lick's chain and Moon River Chicken and Ribs, how long she cooked her fall-off-the-bone sweet ribs.

"Long," she said.

"How long?"

"Really long," she said.

In Carolina, Georgia and Texas, the cooking temperature rarely gets above 200°F (95°C). That's the secret: just enough heat to cook the meat and turn the tough connective tissues to gelatin, but not hot enough to make the muscle contract and get tough.

For healthy appetites, count on a pound of ribs per person.

2 lb	pork spare ribs	900 g
	Dry rub (recipe below)	
½ cup	Barbecue sauce (recipe below)	125 mL

You can grill the ribs on the backyard barbecue if it has a lid. When you lift the lid to baste, a lot of heat escapes. To solve this problem, keep a spray bottle full of water handy. After you've basted, give the coals a quick spray and lower the lid. The steam blasts the meat at about 400°F (200°C) and brings the temperature up quickly again.

Or cook your ribs in the oven. Heat oven to 450°F (230°C). Rub both sides of the ribs with a generous amount of the dry rub. Put ribs on a rack on a roasting pan in the oven for 10 minutes. Lower the heat to 175°F (80°C) for 2 hours and 20 minutes. Baste ribs with sauce while cooking for another 30 minutes; serve with leftover sauce on the side.

Barbecue Sauce

The idea of adding bourbon to a rib sauce comes from John Barrett, chef at Café Nola in Philadelphia.

MAKES: 1 CUP
(250 ML)

¼ cup	ketchup	60 mL
¼ cup	orange juice	60 mL
¼ cup	bourbon (optional)	60 mL
3 tbsp	butter	45 mL
2 tbsp	cider vinegar	30 mL
2 tbsp	Worcestershire sauce	30 mL
3	cloves garlic, finely minced	3
4 tsp	finely minced onion	20 mL
¾ tsp	liquid smoke*	3 mL
½ tsp	hot pepper sauce	2 mL
¼ tsp	salt	1 mL

Mix all the ingredients in a small pot, bring to a boil, lower heat and simmer for 30 minutes. Use to baste ribs.

Dry Rub for Ribs

	Zest of 1 lemon	
2 tbsp	Hungarian paprika	30 mL
1 tbsp	sugar	15 mL
1 tbsp	garlic salt	15 mL
1 tbsp	black pepper	15 mL
1 tsp	ground coriander	5 mL

Combine the ingredients. Store in an old spice jar.

*Liquid smoke is distilled smoke essence you can buy in a bottle at specialty food stores.

Finishing Sauce for Ribs

A finishing sauce is something you put on the meat during the last stages of cooking to give it that gooey, caramelized "finish," or coat. A table sauce is a sauce meant for dipping as you eat, as in the table sauce served with a chopped beef brisket sandwich.

2 tbsp	ketchup	30 mL
2 tbsp	orange juice	30 mL
2 tbsp	Worcestershire sauce	30 mL
2 tbsp	cider vinegar	30 mL
1 tbsp	liquid smoke	15 mL

Combine all ingredients. Cook over low heat for 5 minutes. Paste on ribs during the last 30 minutes of cooking.

Barbecued Brisket

PREPARATION TIME:
5 MINUTES
COOKING TIME:
8 HOURS
SERVES: 10

1	brisket, 6 to 8 lb (2.75 to 3.6 kg)	1
	Dry rub for beef (recipe, p. 210)	
	Buns	
	Finishing sauce for brisket (recipe, p. 211)	

You can barbecue a rib roast, a tenderloin or a sirloin roast (although you really shouldn't) for an hour under intense smoke (which doesn't really make it barbecue) but, really, the brisket is king. Brisket, the wedge-shaped cut that gives us corned beef, has all the credentials for great barbecue. It is from the chest area of the steer, which gets a lot of use, which means it gets a lot of blood flow, which gives it flavor. It is also fatty and has lots of connective tissues that after eight hours of cooking break down into gelatin, giving the meat a luxurious taste and texture.

A brisket has to be smoked in a barbecue, not made in the oven.

When I was a food writer, I publicly announced prejudice against the gas barbecue: wouldn't use, offends my sensibilities. That was before we had children—two of them, hellions both. Suddenly a barbecue I could fire up in a second rather than building a bed of coals for an hour became an attractive alternative. Since then, I have cooked only on gas, an admission that will justify every true barbecuer in calling me a fraud. To them I say, "Well, excuse me. Take my kids for a year. Then we'll talk."

You *can* barbecue smoke with gas—as long as you have enough fuel in that little tank. (You do not want to shock the meat with up-and-down temperatures.)

Okay, so here's how you do it.

You need hardwood, because hardwood, when soaked in water, smokes, and the sweet, pungent smoke permeates the muscle, and especially the fat. Softwood burns at too low a temperature and creates resin in the smoke. Resin tastes awful, unless you like retsina, which is perfectly good wine aged in pine barrels that leach resin and make the wine unpalatable to all but Greeks. I'll get letters about this, I know.

You can buy hardwood in chips, which are good only for the chip companies because they burn up in about ten minutes. Your brisket or pork shoulder will cost you about a bagful, enough to send the chip-company president to South Carolina every day for lunch. What you want are large chunks of hardwood (often called "hunks" by wives not allowed to utter the word in any other context because most barbecuers are paleolithic chauvinists).

Hickory chunks are choice No. 1, which is why Kraft made a fortune on hickory-flavored barbecue sauces. If you can't find hickory, phone your local food writer or barbecue salesperson, or call the neighbor who smells like he's just come from a three-alarm fire.

If you are using a gas barbecue, soak the wood in water for at least a day. (Most people will tell you to soak it "for at least an hour." These people have shares in the wood-chip company.) Trust me, a gas barbecue is not going to go out when wet wood is put on top of those lava rocks. If you are using a traditional charcoal barbecue, soak the wood for four hours.

The theory is this: the fire heats the wood until it smokes but does not burn up because of the water content. Water can only go to 212°F (100°C), after all. With the barbecue lid closed, the smoke circulates around the meat at a temperature that does not exceed 200°F (95°C)—ideally 170°F (77°C).

Place an aluminum-foil tray, or some aluminum foil the size of the brisket, right on top of the lava rocks and right under the grill where you are going to put the brisket. It is there to catch the drips so they will not flare up and scorch the meat. Instead, the drippings will boil. They will rise as steam and flavor the surrounding smoke. Great stuff, eh?

Fire up the barbecue and let it heat up for five to ten minutes, to about 500°F (260°C). I mention this only to avoid threatening letters from do-gooders who worry quite needlessly that the meat will be unsafe (bacteria, salmonella, trichinosis). Barbecuing like this has been going on for centuries without incident, but this fact pales in the face of old wives' tales.

Put the soaked chunks of hardwood at one end of the barbecue. Sprinkle the brisket liberally with the dry rub and work it into the meat with your fingers. Place the meat, fatty side up, above the aluminum drip pan. Close the lid, regulate the temperature to below 200°F (95°C)—ideally 170°F (77°C)—and ignore it until the wood is gone. Replenish the wood, close the barbecue and ignore it again.

This goes on all day. At least eight hours.

When you take the brisket off the barbecue, you will notice that it has a top flap. Slice off the flap, chop it up and dump it on buns slathered with barbecue sauce.

The bottom half is leaner and can be cut into slices. Put the slices on buns and slather them with the barbecue sauce.

Serve with cold beer or root beer, and finishing sauce on the side. Provide serviettes, but post a notice that you will not be held responsible for cleaning bills.

Dry Rub for Beef

5	cloves garlic, finely minced	5
2 tbsp	Hungarian paprika	30 mL
2 tbsp	brown sugar	30 mL
2 tbsp	black pepper	30 mL
	Zest of 1 lemon	
1 tbsp	salt	15 mL

Combine all ingredients. Store in a tightly closed container.

Finishing Sauce for Brisket

½ cup	butter	125 mL	
½ cup	ketchup	125 mL	
¼ cup	lemon juice	60 mL	
¼ cup	bourbon or rye	60 mL	
¼ cup	cider vinegar	60 mL	
3 tbsp	Worcestershire sauce	45 mL	
1	*chipolte* or jalapeño pepper, finely minced (remove seeds if you don't want added heat) 1-inch (2.5 cm) piece of fresh ginger, peeled and finely grated	1	
1 tsp	celery salt	5 mL	
1 tsp	cayenne or hot Hungarian paprika	5 mL	
¼ tsp	salt	1 mL	

PREPARATION TIME:
15 MINUTES
COOKING TIME:
30 MINUTES
MAKES: SAUCE FOR 8 SANDWICHES, MORE IF YOUR GUESTS ARE REALLY NEAT

In a small saucepan over low heat, melt butter. Combine remaining ingredients, add to butter and simmer for 30 minutes.

This sauce can be made in larger quantities, but do not increase the amount of salt. The sauce can be bottled and aged for a week or more, which will make it hotter, especially if you don't remove the seeds from the pepper.

Hush Puppies

For years, John Henry Jackson, a huge man with an even larger smile, ran the Underground Railroad in downtown Toronto. I could never start a meal there without Jackson's hush puppies. Sadly, his restaurant is no more.

PREPARATION TIME:
70 MINUTES
COOKING TIME:
10 MINUTES
SERVES: 8

2 tbsp	unsalted butter	30 mL
1 cup	milk	250 mL
1	large egg	1
1 tsp	lemon juice	5 mL
1 cup	cornmeal	250 mL
1 cup	all-purpose flour	250 mL
2 tbsp	baking powder	30 mL
1 tsp	hot Hungarian paprika or ½ tsp cayenne pepper	5 mL
1 tsp	dried thyme	5 mL
1 tsp	dried oregano	5 mL
½ tsp	salt	2 mL
	Lard for deep frying	

Melt butter. In a separate pan, heat milk. Beat egg, butter and lemon juice into the hot milk and set aside. In a large bowl, sift together cornmeal, flour, baking powder, paprika, thyme, oregano and salt. Add half the milk mixture to the dry ingredients and stir well. When it has combined with the flour mixture, pour in and combine the rest. Cover and refrigerate 1 hour.

In a large frying pan, heat lard to 350°F (175°C). Drop the batter, 1 tbsp (15 mL) at a time, into the hot lard and fry until brown on all sides, about 1 minute. Don't overcrowd the pan, and don't try to make hush puppies larger than 1 tbsp (15 mL), because they won't cook all the way through. Drain on paper towels.

Pork Stuffed Onions

Onions are at the very core of barbecue cooking. My sister, Joan, hates onions. She loves these.

PREPARATION TIME:
30 MINUTES
COOKING TIME:
1 HOUR
SERVES: 8

8	large onions	8
3 tbsp	butter	45 mL
1 cup	fresh bread crumbs	250 mL
¼ cup	whipping cream	60 mL
½ lb	finely ground breakfast sausage meat	225 g
¼ tsp	dried thyme	1 mL
	Pinch dried finely ground sage	
¼ cup	chopped parsley	60 mL
	Salt and pepper to taste	
¼ cup	dry red wine	60 mL
1 cup	beef stock	250 mL
	Butter	
	Chopped parsley for garnish	

Slice the tops off the onions about ¼ inch (5 mm) down. With a knife, chop the insides and then scoop them out with a spoon. Leave the onion shells at least 2 layers thick, strong enough to stand up to cooking. Finely chop the removed onion. In a pan over medium-low heat, melt 3 tbsp (45 mL) butter and slowly sauté chopped onion until it takes on a golden color.

Bring a large pot of water to the boil. As chopped onion sautés, plunge onion shells in boiling water for 3 minutes; remove, drain and dry. In a bowl, soak bread crumbs in the cream.

When the chopped onions are golden, add sausage meat and cook until the meat is no longer pink. Squeeze the cream out of the bread crumbs, discard cream and add bread crumbs to the meat mixture. Add thyme, sage and parsley and combine. Cook for another 3 minutes to soften up dried herbs. Taste and adjust for salt and pepper.

Preheat oven to 350°F (175°C). Place onion shells in a greased ovenproof dish just large enough to hold them in one layer. Stuff each with the sausage mixture (you can mound them up a bit), pour wine and stock around them, dot each with a knob of butter and bake for 45 minutes. When done, carefully remove onions from dish to heated plates. Pour cooking liquid into a small saucepan. Over medium-high heat, reduce it by half, or until it coats the back of a spoon, about 3 minutes. Dribble the sauce over each onion and garnish with parsley.

Grilled Oyster Mushrooms

Oyster mushrooms are white with gills and look like Chinese fans. They have either a silky skin or are slightly slimy, I have never decided which. They are at their best slapped on a very hot barbecue just long enough to turn them golden on both sides.

PREPARATION TIME:
3 MINUTES
COOKING TIME:
5 MINUTES
SERVES: 4

¼ cup	olive oil	60 mL
10	drops Tabasco (optional)	10
24	oyster mushrooms (the biggest you can find)	24
	Salt and pepper	

Mix the oil and Tabasco. Dip mushrooms in mixture to coat them. Slap them on the grill. When golden, about 1 or 2 minutes depending upon the heat, turn them over and cook them on the other side. Salt and pepper, and serve.

Larry Morse's Quesadillas

PREPARATION TIME:
5 MINUTES
COOKING TIME:
2 MINUTES
MAKES: 8 APPETIZER
PORTIONS

Jake Spanner is seventy-eight years old and lives in Los Angeles. Some years back he had to kill a drug dealer named Tony Novallo. "My doctor at the clinic—a thirty-five-year-old with a weight problem, ulcers, fallen arches, a smoker's cough and dandruff—told me to stop eating spicy food. Since that was one of my few remaining real pleasures, I usually ignored the advice… If I were going to go, a lethal chili verde seemed as good a way as any: 'J. Spanner. Suddenly in the night from an exploding burrito.' I could go along with that."

Spanner is the hero of *The Old Dick*, a classic 1981 novel by writer and killer chili cook L.A. Morse. I tracked down Larry Morse in 1985; he cooked some of the explosive concoctions that appear in his books and then kindly gave me the recipes. I have been tinkering with them ever since. The first recipes for quesadillas, the *chili verde*, killer chili, *pozole* and *salsa cruda* were all inspired by Morse.

When making quesadillas, he roasts the jalapeños before he peels and seeds them. I don't. I'm lazy. If you want to go the extra mile, by all means. How to roast them is in the *pozole* recipe.

Jalapeños in a jar are hotter than fresh ones, and I prefer them. If you are seeding only a few fresh jalapeños or chilies, coat your hands with oil first to prevent burning; when you're finished, wash off the oil with warm soap and water. If you are seeding more than a few, put a sandwich bag over your hands or wear rubber gloves. If you want to tame a jalapeño, remove the seeds. If you like it hot, leave the seeds. Don't bother peeling a fresh jalapeño. The skin is not that thick, and you don't eat enough of them to worry about digestion. That, by the way, is why you peel a bell pepper (or red, yellow or orange): most people can't digest the peel.

10	sprigs fresh English parsley	10
¼ cup	Monterey Jack cheese, grated	60 mL
1 tbsp	jalapeño pepper, diced	15 mL
2	flour tortillas (recipe, p. 217)	2
1 tbsp	oil for frying	15 mL
2 tbsp	sour cream or salsa	30 mL

Cut off the stems of the parsley. Throw parsley into a deep-fat frier set at 375°F (190°C) for about 5 seconds; remove and drain. The parsley becomes crisp, slightly darkened in color, and melts in your mouth.

Sprinkle cheese and chopped jalapeño peppers evenly on one tortilla, leaving ½ inch (1 cm) clear at the edge. Cover with second tortilla. Fry the tortilla sandwich in a pan over medium-high heat quickly in a minimum of hot oil. Flip. Brown other side. Place on a plate and cut into eight triangles. Garnish with fried parsley. Serve with sour cream or salsa.

Quesadillas Variations

You can add just about any ingredient to make your own quesadillas. A simple variation is ¼ cup (60 mL) grated Monterey Jack cheese and 3 tbsp (45 mL) *salsa cruda* (recipe, p. 219). Nora Pouillon, chef and owner of Nora in Washington, D.C., makes one with grilled pineapple, Cheddar cheese and black beans. Patricia Williams, executive chef of Restaurant Charlotte in New York, makes a lobster quesadilla—many, actually: she goes through about a hundred and fifty lobsters a week. Sauté lobster meat in garlic butter and shallots with a dash of Tabasco and a squirt of lemon juice.

Or take ¼ lb (115 g) leftover roast beef and marinate it in 2 tbsp (30 mL) lime juice for 2 hours. Drain, then sear beef on a very hot charcoal barbecue to blacken the outside, or sear it in a dry, white-hot cast-iron skillet. Slice it thinly, then mix it with just enough Barbecue Sauce (recipe, p. 207) to bind it. Spread it on a flour tortilla, top with another, fry in oil as in the main recipe, slice the pie into 8 pieces and top with sour cream.

Or use a flour tortilla as the base for a California-style pizza. Wolfgang Puck of Spago, in L.A., gives his famous thin-sliced pizza a whack with what he calls "chili oil." To ¼ cup (60 mL) of the best olive oil, add at least 20 drops of Tabasco sauce. (This is enough oil for 4 to 6 quesadillas.) Paint 1 flour tortilla with the oil. Don't be shy. Cover it with 2 tbsp (30 mL) grated Monterey Jack, 6 very thin slices of onion, 6 very thin slices of tomato, 8 very thin slices of smoked turkey (or pepperoni or duck sausage, as Puck does) and 2 tsp (10 mL) dried or 2 tbsp (30 mL) freshly chopped oregano. Top with a second tortilla, fry both sides, cut pie into eight pieces and serve.

Pepperwood, a restaurant in Burlington, Ontario, makes crab quesadilla with baked tortillas. They spread crab, cheese, peeled, seeded and diced tomatoes, onions and jalapeños on a flour tortilla, place another tortilla on top and bake it at 375°F (190°C) until the tortilla is browned.

Corn Tortillas

PREPARATION TIME:
5 MINUTES
COOKING TIME:
10 TO 20 MINUTES
(DEPENDING ON THE
HEAT OF THE PAN)
MAKES: 10 TORTILLAS

Tortillas are the basis for much adobe food, and corn tortillas are used the most, especially for such delicacies as enchiladas. To make corn tortillas, you use *masa harina*, a corn flour made from hominy (see *pozole*, below), which is hulled and lye-bleached corn kernels. It's available in Mexican, Hispanic and South Asian markets. A tortilla is a dough rolled into circles and dry-fried (baked) in a hot skillet. For enchiladas they are dipped into hot oil, then dipped into a chili sauce, then filled with cheese and onions, rolled up and oven-baked in another sauce. You really have to use corn tortillas right away; otherwise you might as well buy ready-made tortillas at the supermarket. When it comes down to it, you are better off buying the commercial ones. Or you can cheat …

The following recipe is neither mine nor a recipe for true corn tortillas, but it's so simple it can hardly be improved upon. I got it from Bert Greene's *The Grains Cookbook* (Workman Publishing, New York, 1988). I've cut down the amount of water because I use very fine cornmeal and ordinary all-purpose flour.

1 cup	yellow cornmeal	250 mL
½ tsp	salt	2 mL
½ cup	all-purpose flour	125 mL
1	egg, beaten	1
1 ¾ cup	water	415 mL

Sift together the cornmeal, salt and flour. Mix egg and water and whisk into the dry ingredients to produce a very watery batter. Over medium heat, pour ¼ cup (60 mL) of batter into a nonstick fry pan at least 6 inches (15 cm) across. Quickly swirl the batter in the pan to form a large pancake. Fry 1 to 2 minutes (don't let it brown) and flip. Fry another 1 minute and remove to a plate. Repeat until all the batter is used up. Makes about 10 tortillas.

Now you have great-tasting corn tortillas to make anything from quesadillas to enchiladas. Mark McEwan, chef and owner of North 44, in Toronto, makes corn tortillas stuffed with grilled pork and charred tomato salsa.

Flour Tortillas

Since you don't run a restaurant and don't have to pinch pennies, buy tortillas at the supermarket. They are convenient, and the leftovers can be frozen. But, if you want to make them, here's how.

PREPARATION TIME:
30 MINUTES
COOKING TIME:
15 MINUTES
MAKES: 8 LARGE
TORTILLAS

2 cups	flour	500 mL
1 tsp	salt	5 mL
1 tsp	baking powder	5 mL
⅓ cup	bacon fat	80 mL
	Water	

Whirl flour, salt, baking powder and fat in a food processor for a few seconds to combine. Add ¼ cup (60 mL) of the water and whirl. Then, a spoonful at a time, add water and whirl until the flour turns into a ball of dough. (It's amazing how suddenly this happens.)

Grease a bowl, put the dough in it, cover with a wet tea towel, and let it rest for 30 minutes.

Heat a dry cast-iron skillet or a nonstick fry pan at least 8 inches (20 cm) wide over medium heat.

Divide the dough into 8 pieces and roll each piece into a ball. Cover the dough balls with the damp tea towel to keep them moist. Roll 1 ball of dough into a round tortilla ¼ inch (5 mm) thick at most. Slap it into the skillet or pan and dry-fry until bubbles form on top of the dough and the underside is brown in spots, about 1 minute. Flip it over and cook the other side.

Now, here's the chef's trick. As it cooks on the second side, rotate the tortilla a quarter turn, pressing down with the tips of all 5 fingers as you rotate it. A few seconds later, rotate it another quarter turn, then again, then again. It makes the tortilla puff in the middle. That's good.

As soon as the tortilla is done, put it on a plate and cover with plastic wrap. Repeat with the other 7 tortillas.

Chili, Texas Style

PREPARATION TIME:
30 MINUTES
COOKING TIME:
2 HOURS
SERVES: 8

True chili, purists say, don't have no beans. It's beef or venison, maybe a little pork, chili peppers, salt, cumin and tomatoes. But if that's all you put in your chili, you're going to get a bland bowl of slop. This ain't it.

1 lb	top sirloin or round, cut into 1-inch (2.5 cm) cubes	450 g
2 tbsp	flour	30 mL
2 tbsp	butter	30 mL
2 lbs	ground beef	900 g
1 ½ cups	diced onion	375 mL
6	cloves garlic, finely chopped	6
2 tbsp	chili powder*	30 mL
¼ cup	freshly ground cumin	60 mL
2 tbsp	dried oregano	30 mL
1 tsp	salt	5 mL
1 tbsp	freshly ground black pepper	15 mL
2 cups	water	500 mL
3 cups	peeled, seeded and diced tomatoes (about 12 medium tomatoes)	750 mL
2 tbsp	Worcestershire sauce	30 mL
2 tsp	sugar	10 mL
2 tbsp	cornmeal	30 mL
½ cup	or more grated brick or Monterey Jack cheese Crusty bread *Salsa Cruda* (recipe, p. 219)	125 mL

In a plastic bag, toss beef cubes with flour to coat evenly. In a large pot, melt butter over medium heat and brown beef cubes. Remove and reserve. To the pot add ground beef, onions and garlic; cook until beef is browned. Return beef cubes to the pot and add chili powder, cumin, oregano, salt, pepper and water; cover pot and simmer for 1 hour. Add tomatoes, Worcestershire sauce and sugar; simmer,

*Larry Morse's killer chili calls for 3 tbsp (45 mL) mild Mexican chili powder, 2 tbsp (30 mL) each of ground pasilla and *chipolte* chilies and 1 tbsp (15 mL) ground red chilies. He also uses 1 ½ tsp (7 mL) celery seeds.

uncovered, for 30 minutes. Taste and adjust seasonings (more chili powder, cumin, or sugar to suit your taste).* Sprinkle cornmeal on top, fold in and simmer 30 minutes or until the chili thickens. Serve in big bowls with grated cheese on top, with big chunks of fresh, buttered, crusty bread and with *salsa cruda* on the side.

Salsa Cruda

North American supermarkets now sell more salsa than ketchup. It fits the times. Salsa is really just salad in a jar. Delicious salad. "Honey, I tricked the kids" salad.

1 tbsp	olive oil	15 mL
6	jalapeño peppers	6
1	yellow or green bell pepper	1
4	large tomatoes, peeled, seeded and coarsely chopped	4
1	medium onion, coarsely chopped	1
1 cup	coarsely chopped cilantro (coriander or Chinese parsley)	250 mL
1 tbsp	white vinegar	15 mL
	Salt and pepper to taste	

Oil the skins of the jalapeño and bell peppers. Under the broiler, or over the flame on a gas stove or barbecue, char the peppers on all sides; plop them in a paper bag, close the bag and let them steam and cool, about 15 minutes. When cool, peel them, seed them and chop them finely. In a bowl, combine them with remaining ingredients and refrigerate for at least 1 hour before serving.

*Chili powder and cumin lose their potency quickly. If you bought them bottled from a supermarket, chances are they are old. It is much better to have a small spice grinder and grind your own cumin seeds and chili peppers.

Pozole

PREPARATION TIME:

2 DAYS, OR 5 HOURS

IF YOU USE CANNED

HOMINY

COOKING TIME:

4 ½ HOURS

SERVES: 8

"One thing I learned being broke. I'd learned to cook up a storm using spare parts, the kind of stuff that ordinarily went into pet food."

Jake Spanner doesn't have a lot good to say about *pozole*, the Mexican one-dish meal of anything in the leftover bin at the cut-rate butcher shop. Author L.A. Morse, Spanner's creator, disagrees.

Pozole explains the financial mess most restaurateurs get in. They open a restaurant that serves simple, inexpensive dishes like *pozole*, and they sell bankers and backers on the notion that food costs will run at only twenty percent. Accountants love it. The place can't lose! What they're forgetting is the cost of labor.

In a first-class steak and seafood restaurant, the price of the meat and lobster is astoundingly high. But it doesn't take a genius to grill and boil. On the other hand, boeuf bourguignon, pot au feu and *pozole* use relatively cheap but tough cuts of meat, which take hours to cook, which means hours of labor. It also means hiring an expensive chef rather than a cheap cook. In order to make cheap cuts of meat taste good enough to charge enough to cover your labor costs, you need someone who knows what she is doing—and who can teach anyone in the kitchen to do the same. Consistency, after all, is the hallmark of a great restaurant.

Pozole uses dirt-cheap ingredients, takes a long time to cook, but winds up as a wonderful stew of fabulous flavor and aromas. The best is made with whole dried hominy, corn that is soaked in water, lime and lye until the hull splits off and is then dried. When it is ground into flour, it's called *masa harina*, and it's the flour used to make corn tortillas and chips. In Mexican and Hispanic stores, you can also buy it in cans. If you use canned hominy (often labeled *pozole* or *posole*), add it straight to the dish at the end and forget the hominy preparation at the beginning of the recipe.

½ cup	whole dried hominy	125 mL
	Water	
6	jalapeño peppers	6
2	*chipolte* (hot and smoky) peppers, chopped finely	2
1	green bell pepper	1
3 lb	pork hocks	1.4 kg
2 lb	chicken backs	900 g
4 cups	coarsely chopped onion	1 L
16	cloves garlic, peeled	16

1 tsp	salt	5 mL
1 tbsp	whole black peppercorns	15 mL
10 cups	water	2.5 L
1 lb	pork shoulder, cut into 1-inch (2.5 cm) cubes	450 g
1 tbsp	chopped fresh cilantro (coriander or Chinese parsley)	15 mL
1 tbsp	dried oregano	15 mL
1	medium onion, coarsely chopped	1
½	head iceberg lettuce, chopped	½
6	radishes, coarsely chopped	6
1	lime, quartered	1
	Fried flour tortillas	

Put whole dried hominy in a bowl; cover with water and soak overnight. Drain and rinse it at least 3 times. In 3 cups (750 mL) water, bring it to a boil; simmer for 2 ½ hours. Drain. It will yield 2 cups (500 mL) cooked hominy, which will look like white chickpeas.

Place peppers on a barbecue or gas stove on high heat, or broil them in the oven, until the skin is blackened on all sides. Put them in a paper bag, close it up and leave them until they're cool, about 20 minutes. The skins should peel right off. Cut them in half, remove the seeds and chop finely. Reserve.

In a large pot over high heat, combine pork hocks, chicken, onion, garlic, salt, pepper and water. Bring to a boil, skim the top, reduce heat and simmer, covered, for 3 hours. Remove meat, strip it from the bones and reserve. To the stock add the pork shoulder; bring to a boil, reduce heat and simmer for 40 minutes, skimming when necessary. Add hominy, cilantro, oregano and reserved meat; simmer for 20 minutes.

To serve, ladle stew into bowls. Guests may add chopped raw onion, chopped lettuce, chopped radishes and lime juice to taste. Serve with fried flour tortillas.

Caesar Salad

PREPARATION TIME:
15 MINUTES
MAKES: 4 LARGE
SALADS, 8 SMALL
SIDE SALADS

I was introduced to Caesar salad at a restaurant called the Burnham Mansion in the early 1970s. My girlfriend at the time was Sandy. Both of us were reporters with the Peterborough daily; neither had any money. We would eat at my apartment and then go to the Burnham Mansion for a Caesar salad and a bottle of Pouilly-Fuissé. (No wine goes well with salad, but we were young, foolish and in lust.) The waiter made the salad right at the table. I watched, like a virgin at a sex workshop by Don Juan, and eventually perfected it.

Years later I learned from Diana Kennedy's book, *Mexican Regional Cooking*, that the Burnham's Caesar salad was not exactly the original. Indeed, Caesar salad is not an Italian salad at all, but Mexican, having been invented in Tijuana by two transplanted Italian restaurateurs, Alex and Caesar Cardini. (This surprise was equaled only by the discovery that crème brûlée is an English dish with a snooty French name.)

I introduced the original recipe to several restaurants for which I was consulting. The originality of the recipe was proudly proclaimed on the menu. Were the customers impressed? No. Did they notice? Yes! They noticed the price! Because you have to cook it, it had to be priced at least $6.50 to accommodate the labor. On the old menu, Caesar salad had cost $3.50. A near-riot erupted. The heathens wanted the old price back even if it meant the old salad, which came from a plastic jar, the croutons from a box. The heathens got their wish.

My great friend, restaurateur Harry Barberian, just shook his head and shared a wise rule of the business: never put pride before profit.

Caesar salad was invented in two stages. Caesar Cardini began selling a salad with a dressing of olive oil, Worcestershire sauce, lime juice (not lemon), coddled eggs and Parmesan cheese. Then brother Alex arrived and supplied the taste that made the salad famous. He toasted fresh bread in a 300°F (150°C) oven, brushed the bread with olive oil to brown and crisp it, then slathered it with a paste made of anchovy filets, garlic and olive oil. Thus, the timid could have a Caesar salad without the garlic and anchovy whack by passing on the croutons.

Here's my version, which is really only a minor variation on the original (which is in Diana Kennedy's book). The biggest problem with most restaurant Caesars is that the kitchen does not thoroughly dry the romaine lettuce after washing, and this dilutes the dressing. I like a dressing that really coats each leaf. And, I'm ashamed to confess—because it is nowhere in the original—I crumble crisp bacon in my salad.

Anne Rozensweig at New York's Arcadia makes her Caesar with arugula. (It began as a mistake: an apprentice couldn't tell the difference between arugula and romaine.) Of late, however, restaurants have been throwing all sorts of mistakes on a Caesar—shrimp, grilled chicken, even beef. Enough!

1	large head romaine lettuce	1
1	loaf French bread, crusts removed, cut into 1-inch (2.5 cm) slices	1
	Olive oil	
½ tsp	salt	2 mL
4	cloves garlic, crushed	4
2	anchovy filets	2
2	eggs	2
½ cup	good olive oil	125 mL
1 tbsp	coarse-grained mustard (moutarde de meaux)	15 mL
1 tsp	Worcestershire sauce	5 mL
2	dashes Tabasco	2
	Juice of 1 small lime	
⅓ cup	grated *parmigiano reggiano*	80 mL
4	strips bacon, fried crisp and crumbled	4

Rip off the base of the lettuce. (Cutting it with a knife will discolor the leaves.) Wash leaves, dry thoroughly, rip into thirds and set aside.

Preheat oven to 300°F (150°C). Place bread slices on a cookie sheet and bake for 20 minutes. Brush both sides with olive oil; bake for 10 minutes more, or until the bread is golden brown.

Burnham Mansion Caesar: Place salt and garlic in a large wooden salad bowl and crush to a paste with a pestle or the back of a spoon. Add anchovies and crush into the garlic to form a paste. Whisk in the eggs, olive oil, mustard, Worcestershire, Tabasco, lime juice and ¼ cup (60 mL) of the cheese until the dressing is smooth and creamy. Add romaine and toss thoroughly to coat all leaves. At the last minute cut the toasted bread into 1-inch (2.5 cm) cubes. Throw the bacon and croutons into the salad and dust with the remaining cheese.

Original Caesar: In a food processor, process salt, garlic and anchovies into a paste. Slowly add up to ¼ cup (60 mL) olive oil, one spoonful at a time, and process until it is a spreadable paste. Cut the croutons into 1-inch (2.5 cm) cubes and coat them with this paste. Whip eggs in a salad bowl, then add olive oil, mustard, Worcestershire, Tabasco, lime juice and ¼ cup (60 mL) of the cheese—in that order—until the dressing is creamy. Toss with the romaine, add bacon and croutons, dust with more cheese and serve.

Index